The Concurrent C Programming Language

Narain Gehani
William D. Roome

AT&T Bell Laboratories
Murray Hill, NJ 07974

Silicon Press
25 Beverly Road
Summit, NJ 07901
USA

Silicon Press
25 Beverly Road
Summit, NJ 07901

First Edition
Printing 9 8 7 6 5 4 3 2 1   Year 93 92 91 90 89

UNIX is a registered trademark of AT&T

Library of Congress Cataloging in Publication Data

Gehani, Narain, 1947-
  The Concurrent C Programming Language / Narain Gehani, William D. Roome
    p. cm.
  Bibliography p.
  Includes Index.
  ISBN 0-929306-00-7
  1. C (Computer program language) 2. Parallel programming
  (Computer science)   I. Roome, William D. II. Title
  QA76.73.C15G46 1988
  005.13′3--dc19   88-28829
                                                            CIP

To
Indu, Neel and Varun

and

Jan

Contents

Preface

Chapter 1   Basics   1
1. Processes 1
2. Process Parameters 4
3. Process Interaction & Trans. Calls 6
4. Process Declarations 9
5. Process Creation 11
6. Process Values and Process Ids 12
7. Producer-Consumer Example 12
8. Shared Memory Hazards 21
9. Program Organization Suggestions 23
10. Examples 23
11. Exercises 31

Chapter 2   Advanced Facilities   33
1. Process Values & Process Management 33
2. The Delay Statement 36
3. Timed Transaction Calls 38
4. The Accept Statement 39
5. The Select Statement 42
6. Collective Termination 49
7. Transaction Pointers 54
8. Asynchronous Transaction Calls 55
9. Examples 60
10. Exercises 77

Chapter 3   Run-time Environment   79
1. Process Ids 79
2. Process States 79
3. Process Abortion 80
4. Process Priority 81
5. Number of Pending Transaction Calls 82

6. Giving Names to Process Instances   84
7. Processor Selection on a Multiproc.   85
8. Interrupts and Transactions   86
9. Process Stack Size   90
10. C and UNIX Functions   90
11. Exercises   91

Chapter 4   Large Examples   93
1. Protocol Simulation   93
2. Robot Controller   103
3. Concurrent Make   114
4. Window Manager   124
5. Exercises   131

Chapter 5   Concurrent C++   133
1. Brief Summary of C++   133
2. Data Abstraction & Concurrent Prog.   135
3. Summary   151
4. Exercises   152

Chapter 6   Concurrent Programming Models   153
1. Concurrent C Concurrent Prog. Model   153
2. The Producer-Consumer Example   155
3. Concurrent C   157
4. Semaphores   158
5. Critical Regions   159
6. Monitors   160
7. Communicating Sequential Processes   162
8. Distributed Processes   164
9. Ada   165
10. Final Comments   166
11. Exercises   166

Chapter 7   Concurrent Programming Issues   167
1. Message Passing   167
2. Deadlock   181
3. Maximizing Concurrency   185
4. Polling   187
5. Exercises   188

Chapter 8   Discrete Event Simulation   189
1. The Process-Inter. Model of Sim.   190
2. A Two-Stage Queueing Network   192
3. Structure of The Simulation Program   193

4. Process Implementations   198
5. A Feedback Queueing Network   208
6. Extensions and Modifications   209

Appendix A   Concurrent C Reference Manual   211
1. Keywords   211
2. Processes and Process Interaction   211
3. Process Types & Trans. Declarations   212
4. Process Bodies   214
5. Process Creation   214
6. Process Types And Ids   216
7. Transaction Pointers   217
8. Transaction Calls   218
9. Accept Statements   219
10. Delay Statements   221
11. Select Statements   222
12. Preprocessor   223
13. Library Functions   224
14. Syntax Summary   228

Appendix B   Concurrent C: Design and Implementation   231
1. Design   231
2. Implementation Overview   235

Appendix C   Comparison with Conc. Programming in Ada   251
1. Terminology   251
2. The Rendezvous Model   251
3. An Example   252
4. Process Parameters   254
5. Process Specification And Creation   255
6. Synchronous vs. Async. Trans. Calls   255
7. Ordering Process Interaction Req.   256
8. Process Priorities   262
9. Transaction Pointers   262
10. Immediate Alt. of the Select Stmt.   263
11. Collective Process Termination   264
12. Miscellaneous   265
13. Summary   267

Appendix D   C: A Synopsis   269
1. Examples Illustrating the Language   269
2. Types   271
3. Type Declarations   275
4. Definitions   276

5. Operators   279
6. Control Structures   281
7. Functions   285
8. Source File Organization   286

Annotated Bibliography   287

Index   297

Preface

Concurrent programming is becoming increasingly important because multicomputer architectures, particularly networks of microprocessors, are rapidly becoming attractive alternatives to traditional maxicomputers. Concurrent programming is important for many reasons [Hoare 1978; Gehani 1984a]:

- Concurrent programming facilities are notationally convenient and conceptually elegant for writing systems in which many events occur concurrently, for example, operating systems, real-time systems, and database systems.

- Inherently concurrent algorithms are best expressed when the concurrency is stated explicitly; otherwise, the structure of the algorithm may be lost.

- Efficient utilization of multiprocessor architectures requires concurrent programming.

- Concurrent programming can reduce program execution time even on uniprocessors, by allowing input/output operations to run in parallel with computation.

The only disadvantage is that concurrent programming adds complexity to a programming language. For example, a concurrent programming language introduces additional syntax and semantics for defining program components that can run in parallel and for controlling how they interact. However, remember that anyone who implements a parallel application in a sequential language must write code to simulate these concurrent facilities. This may be much more work than you expect. The amount of work involved is non-trivial, and it requires knowledge of the hardware, the operating system and the inter-processor communication facilities. In addition, it is likely that the code will be difficult to port to a different computer system.

As an analogy, consider the function call mechanisms in most programming languages. Neophyte programmers are often confused by these mechanisms (call-by-value vs. call-by-reference, arguments vs. parameters, etc.). In theory, function call mechanisms are not necessary; any program which uses functions can be converted into one which does not. But although they are complicated, function call mechanisms exist in programming languages because once programmers have invested the time to learn these mechanisms, they make it easier for programmers to write, understand, and modify programs. We feel that adding concurrent programming facilities to a programming language can have a similar effect: programmers will find it easier to write concurrent programs, and the resulting programs will be much easier to understand and modify.

1. Concurrent C

We picked C as the basis for our work on parallel programming because (a) it is an immensely popular language, (b) it does not have parallel facilities, and (c) we use it. We had several objectives in enhancing C with concurrent programming facilities:

1. To provide a concurrent programming language that can be used for writing systems on genuinely parallel hardware, such as a network of microprocessors or workstations.

2. To provide a test bed for experimenting with a variety of high-level concurrent programming facilities.

3. To design a practical concurrent programming language that can be implemented on a variety of currently available multiprocessor architectures.

Concurrent C is the result of an effort to enhance C so that it can be used to write concurrent programs that can run efficiently on single computers, on loosely-coupled distributed computer networks, or on tightly-coupled multiprocessors. Concurrent C is an upward-compatible extension of C. These extensions include mechanisms for the declaration and creation of processes, for process synchronization and interaction, and for process termination and abortion.

C++ is an extension of C that provides data abstraction facilities [Stroustrup 1986]. Concurrent C does not provide data abstraction facilities but its parallel programming facilities can be used in conjunction with C++. The resulting language is called Concurrent C++. The Concurrent C compiler, as a compile-time option, accepts Concurrent C++.

Concurrent C was first designed and implemented circa 1984-1985. Concurrent C implementations are available for several versions of the UNIX® system: System V, BSD 4.2, and NRTX [Kapilow 1985] (a stripped-down real-time version of UNIX) running on a variety of computers, including VAX† computers, AT&T 3B computers and SUN workstations. These are uniprocessor implementations, in that the Concurrent C program runs as one

---

† VAX is a trademark of Digital Equipment Corporation.

UNIX process; the Concurrent C run-time library provides a scheduler that switches between Concurrent C processes as needed.

Concurrent C has also been implemented on several types of multiprocessors. One is a loosely-coupled network of independent computers connected by local area network (Ethernet), each running the UNIX operating system. Here both the hardware and software are loosely coupled. The second system, the AT&T 3B4000, also has several UNIX processors connected via a bus, but this system looks like one virtual UNIX system; for example, the file system is shared among all processors. In this system, the hardware is loosely coupled but the operating system software is tightly coupled. And the last system is a shared-memory multiprocessor; here Concurrent C is implemented on top of a real-time multitasking kernel [Roome 1986b]. In this system, both the hardware and the software are tightly coupled.

The uniprocessor version of Concurrent C has been used for several projects (primarily research) and for teaching and research at many universities. Experience with the multiprocessor versions is rather limited at this time, but this is likely to change rapidly as soon as the multiprocessor implementations of Concurrent C are made available to users.

2. About This Book

This book is both about concurrent programming and about Concurrent C. We will discuss concurrent programming in general, describe Concurrent C, use Concurrent C to illustrate concurrent programming, discuss issues related to concurrent programming, discuss the design and implementation of Concurrent C, and compare Concurrent C with Ada.

We believe that programming is learned best from example. Consequently, we will include numerous "real" examples, both short and long ones. We encourage the reader to compile and run the programs shown in this book. Of course, the size of the book imposes a constraint on the number and length of the long examples.

Now for the organization of the book. A chapter (or an appendix) will be devoted to each of the following topics:

- Basics: the process model, process creation, synchronous transaction calls, process ids.

- Advanced facilities: *select* statements, timed transaction calls, mutual termination, transaction pointers, asynchronous transactions.

- Run-time environment (library functions).

- Large Examples: protocol simulator, robot controller, Concurrent Make, window manager.

- Concurrent C++.

- Concurrent programming models.

- Concurrent programming issues.

- Discrete event simulation.

- Concurrent C reference manual.

- Design of Concurrent C and an overview of its implementations.

- Comparison with concurrent programming in Ada.

- C: A synopsis.

- Bibliography.

3. Audience

The book is intended for people interested in learning about Concurrent C or concurrent programming or both. It can be used as a text book for a course on Concurrent C or concurrent programming. It is also suitable as a supplementary text book for courses on programming languages or operating systems.

We assume that the reader is familiar with a high-level language such as C, Pascal, Modula, or Ada. We also assume that the reader has some experience with C. If you are not familiar with C, or if your C is rusty, Appendix D gives a summary of the C language. For a more detailed description of C, see books such as those by Kernighan & Ritchie [1978] or Gehani [1985, 1988].

The reader familiar with concurrent programming will find this book a good introduction to Concurrent C and its facilities. The reader who has had to write concurrent programs in a sequential programming language will quickly appreciate the value of the parallel programming facilities. For example, a typical way to do concurrent programming with a sequential language is to use operating system calls to create processes and to pass messages between processes. We have found that a Concurrent C program can take an order of magnitude less code than an equivalent sequential program which uses operating system calls.

4. Notation

We shall use the constant-width (typewriter) font for C program fragments and the italic font for emphasis, abstract instructions and syntactic terms (e.g., *divide and conquer* strategy, *print error message* and *declarations*). Using the constant-width font for C program fragments conforms with "C style" [Kernighan & Ritchie 1978]. Also, we will often present Concurrent C source files by enclosing them in a box, with a tag indicating the file name, as in

```
                                                           File: hello.cc
#include <stdio.h>
main()
{
    printf("Hello, world\n");
}
```

Finally, sometimes we use a smaller point size to ensure that a program component fits on the current page instead of "floating" over to the next page.

5. Preparation of the Book

This book was prepared using the extensive document preparation tools such as *pic* (preprocessor for drawing figures), *tbl* (preprocessor for making tables), *eqn* (preprocessor for formatting equations), *mm* (collection of *troff* macros for page layout) and *troff* (formatter), which are available on the UNIX operating system.

6. Acknowledgments

We would like to thank the early users of Concurrent C for their helpful comments (and patience!); these include A. S. Krishnakumar, B. Smith-Thomas, H. Townsend, V. Wallentine, and N. S. Woo. We would also like to thank B. Stroustrup letting us use *cfront* (the C++ to C translator) as the basis for our Concurrent C to C translator, and R. F. Cmelik for modifying *cfront* and for implementing the Concurrent C run-time library. And finally, we would like to thank the people who read a draft of this book, including S. Arevalo, R. F. Cmelik, I. J. Cox, A. R. Feuer, G. J. Dafni, S. Lally, E. D. Petajan, V. E. Wallentine, and N. S. Woo.

Murray Hill, NJ 07974   Narain Gehani
January 1989   William D. Roome

Chapter 1

Basics

Concurrent programming is essential for the efficient utilization of multiprocessor architectures. It is notationally convenient and conceptually elegant when writing systems in which many events occur concurrently. Just as the lack of recursion in FORTRAN discourages FORTRAN programmers from inventing recursive solutions, a programming language that lacks concurrent programming facilities discourages programmers from inventing concurrent solutions for their problems. Besides Concurrent C, several other languages provide high-level concurrent programming facilities, e.g., Concurrent Pascal, Concurrent Euclid, Modula-2 and Ada.

We assume that you are familiar with the C language because in this book we will describe only the Concurrent C extensions to C. If you are not familiar with C, we suggest that you read Appendix D before proceeding. In this chapter we will gradually introduce you to concurrent programming in Concurrent C by means of simple examples.

1. Processes

A Concurrent C program consists of one or more processes. Processes are the building blocks of concurrent programs. Each process is a sequential program component that has its own "flow-of-control," or "thread-of-execution," and has its own stack and machine registers. In theory, these processes all execute in parallel. In reality, if there is only one physical processor, then only one process will be able to run at any given time; an underlying scheduler multiplexes the processor among the processes. That is, the scheduler runs one process for a while, then suspends it and saves its state e.g., program counter and registers, and then picks another process and lets it run for a while. The details of the scheduling policy—how long a process can run, which process runs next, etc.—are left to the implementation.

Processes can actually run in parallel if the Concurrent C program is run on a multiprocessor system. In some multiprocessor implementations, each processor is shared among a set of processes, and each processor has its own scheduler. Again, this depends on the implementation; a different implementation could dedicate one processor to each process.

For now, the important things to remember are (a) you should think of all the processes as running in parallel, and (b) the Concurrent C implementation handles scheduling of these processes.

When a Concurrent C program starts executing, there is only one active process. This process is called the `main` process and it calls function `main`. Thus the simplest Concurrent C program is also an ordinary C program:

File: `hello.cc`

```
#include <stdio.h>
main()
{
    printf("Hello, world\n");
}
```

This program just prints "Hello, world" on standard output. The `main` process terminates when the `main` function returns, thus terminating the Concurrent C program.

The Concurrent C compiler on the UNIX system [AT&T UNIX 1983; Berkeley UNIX 1983] is named `CCC`. Its compiler options are like those of the C compiler. Concurrent C files must have the suffix `.cc` and the object files produced by `CCC` have the suffix `..o`. Like the C compiler, the executable file produced by `CCC` is named `a.out`. The above program, which is stored in the file `hello.cc`, can be compiled and executed with the following commands:

```
$ CCC hello.cc
$ a.out
Hello, world
$
```

Note that the character `$` is the UNIX system prompt.

Let us now look at the following program in which the `main` process creates another process which also prints messages:

File: `printer1.cc`

```
#include <stdio.h>

process spec printer();      /* process type */
process body printer()       /* process body */
{
    printf("Hi from printer process\n");
}

main()
{
    printf("Hi from main\n");
    create printer();
    printf("Bye from main\n");
}
```

The `create` operator, in this program, creates a new process of type `printer`. This new process executes the statements in its body and becomes eligible to run—that is, it can start executing—immediately after the `create` operator is executed. Thus if the scheduler runs the new process as soon as it is created, this Concurrent C program will print

```
Hi from main
Hi from printer process
Bye from main
```

However, if the newly created process does not run immediately, the program will print

```
Hi from main
Bye from main
Hi from printer process
```

Both outputs are correct. In theory, the last two lines could be scrambled on a character-by-character basis. That is, the `main` process might print a few characters, then the `printer` process might print a few characters, and so on until they finish. In practice, that does not happen because most implementations allow `printf` to write its output as a single atomic action.

The `printer` process terminates when it runs off the end of its body. As before, the `main` process terminates when the `main` function returns. The Concurrent C program terminates when both of these processes terminate, i.e., when no processes are left.

The `printer` process is a child of the `main` process because it is created by the `main` process; the `main` process is its parent. All processes with the same parent are called siblings. When a Concurrent C program starts, the `main` process is the only active process, so it must create all processes in the program, either directly or indirectly.

The definition of the `printer` process consists of two parts: a *type* (or *specification*) and a *body* (or *implementation*). A process definition consists of two parts to simplify construction and maintenance of large programs. The process type is the public part of a process definition. Only the information specified in the process type is visible to other processes. The process type contains all the information necessary to create and interact with processes of this type. A process body contains the code that is executed by each process of the associated type. Internal details of a process body are of no relevance to other processes.

A *process* is the instantiation of a process definition. Thus a process definition is Concurrent C code, while a process itself is an active entity that executes this code. It helps to draw an analogy between processes in Concurrent C and functions in sequential C. A process body is similar to a function body and a process type is similar to a function declaration (e.g., a declaration that the function `malloc` returns a value of type `char *`). A process body is a passive, static entity, just as a function body is a static block of code. There is only one process body for each process type in a program, just as there is only one function body for each function, and this process body exists for the life of the program. A process is an instantiation of a process type: that is, a process is a flow-of-control that executes the statements in a process body. A process is analogous to an activation, or call, of a function. Thus a process is a dynamic entity; processes can be created and they can terminate, just as functions can be called and they can return. There can be many processes of the same type, just as there can be many activations of a recursive function. The distinction between a process and a process definition is important when several processes of the same type are created. But when the meaning is clear, we will use "process" to refer to either a process definition or to an instance of a process definition.

A process body can have variable declarations; as in a function, each process gets its own copy of these variables. Functions, such as `printf`, can be called from a process body. The function is considered to be executing on behalf of this process (here we mean "instance of a process").

2. Process Parameters

A process can have parameters; they are used to pass information to the process when it is created, so that this information is available to the new process when it starts execution. Process parameters behave very much like function parameters, and are also passed by value.

A process does not return information to its parent upon completion. If a process must pass information to its parent process, or, in general, if two processes have to exchange information, then they must use transactions. Transactions are discussed later, but for now let us take a further look at our previous example.

Suppose that we have created two instances of the printer process. Then they will print identical output, and we will not be able to tell which was which. We can distinguish the outputs of the two processes by printing an identifying number along with the message. In the following example, the parent process provides such an identification number as a process argument when it creates a printer process:

File: `printer2.cc`

```
#include <stdio.h>

process spec printer(int id);
process body printer(id)
{
    printf("Hi from printer process %d\n", id);
}

main()
{
    process printer p0, p1;

    printf("Hi from main\n");
    p0 = create printer(0);
    p1 = create printer(1);
    printf("Bye from main\n");
}
```

Executing the above program produces the following output:

```
Hi from main
Hi from printer process 0
Bye from main
Hi from printer process 1
```

In the above program, the printer process' parameter is called id and it's type int. This parameter can be used as an ordinary variable within the body of the process—just as a function parameter can be used as an ordinary variable within the body of the function.

This program illustrates a new feature. The main process declares two variables, p0 and p1, of type process printer. These are process variables, and they can hold process values, or "process ids," for any process of type `printer`. The `create` operator returns a process id every time it creates a process. The `main` process saves the two process ids returned by the `create` operator in p0 and p1. A process id can be used to interact with a process, as we will show in the next section. A process id can also be used to abort a process, change its priority, determine its status, etc.

3. Process Interaction and Transaction Calls

Processes interact by means of *transactions*. Such an interaction involves two processes. One process initiates the interaction and is called the *caller*. The initiating process waits for the interaction, and is called the *receiver*. Sometimes we call these processes the *client* and *server*, because the two processes often play these roles. The interaction is called a *transaction call*.

There are two types of transactions: *synchronous* and *asynchronous* transactions. In a synchronous transaction, the caller sends some data to the receiver, and waits for the receiver to accept this transaction. Eventually the receiver does this, performs some actions, and returns some data to the caller. At this point the caller resumes execution. Thus a synchronous transaction involves both synchronization between two processes and a bi-directional exchange of information between them. The following "time-line" diagram illustrates what happens during a synchronous transaction call; a solid line indicates that the process is running while a dotted line indicates that it is waiting:

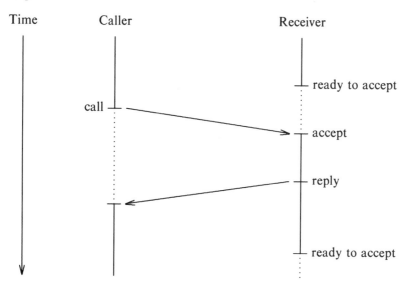

Note that even if a synchronous transaction does not return a value—that is, even for a `void`-valued transaction—the caller still waits for the called process to accept and complete the transaction call.

In an asynchronous transaction, the caller sends information to the receiver and continues. The caller does not wait for the receiver to accept the transaction and manipulate the data sent; the caller also does not get back any data. Thus an asynchronous transaction involves a uni-directional exchange of information and does not involve synchronization. In this chapter, we will describe synchronous transactions; asynchronous transactions are described later.

For each type of transaction, the receiver's process type defines both the data that the caller sends to the receiver and the data that the receiver returns to the caller. The process type also gives a name for each transaction. In general, each transaction corresponds to some type of service which the receiving process can perform when requested by a calling process. To illustrate transaction calls, we will modify our printer process so that it accepts print-string requests (transactions). Here is the revised process type:

File: `printer3.h`

```
process spec printer(int id)
{
    trans void print(char *msg);
};
```

This specification says that a process of type `printer` can accept one type of transaction, `print` that has one `char *` parameter; the `void` result type specifies that `print` does not return a value to the caller.

Here is the rest of this program:

File: `printer3.cc`

```
#include "printer3.h"
main()
{
    process printer p0, p1;       /*process ids  */
    p0 = create printer(0);       /*create procs,*/
    p1 = create printer(1);       /*and save ids */
    p0.print("Good Morning!");    /*call trans   */
    p1.print("Good Morning!");
    p0.print("");
    p1.print("");
}

process body printer(id)
{
    for(;;)
        accept print(msg) {
            if (*msg == 0)        /*if msg is "",*/
                break;            /*stop process */
            printf("%d: %s\n", id, msg);
        }
}
```

The output produced by this program is

```
0: Good Morning!
1: Good Morning!
```

As in our previous example, the `main` process creates two `printer` processes and saves their process ids in the variables `p0` and `p1`. Next, the `main` process uses these variables to call the `print` transactions of the two `printer` processes (lines 7-10). A transaction call is similar to a function call except that the function name is of the form *pid.tname*, where *pid* is a process id, and *tname* is a transaction name. After the `main` process issues a transaction call, it is made to wait until the `printer` process accepts and completes the transaction call.

A transaction call specifies values for the transaction's parameters. Like function arguments, transaction arguments are passed by value. Unlike function calls, the number and types of the arguments in a transaction call must match the number and types of the transaction parameters as declared in the process type. In general, a transaction call can be used wherever a function call with the same return value type can be used.

The `printer` process accepts a transaction call by executing an *accept* statement. This statement has the form

> `accept` *transaction-name* (*parameter-name-list*)
> *statement*

statement can be a simple or a compound statement; we call it the *body* of the *accept* statement.

Each `print` transaction call in the `main` process *synchronizes* with the corresponding *accept* statement in the `printer` process. The first process to arrive at the synchronization point waits for the other to arrive. When this happens, the `printer` process executes the body of the *accept* statement. Within the body of the *accept* statement, the `msg` parameter is a local variable, and its initial value is the value of the argument supplied by the caller. After the `printer` process exits the body of the *accept* statement, which it does by either executing the *break* statement or by running off the end of the *accept* body, both it and the `main` process can resume executing independently.

In this example, the transaction does not return a result. If a transaction returns a result, then the *treturn* statement must be used in the corresponding *accept* statement to return the result. The *treturn* statement also completes execution of the *accept* statement.

Note that we put the process type in a separate file, called `printer3.h`. Because this was a small program, we put the bodies of the `main` process (the `main` function, to be precise) and the `printer` process in one file. Had these processes been more complicated, it would have been more appropriate to put their bodies in separate files, say `printer3.cc`, and `main3.cc`. Both of these files would then include `printer3.h`: `main3.cc` because it calls `printer` processes, and `printer3.cc` because it contains the body for the `printer` process. Files `printer3.cc` and `main3.cc` can then be separately compiled and linked together to produce the executable file `a.out`:

```
$ CCC -c printer3.cc
$ CCC -c main3.cc
$ CCC printer3..o main3..o
$ a.out
0: Good Morning!
1: Good Morning!
```

4. Process Declarations

In the previous section, we gave an informal description of processes. Now we will give a more formal definition of the syntax of process types, transaction declarations, and process bodies.

4.1 Process Type (Specification)

A process type (specification) has the form[1]

> process spec *process-type-name*(*parameter-declarations$_{opt}$*)
>   {*transaction-declarations*}$_{opt}$;

parameter-declarations is a comma-separated list of parameter declarations, as in

> process spec multiplexor(int number, int max);

The names in the parameter declarations are optional, but recommended; mnemonic names can improve readability by indicating the purpose of each parameter. Although not required, it is a good idea to have the names in the process type match those in the corresponding process body.

Sometimes we will refer to the process type as a process specification because it specifies the interface for processes of this type.

4.2 Transaction Declarations

As mentioned earlier, Concurrent C processes interact by means of transactions. A process type must contain a transaction declaration for each of the process' transactions. A transaction declaration is like a function declaration except that it is preceded by the keyword trans, and its parameters are explicitly declared. The form of a transaction declaration is

> trans *return-type tname*(*parameter-declarations$_{opt}$*) ;

tname is the name of the transaction being declared; In case of a synchronous transaction, *return-type* specifies the type of the value returned by the transaction; in case of an asynchronous transaction, *return-type* is the keyword async (an asynchronous transaction does not return a value). *parameter-declarations* consists of a comma-separated list of parameter declarations. The parameters are the data that a caller gives to the called process; the return type is the type of the value that the called process returns to the caller. As with process parameters, transaction parameter names are optional but recommended.

A transaction name is only meaningful in the context of a specific process type. The same transaction name can be used in several process types, and these transactions can have different argument types and different return value types.

---

1. Subscript *opt* associated with an item indicates that the item is optional.

4.3 Process Bodies

A process body has the form

> `process body` *process-type-name* (*parameter-names$_{opt}$*)
> *compound-statement*

The process body specifies the statements to be executed by each process of the associated process type. Each process is a sequential program component that runs independently and in parallel with other processes. The process body is a compound statement, and it can have automatic variables; each process of that type receives its own set of variables. *parameter-names* is a comma-separated list of names of the parameters of this process. The number of names must match the number of process parameters declared in the process type. These process parameters behave like local variables in the process body, and have the types given in the process type. The initial values of the process parameters are those given as arguments when the process is created.

Process bodies can contain any legal C statement, plus Concurrent C extensions, such as *accept* and *select* statements, which are described later. Functions can be called from a process body; the function is considered to be executing on behalf of the process.

A process can terminate in three ways: either by running off the end of the process body, by executing the *return* statement, or by executing the *terminate* alternative.

5. Process Creation

The `create` operator creates (instantiates) a new process. The created process is called a *child* process of the creating, or *parent*, process. Processes that have the same parent process are called *sibling* processes. The `create` operator has the general form

> `create` *process-type-name* (*arguments$_{opt}$*)
> `priority(` *p* `)`$_{opt}$ `processor(` *n* `)`$_{opt}$

where *arguments* is a comma-separated list of expressions. The `create` operator returns a process identifier value (process id) that identifies the created process.

Process arguments are passed by value. The number of arguments and their types must match the number of parameters and their types as specified in the process specification.

The optional `priority` clause specifies that the new process' priority is to be *p* (an integer expression). A positive *p* gives the new process a higher priority; a negative *p* gives it a lower priority. If the priority is not specified, the new process is assigned priority zero.

The optional `processor` clause specifies that the new process is to be assigned to processor *n* (an integer expression). This applies only to multiprocessor implementations, and is ignored by the uniprocessor implementations. If omitted, the implementation can assign the new process to any available processor. Chapter 3 contains more details about process priorities and processor assignments.

6. Process Values and Process Ids

The `create` operator returns a *process value* identifying the newly created process. A process value is an identifier (id), or an alias, for a specific process. A process value can be stored in a process variable of the same type, as in

```
process printer b;
b = create printer(6);
```

Concurrent C programs can have arrays of process ids, structures whose members are process ids, or pointers to process ids, as in

```
process printer prtarr[10], *pprt;
```

If the same process id is stored in several process variables, then all of these variables refer to the same process. Provided the types match, process ids can be used in the following ways:

- As arguments to functions, transactions, or processes.
- As values returned by functions or transactions.
- In assignment to process variables.
- In equality or inequality tests.

7. Producer-Consumer Example

So much for formal descriptions; it is time for another example. We will present a Concurrent C program which reads data, transforms it and then prints the results. For this example, the data is a stream of characters, and the transformation converts lower-case letters to upper-case letters. The purpose of the example is to show how to connect processes together, not how to do interesting transformations.

The Concurrent C program will be structured as follows: one process, called the "producer", reads the data from the standard input and sends it to another process, called the "consumer". The consumer process converts the data to upper case and then prints it on the standard output. This problem is an example of a general class of problems often called "producer-consumer" problems.

This chapter presents two versions of this program. In the first version, the producer process uses a synchronous transaction to send the data directly to the consumer process without any intermediate data buffering. The second version uses an extra process to buffer the transfer of data from the producer process to the consumer process.

Chapter 2 presents a third version, which uses asynchronous transactions. However, that version is considerably more complicated than either of the versions presented here.

7.1 Synchronous Producer-Consumer Solution

The synchronous solution to this producer-consumer problem can be described pictorially as

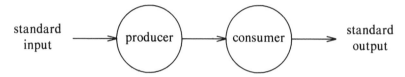

The solution has two process types, `consumer` and `producer`. The `consumer` process has one transaction, `send`, which the `producer` process calls to send one character to the `consumer`:

	File: pc-sync.h

```
process spec consumer()
{
    trans void send(int c);
};
process spec producer(process consumer cons);
```

Here is the rest of the program:

```
#include <stdio.h>
#include "ctype.h"    /*for islower(), toupper()*/
#include "pc-sync.h"
process body producer(cons)
{
    int c;
    while ((c = getchar()) != EOF)
        cons.send(c);
    cons.send(EOF);
}
process body consumer()
{
    int xc;
    for (;;) {
        accept send(c)
            xc = c;
        if (xc == EOF)
            break;
        if (islower(xc))
            xc = toupper(xc);
        putchar(xc);
    }
}
main()
{
    create producer(create consumer());
}
```

The main process creates the consumer and producer processes; it also passes the id of the consumer process to the producer process so that the producer process knows the id of the process to which it must send the data. The producer process reads characters from the standard input, and sends each character to the consumer process by calling its send transaction. The consumer process accepts each call by executing an *accept* statement. The consumer process saves the character sent by the producer process in a variable and exits the body of the accept statement, which allows the producer to continue. The consumer then converts the character to upper case (if appropriate) and outputs it. Notice that while the producer reads the next character, the consumer process transforms and prints the previous character.

Note that the value passed between the processes is declared to be an integer, not a character. The reason is that the value EOF is defined as −1. We use integers so that EOF will be distinct from the legal character codes.

The two processes synchronize on each character: the transaction call in the producer process synchronizes with the *accept* statement in the consumer process. Thus the two processes run in lock-step; the producer process cannot get more than one character ahead of the consumer process.

In the consumer process, we put the putchar call outside the body of the *accept* statement. If we had placed it inside, the producer process would wait until the output was completed. This would reduce parallelism, because the producer process would not be able to read input while the consumer process was writing output. Of course, in this program, the increase in parallelism is trivial. But this is not always the case. For example, suppose that putchar writes directly to the output device, and that it waits until that device has accepted the output character. In this case, a putchar call could take a significantly longer.

Consequently, to maximize parallelism, it is best to design a process to minimize the time it takes to accept a transaction call, and to minimize the time it spends executing the statements in the body of each *accept* statement. The body should contain only those statements that require the calling process to wait. For example, in some cases it may be sufficient just to copy the parameter values into variables global to the *accept* statement.

7.2 Buffered Producer-Consumer Solution

In our synchronous producer-consumer solution, the two processes operate in lock-step, in that the speed of one process depends upon the speed of the other process. For example, the producer process cannot pass a large number of characters to the consumer process in quick succession. The producer process must wait for the consumer process to convert and print each character before it can send the next character. We can decouple the interaction between the two processes by interposing a "buffer" process between these two processes:

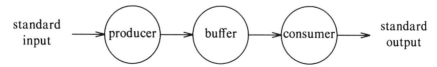

The arrows indicate the direction of data flow. The direction of transaction calls is shown below:

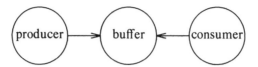

The sole purpose of the `buffer` process is to take characters from one process and give them to another process. Now the `consumer` process cannot slow down the `producer` process; the `producer` is free to read more characters and put them into the buffer. If the `producer` process slows down after sending a large number of characters, the `consumer` process can keep on processing the buffered characters.

This buffering is helpful only if the two processes run at the same average speed, but their speeds vary a lot from this average. Buffering allows one process to run at full speed while the other is temporarily running slowly, and vice versa. Buffering will not be of much help if the `producer` process has a higher average speed than the `consumer` process, because the buffer will just fill up. The `buffer` process smooths the variations in speed of two processes. The amount of smoothing depends upon the size of the buffer; the larger the buffer, the more smoothing. This is an example of a trade-off between memory and execution speed.

One final comment: buffering does not come for free; the extra process does take up some CPU cycles. The advantages of buffering may not be apparent in this simple example. However, in many applications, the cost of buffering will be small compared to the advantages of decoupling two interacting processes.

Here is the specification of the process that manages the buffer:

File: `buffer.h`

```
process spec buffer(int max)
{
    trans void put(int c);
    trans int get();
};
```

The `buffer` process has two transactions:

    `put:`   This transaction puts a character into the buffer. If the buffer is full, this transaction is not accepted until space becomes available.

    `get:`   This transaction takes a character from the buffer and returns it. If the buffer is empty, this transaction is not accepted until a character is available.

The direction of information transfer is independent of which process makes the transaction call. For example, the process calling transaction `put` sends information to the buffer process while the process calling get gets information from the buffer process.

The buffer process implements a circular buffer:

```
                                                File: buffer.cc
#include "buffer.h"

process body buffer(max)
{
    int *buf;       /*circular buffer of size max*/
    int n = 0;      /*number of chars in buffer*/
    int in = 0;     /*index of next empty slot*/
    int out = 0;    /*index of next character*/
    char *malloc();

    buf = (int*) malloc(max*sizeof(int));
    for (;;)
        select {
            (n < max):
                accept put(c)
                    buf[in] = c;
                in = (in + 1) % max;
                n++;
        or
            (n > 0):
                accept get()
                    treturn buf[out];
                out = (out + 1) % max;
                n--;
        }
}
```

The buffer process allocates space for the buffer, and then repeatedly executes a *select* statement. This statement has two alternatives, separated by the keyword or. Each alternative starts with a Boolean test and is followed by an *accept* statement. The Boolean test is called a *guard* and it gives the conditions under which that alternative can be chosen. For example, the guard for the first alternative is true whenever the buffer process has space to store a character, and the guard for the second alternative is true whenever the buffer process has characters to give out.

When the above *select* statement is executed, it selects one of the alternatives, executes all statements in that alternative, and skips the other alternative. For an *accept* alternative to be selected, (a) its guard must be true and (b) there must be a pending transaction call which satisfies the leading *accept* statement.

If both alternatives are eligible, the *select* statement picks one non-deterministically. If both guards are true but no transaction calls are waiting, the *select* statement waits for the first call of either type.

Initially the buffer is empty, and only the first guard is true. Consequently, the *select* statement waits for a `put` transaction call to arrive, and then executes the first alternative. This alternative accepts the call, saves the character in the buffer, and updates the indexes. The `buffer` process then loops back and executes the *select* statement again. Now both guards are true, so it waits for the next `put` or `get` transaction call to arrive.

In general, a *select* statement can have an arbitrary number of alternatives, not just two alternatives as shown here. Furthermore, it can wait for events other than the arrival of a transaction call. In Chapter 2 we will give more information about the *select* statement.

Here are the specification and the body of the `producer` process:

File: `producer.h`

```
process spec producer(process buffer buf);
```

File: `producer.cc`

```
#include <stdio.h>
#include "buffer.h"
#include "producer.h"
process body producer(buf)
{
    int c;

    while ((c = getchar()) != EOF)
        buf.put(c);
    buf.put(EOF);
}
```

This `producer` process is similar to the one shown before, except that its parameter is now the id of a `buffer` process. The `producer` process does not interact with the `consumer` process directly, and in fact does not even know which process (or processes) are consuming the data it gives to the `buffer` process.

Here are the specification and the body of the `consumer` process:

File: `consumer.h`

```
process spec consumer(process buffer buf);
```

File: consumer.cc

```
#include <stdio.h>
#include "ctype.h"
#include "buffer.h"
#include "consumer.h"
process body consumer(buf)
{
    int c;

    while ((c = buf.get()) != EOF) {
        if (islower(c))
            c = toupper(c);
        putchar(c);
    }
}
```

The differences between this version of the consumer process and the previous version are that this version has one parameter (the id of the buffer process) and that it does not have any transactions; instead, now the consumer process gets the characters by calling transaction get of the buffer process.

Note that the buffer process can be classified as a "server" process because its only role is to "service" the requests of the "client" producer and consumer processes.

The main process now creates three processes, and passes the id of the buffer process as a parameter to the other two processes:

File: pc-main.cc

```
#include "buffer.h"
#include "producer.h"
#include "consumer.h"
#define BUFFER_SIZE 32
main()
{
    process buffer buf;

    buf = create buffer(BUFFER_SIZE);
    create consumer(buf);
    create producer(buf);
}
```

We have placed the source for the various processes in separate files to illustrate techniques for maintaining large concurrent programs. For a simple

program like this, it does not make much difference. But such techniques can
be very helpful for large programs which have tens of process types, each of
which provides five or ten different transactions and has hundreds of lines of
code.

There is one problem with this example: the program never terminates because
the buffer process never terminates. After the producer and
consumer processes get an end-of-file (EOF) and terminate, the Concurrent
C run-time system will print a diagnostic saying that the program has
"deadlocked", i.e., the program has not terminated but it cannot proceed
further. In fact, here is the diagnostic output produced by one Concurrent C
implementation as a result of running the buffered version of the producer-
consumer program (a.out is the name of the executable file):[2]

```
a.out: deadlocked
_Null/10000:
          parent    _Null/10000
          child     main/20001 _Null/10000
          prty      -2147483648
          state     current ready
main/20001:
          parent    _Null/10000
          child     buffer/30002
          state     completed
buffer/30002:
          parent    main/20001
          state     wait-event put()
```

This diagnostic output says that the buffer process is waiting for a put
call, and the main process is waiting for the buffer process to complete.

We will present a general process-termination mechanism in the next chapter.
But it is easy to fix the above program so that the buffer process terminates.
All we need to do is to modify it to terminate after the get transaction returns
EOF.

---

2. The _Null process is a low priority process which is part of our Concurrent C
    implementation's run-time system; it runs when no other processes are active.

8. Shared Memory Hazards

In some implementations of Concurrent C, processes can use shared memory to communicate—they reference the same global variables or they use pointers that refer to the same locations. However, remember that this depends on the implementation. An implementation that does not provide shared memory will still allow processes to refer to global variables—but each process might have its own copy of these "global" variables. Consequently, although you might think that you are sharing data by referring to the same variables, you are actually using different variables that happen to have the same names.

Even if you have shared memory, you must use it with care. As an example, consider two processes that reference and update the same variable:

File: shared.cc

```
#include <stdio.h>
int x = 0;
process spec share(int id);
process body share(id)
{
    x = x + 2;
    printf("%d: x = %d\n", id, x);
}
main()
{
    create share(0);
    create share(1);
}
```

The desired output of this program is probably

```
0: x = 2
1: x = 4
```

However, depending on how the processes are scheduled, we could also get

```
0: x = 2
1: x = 2
```

or

```
0: x = 4
1: x = 4
```

Which scenario occurs depends upon how the two processes execute. Suppose process 0 fetches the value of x, which is 0, stores it in a register, and then increments the register by 2 (remember that each process has its own set of registers; the scheduler saves and restores them when it switches among processes). But before process 0 can store the register back into **x**, suppose that it is interrupted by the scheduler and suspended. The scheduler then runs process 1. Process 1 fetches the value of **x**, which is 0, increments it by 2, stores 2 back in **x**, and completes execution. Now process 0 is rescheduled. It stores the value in its register in **x**, and completes. The result is that x has the value 2 instead of 4.

Shared memory can be beneficial because it avoids copying large amounts of data between processes. However, shared memory accessed by multiple processes can lead to inconsistent results. To avoid inconsistencies, some synchronization mechanism must be used. Chapter 2 gives some examples of how to construct such synchronization mechanisms in Concurrent C.

If only one process references and updates each global variable (either directly or through function calls), then things will work as you expect. Thus a process can use global variables for accessing large amounts of data or to communicate with the functions that it calls. For example, in the following program, process `itemManager` calls the `qsort` function to sort an array of items; this array is shared by `itemManager` and `qsort`:

File: `item-mngr.cc`

```
typedef struct {      /*item: key and value*/
    int   key, value;
} ITEM;
int   Nitems;
ITEM Items[1000];

process spec itemManager();
process body itemManager()
{
    read items into array Items;
    set Nitems to number of items;
    qsort(Items,Nitems,sizeof(ITEM),cmpitems);
    process the sorted array;
}

main()
{
    create itemManager();
}
```

Function `cmpitems` compares two items, say a and b, of type `ITEM` and returns −1, 0 or 1 depending upon whether a is less than, equal to, or greater than b, respectively.

Note that if the `main` process also accesses the array `Items`, or calls a function which does, the results will depend on the Concurrent C implementation. If the implementation provides shared memory, then they will see the same array. However, if the implementation does not provide shared memory, then the `main` process will see another array, which does not have the values set by the `itemManager` process. Of course, you will get even stranger results if the `main` process creates two instances of the `itemManager` process.

Consequently, you can get surprising results if you do not use shared memory carefully. For now, the moral is

> **Be very careful if you share variables between processes!**

9. Program Organization Suggestions

In any Concurrent C program, a process specification must precede

a. the corresponding process body,
b. any call of one of that process' transactions (except those made by using transaction pointers which are discussed later),
c. any declaration or definition which uses that process specification, or
d. any attempt to create a process of that type.

The process body must exist in some file that is compiled with the program, but other processes do not need to see the body. A common technique is to put the specification for a process in one file, and its body in a separate file. All files which use the process type include its specification file, as does the file containing the process body. The file containing the process body can be compiled separately.

10. Examples

10.1 The Betting Processes

Normally, Concurrent C requires that all objects be declared or defined before they can be used. There is one exception to this rule. To allow two processes (whether of the same type or of different types) to call each other's transactions, a process type can be used within its own declaration, and variables and parameters can be declared as process values for some as yet undefined process type. The following example illustrates the former situation which occurs when two processes, of the same type, call each other's transactions.

We will write a Concurrent C program to model a very simple two-person betting game. Each person is modeled as a process of type `bettor`. The two processes take turns betting. To place a bet, one process calls the other with its bet. A player's bet is his opponent's last bet plus a random number between 1 and 100, provided the total does not exceed the player's betting limit. If it does, the player gives 0 as a bet, signifying that he has lost. One process is designated as the first bettor, and initially calls the other with a bet of 1. After this, the processes alternate between waiting for the next bet (waiting for a transaction call) and placing a bet (making a transaction call). The processes continue until one of them places a bet of 0. The first bettor prints the results.

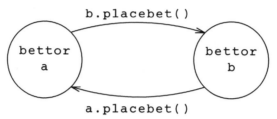

Here is the specification of the `bettor` process. Notice how the process type `bettor` is used within its definition to specify the type of transaction `playwith`'s parameter:

```
                                                    File: bettor.h
process spec bettor(int first, int limit)
{
    trans void playwith(process bettor player);
    trans void placebet(int bet);
};
```

Here is the body of the `bettor` process:

File: `bettor.cc`

```
#include "bettor.h"
process body bettor(first, limit)
{
    int mybet = 1, hisbet = 1;
    process bettor opponent;

    accept playwith(player)
        opponent = player;
    if (first)
        opponent.placebet(mybet);
    while (mybet > 0 && hisbet > 0) {
        accept placebet(bet)
            hisbet = bet;
        if (hisbet > 0) {
            mybet = hisbet + 1 + rand()%100;
            if (mybet > limit)
                mybet = 0;
            opponent.placebet(mybet);
        }
    }
    if (first)
        if (mybet > 0)
            printf("I won; last bet %d\n",mybet);
        else
            printf("I lost; last bet %d\n",hisbet);
}
```

Finally, here is the `main` process:

File: `bet-main.cc`

```
#include "bettor.h"
#define BETTING_LMT 1000
#define FIRST_PLAYER  0

main()
{
    process bettor a, b;
    srand(time(0));      /* set seed for rand() */
    a=create bettor(FIRST_PLAYER==0,BETTING_LMT);
    b=create bettor(FIRST_PLAYER==1,BETTING_LMT);
    a.playwith(b); b.playwith(a);
}
```

Although we have shown you a very simple example of a game playing program, this program structure can be used for implementing more sophisticated game playing programs. For example, you can use this structure to make a chess program play against itself; alternatively, you can make variations of chess programs play against each other to try out different game playing strategies.

10.2 The Mortal Dining Philosophers

Five philosophers spend their lives eating spaghetti and thinking [Dijkstra 1971, Gehani 1984a]. They eat at a circular table in a dining room. The table has five chairs around it and chair number i has been assigned to philosopher number i $(0 \leqslant i \leqslant 4)$. Five forks have also been laid out on the table so that there is precisely one fork between every two adjacent chairs. Consequently there is one fork to the left of each chair and one to its right. Fork number i is to the left of chair number i. Before eating, a philosopher must enter the dining room and sit in the chair assigned to her. Each philosopher must have two forks to eat (the forks placed to the left and right of every chair). If a philosopher cannot get two forks immediately, then she must wait until she can get them. The forks are picked up one at a time. When a philosopher has finished eating (after a finite amount of time), she puts the forks down and leaves the room.

Each of the five philosophers and five forks is implemented as a process. On activation, each `philosopher` process is given an identification number (0-4), and the process ids of her `fork` processes. Each philosopher is mortal and passes on to the next world soon after having eaten 100,000 times (about three times a day for 90 years).

The specifications of the `philosopher` and `fork` processes are

File: `fork.h`

```
process spec fork()
{
    trans void pickUp(), putDown();
};
```

File: `phil.h`

```
process spec philosopher(int id,
                         process fork left,
                         process fork right);
```

The body of the `fork` process is

File: `fork.cc`

```
#include "fork.h"
process body fork()
{
    for (;;) {
        accept pickUp();
        accept putDown();
    }
}
```

The body of the `philosopher` process is

File: `phil.cc`

```
#include "fork.h"
#include "phil.h"
#define LIMIT 100000
process body philosopher(id, left, right)
{
    int nmeal;
    for (nmeal = 0; nmeal < LIMIT; nmeal++) {
        /*think; then enter dining room */
        /*pick up forks*/
          right.pickUp(); left.pickUp();
        /*eat*/
          printf("Phil. %d: *burp*\n", id);
        /*put down forks*/
          left.putDown(); right.putDown();
        /*get up and leave dining room*/
    }
    printf("Phil. %d: That's all, folks!\n", id);
}
```

Finally, the `main` process is

File: `dining.cc`
```
#include "fork.h"
#include "phil.h"
main()
{
   process fork f[5]; int j;
 /*create forks, then create philosophers*/
   for (j = 0; j < 5; j++)
      f[j] = create fork();
   for (j = 0; j < 5; j++)
      create philosopher(j, f[j], f[(j+1) % 5]);
}
```

The program given above will deadlock if each philosopher picks up one fork. One way of avoiding this deadlock is to allow at most four philosophers to sit at the table at any given time. This can be enforced by a gatekeeper process.

Note that the program will not terminate because the `fork` processes do not terminate. The Concurrent C run-time system may print a "deadlock diagnostic" because after the philosophers die, no further execution is possible. We will discuss a mechanism that simplifies process termination in the next chapter.

10.3 Parallel Quicksort

Consider the following sequential `quicksort` [Hoare 1962] function:

File: `quicksort.c`
```
void quicksort(a, lb, ub)
   float a[];
   int lb, ub;
{
   int i, j;
   float temp;
   void partition();

   if (ub-lb == 1 && a[ub] < a[lb]) {
      temp = a[lb]; a[lb] = a[ub]; a[ub] = temp;
   } else if (ub-lb > 1) {
      partition(a, lb, ub, &i, &j);
      quicksort(a, lb, j); quicksort(a, i, ub);
   }
}
```

The problem is to write a parallel version of `quicksort` in which the two recursive calls to `quicksort` are executed in parallel. Note that these two recursive calls operate on disjoint portions of the array `a`, as divided by function `partition`. The function call

```
partition(a, lb, ub, &i, &j)
```

divides array `a` with lower and upper bounds `lb` and `ub` into two partitions, left and right, such that

1. the left partition elements `a[lb]`, `a[lb+1]`, ..., `a[j]` are all less than or equal to some value r, and
2. the right partition elements `a[i]`, `a[i+1]`, ..., `a[ub]` are greater than or equal to r, and
3. `i > j`.

Here is function `partition` [Gehani 1985]:

File: `partition.cc`
```
void partition(a, lb, ub, pi, pj)
    float a[];
    int lb, ub, *pi, *pj;
{

    float r, temp;
    int i, j;

    r = a[(lb+ub)/2];      /* middle element */
    i = lb; j = ub;
    while (i <= j) {
        while (a[i] < r)
            i++;
        while (a[j] > r)
            j--;
        if (i <= j) {
            temp=a[i]; a[i]=a[j]; a[j]=temp;
            i++; j--;
        }
    }
    *pi = i; *pj = j; /*partition points*/
}
```

The two recursive calls to `quicksort` in function `parQuicksort` can be executed in parallel by creating two processes, of type `sort`, each of which calls `parQuicksort`, the parallel version of the quicksort function:

File: parQuicksort.cc

```
#include "sort.h"
void parQuicksort(a, lb, ub)
    float a[];
    int lb, ub;
{
    int i, j;
    float temp;
    process sort p, q;
    void partition();

    if (ub-lb == 1 && a[ub] < a[lb]) {
        temp = a[lb];
        a[lb] = a[ub];
        a[ub] = temp;
    } else if (ub-lb > 1) {
        partition(a, lb, ub, &i, &j);
        p = create sort(a, lb, j);
        q = create sort(a, i, ub);
        p.done(); q.done();
    }
}
```

After creating the two `sort` processes, function `parQuicksort` waits until both processes have finished. It does that by calling the transaction `done` of each process.

Now here is the specification and body of `sort`:

File: sort.h

```
process spec sort(float a[], int lb, int ub)
{
    trans void done();
};
```

File: sort.cc

```
#include "sort.h"
process body sort(a, lb, ub)
{
    parQuicksort(a, lb, ub);
    accept done();
}
```

Note that each instance of `sort` is given a pointer to the array to be sorted; the underlying assumption is that the processes share memory. There is, however, no need for synchronizing accesses to this shared memory because each `sort` process operates on a disjoint portion of the array.

11. Exercises

1. Use the Concurrent C compiler on your system to compile and execute the printer examples and the producer-consumer example.

2. In the betting processes example, information about which process was first and which was second, along with their betting limits, was passed as process parameters at process creation time. However, the transaction `playwith` was used to tell each process about who its opponent process was. Why was it necessary to use a transaction do this? Could not this information have been passed at process creation time?

3. Write a program to simulate the following game: three players pick 1, 2 or 3 coins from a pile of 20 coins. The player forced to pick up the last coin loses the game [Brinch Hansen 1986]. You should consider the following strategies for structuring the program and discuss their pros and cons:

   1. Implement the pile as a data structure that is passed around between the players.
   2. Implement the pile as a shared variable.
   3. Implement a banker who manages the pile.

   Your program should print the name of the winning player.

4. Avoid the possible deadlock in the dining philosophers program by adding a gatekeeper process, which will allow at most four philosophers to sit at the table at one time.

5. Can you think of other ways of avoiding deadlock in the dining philosophers program?

6. Modify the dining philosophers problem so that all of the processes terminate. As shown, the `fork` processes do not terminate.

7. The number of `sort` processes created in the parallel quicksort program can be large; in fact, in the worst case, the number of processes created can equal the number of elements in the array being sorted. Can you explain how this can happen? Modify the parallel quicksort to limit the number of processes that may be created.

Chapter 2

Advanced Facilities

In the first chapter we gave you a quick overview of some of the basic concurrent programming facilities provided by Concurrent C. In this chapter, we will elaborate on some of the facilities discussed in the first chapter and discuss some of the more advanced facilities.

1. Process Values and Process Management

1.1 Built-In Functions

The Concurrent C run-time system provides a number of built-in functions. Chapter 3 describes all of these functions, but there are two which we will need in this chapter. Function `c_mypid` returns the process id for the currently running process, as in

```
process body buffer( )
{
    process buffer me;
    ...
    me = c_mypid( );
    ...
}
```

Global names that start with `c_` are reserved for the Concurrent C run-time system. Users should not define process type names, function names, or global variable names that start with `c_`.

The built-in function `c_abort` kills a process and all of its descendants (its children, their children, their children's children, etc.). For example, the following function prints an error message and then terminates the calling process:

```
                                                  File: mypanic.cc
#include "concurrentc.h"
void mypanic(msg)
    char *msg;
{
    printf("mypanic called: %s\n", msg);
    c_abort(c_mypid());
}
```

Note that this function includes the header file concurrentc.h, which contains the declarations of the return-value types of the built-in functions. This header file is provided by the Concurrent C implementation.

1.2 Null Process Value

The value 0 is an invalid process value. It can be either assigned to process variables or compared to them. The header file concurrentc.h defines c_nullpid to be 0. As an example illustrating the use of the null process value, consider the following function that sometimes needs to create a server process. If it does, it kills the server before returning:

```
    ...
void dowork()
{
    process server myserv = c_nullpid;
    ...
    if (need server)
        myserv = create server();
    ...
    if (myserv != c_nullpid)
        c_abort(myserv);
}
```

In short, the null process value (0) is to process values as the null pointer value (0) is to pointer values in C.

1.3 Process Completion, Process States

Earlier we said that a process terminates by running off the end of its body. This is a slight simplification. If the process does not have any children, or if all its children have terminated, then the process does indeed terminate when it runs off the end.

However, if a process, say P, has children when it runs off the end of its body, then P does not terminate immediately. Instead, P enters the *completed* state, and it stays in this state until all of its children have terminated. When the children terminate, P finally terminates. A process in the completed state is in limbo: its process value exists as a placeholder, but it cannot be reactivated or called.

Note that c_abort forces a process to terminate by killing all of the process' children as well as the process itself. Thus if a process is in the completed state, calling c_abort on that process also kills all of its children.

1.4 Process Anytype

In Concurrent C, process values are strongly typed in that the process types must match when used in assignments, comparisons, transaction calls, etc. For example, the compiler will not allow the following:

```
process spec buffer()
   { trans void put(int c); ... };
process spec printer();
process buffer buf;
process printer prt;
...
buf = prt;        /* illegal: type mismatch */
prt.put('x');     /* illegal: trans mismatch */
```

One way around the strong type checking is to use the predefined type process anytype. This is a "wild card" process type: it is an alias for a process value of an unknown type. It is useful when the process type is not known at compile time. For example, function c_mypid is declared as

```
process anytype c_mypid();
```

In general, any specific process-valued expression can be used wherever a process anytype value is expected. Similarly, a process anytype value can be used wherever a specific process type is expected. Here are some examples:

```
process buffer buf; process anytype p;
p = buf;
...
buf = p;
```

However, a transaction call requires an explicit cast:

```
process anytype p;
...
((process buffer) p).put(c);   /* good */
p.put(c);                       /* illegal */
```

Concurrent C guarantees that a value of a specific process type can be converted to process anytype and can then be safely converted back to the original process type. However, the results of converting to some different process type are undefined.

This wild-card process type provides an escape from type checking. For example, it allows us to write a general "process name server," which maintains a table of pairs of process values and symbolic names. If we did not have the wild-card mechanism, the name server would have to know every possible process type. This would require revising the name server every time it has to handle a new process type.

2. The Delay Statement

The *delay* statement suspends the calling process for a specified time period. Other Concurrent C processes are allowed to run. This statement has the form

```
delay d;
```

The floating point expression *d* specifies the delay time, in seconds. Integer expressions are allowed and are automatically converted to floating point.

As an example, the following process controls a sign that flashes the time, temperature, and an advertisement:

File: flash-sign.cc

```
process spec display();
process body display()
{
    for(;;) {
        clear(); show_time(); delay 15.0;
        clear(); show_temp(); delay 15.0;

        clear();
        show_ad("Toaster Free With New Account");
        delay 30.0;
    }
}
```

Although you can ask for a fractional-second delays, not all implementations can provide such resolution. For example, the UNIX implementations of Concurrent C generally cannot provide a resolution of less than one second; the requested delay is rounded up to the next second. Of course, if the underlying operating system does provide fractional-second delays, then the Concurrent C implementation can provide better resolution.

Here is another example, taken from telephone switching. Process `getno` collects the number dialed by a customer. However, if the customer does not dial all the digits within the specified time limit, then `getno` cancels the call.

getno has two parameters: the number of digits needed and the time limit for the customer to dial them; it also has three transactions. The parent process of getno calls transaction result of getno to get the result; this returns either a telephone number, or else a timeout indication. Some other process calls transaction digitReady when the customer dials a number and presents the new digit. Finally, an alarm clock process calls transaction timeout if and when the time limit expires:

File: getno.cc

```
#include <concurrentc.h>
typedef struct {      /*dialed number*/
    char timeout;     /*!= 0 means got timeout*/
    char digits[10]; /*actual number*/
} telno;
process spec getno(int ndigit, float tlimit)
{
    trans telno result();
    trans void  digitReady(char d), timeout();
};
process spec alarm(process getno p, float del);

process body getno(ndigit, tlimit)
{
    telno t; int i; process alarm alarmpid;
    alarmpid = create alarm(c_mypid(), tlimit);
    i = 0; t.timeout = 0;
    while (i < ndigit && !t.timeout)
        select {
            accept digitReady(d)
                t.digits[i++] = d;
        or
            accept timeout()
                t.timeout = 1;
        }
    accept result()
        treturn t;
    if (!t.timeout)
        c_abort(alarmpid);
}
process body alarm(p, del)
{
    delay del;  p.timeout();
}
```

Process `getno` starts by creating process `alarm` and then accepts digits until it either gets all the digits or it gets a call from `alarm`. Note how we abort the alarm clock process if we get all the digits within the time limit.

Using delays requires some care, however. Suppose that we want to perform some action periodically—say every minute, on the minute. At first, it seems that the following program fragment would do this:

```
delay 60 - clock()%60;   /*wait for next minute*/
for (;;) {
    do action;
    delay 60;
}
```

Function `clock` returns the current time, in seconds (on a UNIX system, this can be implemented by calling function `localtime` [AT&T UNIX 1983]).

Unfortunately, in the long run, this will not perform the action every minute on the minute. The problem is that the interval between actions is really more than 60 seconds; the actual interval also includes the time to execute the action, plus the time delay before this process gets scheduled again. Even if the extra time is small, the error is cumulative. For example, if the extra time is half a second, the cumulative error after an hour will be 30 seconds.

Instead, we need to adjust the requested delay to account for the scheduling delays and the time to execute the action. Here is one way to do this [Barnes 1980]:

```
double nextTime;
nextTime = (clock()/60)*60;
for (;;) {
    nextTime += 60;
    delay nextTime - clock();
    do action;
}
```

3. Timed Transaction Calls

A process making a transaction call is blocked until the call is accepted. Sometimes this is not acceptable because the caller does not want to wait for an arbitrary length of time. A timed transaction call allows the calling process to withdraw a transaction call if the called process does not accept the call within the specified time period. A timed transaction call is an expression of the form

within *duration* ? *p.t(arguments)* : *expr*

where *duration* is a floating-point expression specifying the time in seconds, *p* is a process-valued expression and *t* is a transaction name. If process *p* accepts this transaction call within *duration* seconds, the value returned by *p* becomes the value of the timed transaction call expression. In this case, *expr* is not evaluated. Otherwise, the transaction call is withdrawn, *expr* is evaluated, and its value becomes that of the timed transaction call expression. The transaction call is withdrawn atomically: Concurrent C guarantees that the server process *never* accepts a call that has been withdrawn by the client. The type of *expr* must match the transaction's return value type.

As an example, consider a `reactor` process that has a transaction `temp`, which returns the reactor's current temperature. The following program segment monitors the temperature, and alerts the operator if the `reactor` process does not respond within 0.1 seconds:

```
for ( ; ; ) {
    t = within 0.1?reactor.newTemp():BAD_TEMP;
    if (t == BAD_TEMP)
        operator("Cannot read temperature");
    ...
}
```

Here `BAD_TEMP` is a value, such as −1, which will never be returned as a valid temperature.

The timeout applies to the waiting time until the server *accepts* the call, not to the time until the server completes execution of the transaction call. Once the called process has accepted a transaction call, this call cannot be withdrawn. Also, the timeout is a lower bound on the waiting time before the call can be withdrawn; the Concurrent C implementation will always wait at least the specified time before withdrawing the call.

4. The Accept Statement

In the last chapter, we presented the simple form of the *accept* statement. We will now show you the general form of this statement, which allows you to select calls that can be accepted and specify the order in which they are accepted:

```
accept transaction-name(parameter-name-list)
                        suchthat(tst)opt     by(prty)opt
        statement
```

Here *parameter-name-list* is a comma-separated list of names for the parameters for this transaction, *tst* is a Boolean expression and *prty* is an arithmetic expression. These expressions should involve the parameters of this transaction. The *statement* can be a simple or compound statement; this is the *body* of the *accept* statement.

As described before, an *accept* statement can only appear in the body of a process whose process type has a transaction declaration with the specified name. The parameter names become variables whose scope is the body of the *accept* statement. Their types are taken from the transaction declaration in the process type, and the number of parameters must match the number given in the transaction declaration. When a process executes an *accept* statement, the process waits until an appropriate matching call arrives, at which point the body is executed. Within the body, the parameter variables have the values provided by the caller. When the process exits the body, the calling process becomes eligible for execution.

If the `suchthat` and `by` clauses are omitted, then the pending transaction calls are accepted in first-in-first-out (FIFO) order. If there is a `by` clause, then expression *prty* is evaluated for each pending transaction call, and the call with the minimum value for *prty* is accepted. For example, in a disk scheduler process, the following statement accepts the `diskop` transaction for the cylinder nearest to the current position of the disk arm:

```
accept diskop(cyl, ...) by(abs(cyl-curpos)) {...}
```

If there is a `suchthat` clause, then we consider only those transaction calls for which the expression *tst* is true. If more than one call is satisfactory, we accept them in the order specified by the `by` clause, or else in FIFO order if there is no `by` clause. If none of the pending calls are satisfactory, then we wait until such a call arrives. Pending transaction calls for which *tst* is false are not discarded; they are held, and may be accepted at some later time. As an example, the following statement accepts the first call whose argument is "free":

```
accept lock(id) suchthat(isfree(id)) {...}
```

The `suchthat` and `by` expressions can contain function calls. However, there are no guarantees on how often these expressions will be evaluated, so side-effects should be avoided. You cannot call transactions, or create or abort processes, from within a `suchthat` or a `by` expression.

4.1 A Lock Manager

This example presents a process that manages locks for a large collection of items. Client processes can lock and release these items. If an item is already locked, a process requesting a lock on this item waits until the item is released. Here is the specification of the `lockMngr` process:

File: `lock.h`
```
typedef long lockid;        /*lock identifier*/
process spec lockMngr()
{
    trans void lock(lockid id);  /*wait if busy*/
    trans void release(lockid id);
};
```

Now here is the body of the lockMngr process:

File: `lock.cc`
```
#include "lock.h"
process body lockMngr()
{
    lockid xid;

    for (;;)
        select {
            accept lock(id) suchthat(isfree(id))
                xid = id;
            lock(xid);
        or
            accept release(id)
                xid = id;
            unlock(xid);
        }
}
/*isfree(id) returns true if id is unlocked*/
/*lock(id) locks id*/
/*unlock(id) unlocks id*/
```

The lockMngr process accepts a lock request whenever the requested item is free, and always accepts release requests. Functions isfree, lock, and unlock manipulate a lock table.

4.2 A Simple Disk Scheduler

Now we will show how to write a disk scheduler that uses the "shortest seek time first" algorithm. That is, when getting the next request, the scheduler picks the one which is nearest to the current position of the disk arm.[1] Here is its specification; the `blkno` parameter is the logical disk block number for the block to be read or written:

File: `disk.h`

```
typedef enum {D_READ, D_WRITE} opcode;
process spec diskScheduler()
{
    trans void request(long blkno,
                       opcode op, char *buf);
};
```

Here is its body:

File: `disk.cc`

```
#include "disk.h"
#define BLK_CYL (19*32)          /*blocks per cyl*/
#define CYL(x)  ((x)/BLK_CYL)  /*cyl number*/
#define ABS(x)  ((x)>0?(x):-(x))
process body diskScheduler()
{
    int pos = 0;

    for (;;) {
        accept request(blkno, op, buf)
                    by(ABS(CYL(blkno)-pos)) {
            pos = CYL(blkno);
            seek to pos;
            start disk operation;
            wait for disk operation to complete;
        }
    }
}
```

5. The Select Statement

In Chapter 1, we showed how to use the *select* statement to wait for the arrival of the first of several different types of transaction calls. Now we will show how you can use it to take an alternative action if no calls are pending or to wait for a time out or for collective termination. The *select* statement has the

---

1. This scheduling algorithm performs poorly because it penalizes requests for cylinders at the ends of the disk. Later we will present a better disk scheduler, which uses the "elevator" algorithm.

general form:

```
select {
    ( guard₁ ) : opt     alternative₁
or
    ( guard₂ ) : opt     alternative₂
or
    ...
or
    ( guardₙ ) : opt     alternativeₙ
}
```

An *alternative* is a set of Concurrent C statements. The first statement determines the type of the alternative:

1. an *accept* alternative: an *accept* statement, optionally followed by other statements,

2. a *delay* alternative: a *delay* statement, optionally followed by other statements,

3. a *terminate* alternative: the keyword `terminate` followed by a semicolon, or

4. an *immediate* alternative: a list of statements not beginning with any of the above.

Each alternative can be prefixed by a guard, which is a Boolean expression. An alternative is *open* if its guard is true (non-zero) or if it has no guard. An alternative is *closed* if its guard is false. At least one of the guards must be true; if not, the Concurrent C implementation will print an error message.

The *select* statement executes one and only one of the alternatives. Once chosen, all statements in the selected alternative are executed, and execution resumes after the *select* statement. The following rules determine which alternative will be taken. Only open alternatives are considered; closed alternatives are ignored:

1. If there is an open *accept* alternative (one with a non-zero guard or one without a guard), and if there is a pending call for this transaction, accept that call and take this alternative. If there is a `suchthat` clause, take the alternative only if there is a call that satisfies the `suchthat` clause.

2. Otherwise, if there is an open *immediate* alternative, take it.

3. Otherwise, if there are no open *delay* or *terminate* alternatives, wait for the arrival of a transaction call that satisfies one of the open *accept* alternatives.

4. Otherwise, if there is an open *delay* alternative but no open *terminate* alternative, let *x* be the specified delay. If an acceptable transaction call arrives within *x* seconds, take the corresponding *accept* alternative. If none arrive within *x* seconds, take the *delay* alternative. If there are several open *delay* alternatives, ignore all but the one with the lowest delay value.

5. Otherwise, if there is an open *terminate* alternative and there is no open *delay* alternative, then wait for the first of the following events:

   i. A transaction call arrives that can be accepted, in which case we take the corresponding *accept* alternative.
   ii. The program enters a state in which all other processes have either completed or are waiting at a *select* statement with an open *terminate* alternative, in which case we terminate the entire Concurrent C program.

6. Otherwise, there must be both open *terminate* alternatives and *delay* alternatives. In this case, the Concurrent C implementation can choose one of the following strategies. First, the implementation can choose to combine the test for termination with the delay. That is, the implementation waits for the first of the following events:

   i.   An acceptable transaction call arrives, in which case we take the corresponding *accept* alternative.
   ii. The program enters a state in which all other processes have either completed or are waiting at a *select* statement with an open *terminate* alternative, in which case we terminate the entire Concurrent C program.
   iii. The time limit expires, in which case we take the *delay* alternative.

   Alternatively, the implementation can choose to ignore the *terminate* alternative. That is, if an acceptable transaction call arrives within the specified time limit, take the *accept* alternative; otherwise take the *delay* alternative.

We will now conclude the discussion of the *select* statement with a few notes:

- The order in which guards are evaluated is unspecified, and there is no guarantee that all the guards will be evaluated. Consequently, side effects should be avoided in guards. You cannot call transactions, or create or abort processes, from within a guard.
- If there is an open *immediate* alternative, any *delay* alternatives or *terminate* alternatives will be ignored.
- The order in which the alternatives appear does not matter. In particular, if there are pending calls for several *accept* alternatives, the implementation can take any one of these alternatives.

- Concurrent C implementations are free to select any strategy for implementing the *select* statement, provided the semantics of the implementation are equivalent to those described above. For example, an implementation might not evaluate all the guards.
- An *accept* alternative can have suchthat and/or by clauses. The alternative will be chosen only if there is a transaction call that satisfies the suchthat expression. Once the *accept* alternative has been chosen, the by clause determines which of the pending calls will be accepted. The by clause does *not* determine whether or not the alternative is taken.

We have already shown you examples of the *select* statement with *accept* alternatives. We will now give examples of the *delay* and the *immediate* alternatives. Section 6 contains examples of the *terminate* alternative.

5.1 Chain Printer Controller

We shall illustrate the use of the *delay* alternative by writing a device driver for a chain line printer [Gehani 1984a]. Printer chain wear and tear is minimized by stopping the chain when the printer is not being used. If the printer is idle for 10 seconds, the driver stops the chain. The chain is restarted when a print request arrives.

Here are the specification and body of a process for controlling the printer:

File: printer.cc

```
process spec printer()
    { trans void print(char *line); };
process body printer()
{
    char buffer[128]; int chainRunning = 0;
    for (;;)
        select {
            accept print(line)
                strcpy(buffer, line);
            if (!chainRunning) {
                startChain();
                chainRunning = 1;
            }
            printLine(buffer);
        or (chainRunning):
            delay 10.0; stopChain();
            chainRunning = 0;
        }
}
```

We use the *delay* alternative in the *select* statement to stop the chain if we have not received a request for 10 seconds. Also note how we use a guard to ignore the *delay* alternative when the chain is not running.

5.2 Priority Scheduler

Consider the following priority scheduler that manages a resource, such as a tape drive, that is used by a number of clients [Welsh & Lister 1981]:

File: prty-sched.h

```
process spec prtySched()
{
    trans int   request(parameters);
    trans void acquire(int ticket);
    trans void release();
};
```

```
#include "prty-sched.h"
process body prtySched()
{
    declarations for waiting set;
    int curUser = NONE, nextUser = UNKNOWN;
    for(;;)
       select {
           accept request(parameters) {
               add request to waiting set;
               treturn ticket for request;
           }
           nextUser = UNKNOWN;
       or (curUser==NONE && nextUser!=UNKNOWN):
           accept acquire(ticket)
                  suchthat(ticket==nextUser);
           curUser = nextUser;
           nextUser = UNKNOWN;
           delete curUser from the waiting set;
       or (curUser!=NONE):
           accept release();
           curUser = NONE;
       or (nextUser==UNKNOWN && waiting set not empty):
           nextUser = highest priority user in waiting set;
       }
}
```

Client processes call transaction `request` to request that they be allowed to use the resource. The scheduler gives the client a "ticket" which identifies the client's position in the queue of processes waiting to use the resource. The client then calls transaction `acquire`, using this ticket. The scheduler accepts this call when the resource is available. When a client process has finished using the resource, it calls the `release` transaction. Here is an example illustrating interaction with the priority scheduler:

```
process prtySched s;
s.acquire(s.request(arguments));
use resource;
s.release();
```

5.3 Disk Scheduler Based on the Elevator Algorithm

A better disk scheduling algorithm than the one used for the disk scheduler in Section 4.2 is the "elevator" algorithm. This algorithm accepts all requests for cylinders in the current direction in which the disk head is moving. When there are no more such requests, it changes direction and accepts requests in the new direction. The elevator algorithm does not lead to arbitrarily long delay requests for cylinders at the edges of the disk.

The Concurrent C implementation of this scheduling algorithm has two phases. In phase 1, the scheduler does not have a current direction. The scheduler starts in phase 1, and returns to phase 1 when it has no pending requests. In phase 1, the scheduler accepts the request for the cylinder nearest to the current disk head position. The scheduler moves the disk head in the appropriate direction, handles the request, and enters phase 2. In phase 2, the scheduler has a current direction; it moves the head in this direction, accepting requests as it goes.

Here is our modified version of the `diskScheduler` process. This version has the same specification as our earlier scheduler but it has a different process body:

```
#include "disk.h"
#define BLK_CYL ( 19*32)        /*blocks per cyl*/
#define CYL(x)   ((x)/BLK_CYL)   /*cyl number*/
#define ABS(x)   ((x)>0?(x):-(x))
process body diskScheduler()
{
    int pos = 0, phase = 1, dir;

    for (;;)
        select {
            accept request(blkno, op, buf)
                   suchthat(phase == 1
                       || CYL(blkno) == pos
                       || CYL(blkno)>pos == dir)
                   by(ABS(CYL(blkno)-pos)) {
                if (CYL(blkno) != pos) {
                dir = CYL(blkno) > pos;
                phase = 2;
                pos = CYL(blkno);
                seek to pos;
                }
                start disk operation;
                wait for disk operation to complete;
            }
        or (phase == 2):
            phase = 1;
        }
}
```

Variable `phase` indicates the current phase, and in phase 2, variable `dir` indicates the current direction. The *select* statement has two alternatives: an *accept* alternative and a guarded *immediate* alternative. The *accept* alternative has a `suchthat` clause. In phase 1, any request satisfies this clause. In phase 2, only requests for the current cylinder or those for cylinders in the current direction satisfy it. Of those requests which satisfy the `suchthat` clause, the `by` clause selects the one which is nearest to the current cylinder. Once a request has been accepted, if it involves disk movement, the scheduler sets the current direction and shifts to phase 2. The scheduler then does the disk operation. The *immediate* alternative is executed only when the scheduler is in phase 2 and when there are no pending requests which satisfy the `suchthat` clause (*accept* alternatives have priority over *immediate* alternatives). The *immediate* alternative returns the scheduler to phase 1.

Note that the scheduler does not poll. If the scheduler is in phase 1 and there are no pending requests, the scheduler waits for the next request to arrive. When the scheduler is in phase 2, the *immediate* alternative is open, and will be taken when there are no requests which satisfy the *accept* alternative. This *immediate* alternative returns the scheduler to phase 1. This closes the *immediate* alternative and causes the scheduler to wait for the next `request`.

6. Collective Termination

6.1 The Terminate Alternative of the Select Statement

The *terminate* alternative provides a simple and elegant mechanism for automatic program termination based on a collective decision to terminate by all the processes in a program. It is often used in server processes to terminate them (and therefore the whole program) when all their clients have terminated. In our solution of the dining philosophers problem (Chapter 1), the `fork` processes do not terminate after the `philosopher` processes have terminated. Here is our original version of the `fork` process:

File: `fork.cc`

```
#include "fork.h"
process body fork()
{
    for (;;) {
        accept pickUp();
        accept putDown();
    }
}
```

We can use the *terminate* alternative to make the `fork` processes terminate:

File: `fork-term.cc`

```
#include "fork.h"
process body fork()
{
    for (;;)
        select {
            accept pickUp();
            accept putDown();
        or
            terminate;
        }
}
```

If we use this version of the process body, the program will terminate normally. To see how, suppose that all the philosopher processes have terminated. Then the remaining processes are the five fork processes, which are all waiting at a *select* statement with a *terminate* alternative, and the main process, which is in the completed state and is waiting for its remaining children, i.e., the fork processes, to terminate. According to the definition of the *select* statement, that means that all processes can terminate.

As another example illustrating the use of the *terminate* alternative, consider the buffer process of the "buffered producer-consumer" example given in the last chapter. As shown initially, the buffer did not terminate, so the whole program never terminated. We suggested that this problem could be solved by having the buffer process check for a special *end-of-transmission* value, and then terminate after giving this value to the consumer process. There are two disadvantages to this solution: first, it should not be the role of the buffer process to check for special values indicating end-of-transmission, and secondly, it makes the buffer process dependent on the special end-of-transmission value. The buffer process is a server process. It should terminate when it has no more clients. The *terminate* alternative allows us to do precisely this. Here is the modified version of the buffer process:

File: buffer-term.cc

```
#include "buffer.h"
process body buffer(max)
{
    int *buf;     /*circular buffer of max bytes*/
    int n = 0;    /*number of chars in buffer*/
    int in = 0;   /*index of next empty slot*/
    int out = 0;  /*index of next character*/
    char *malloc();

    buf = (int*) malloc(max*sizeof(int));
    for (;;)
        select {
          (n < max):
              accept put(c)
                  buf[in] = c;
              in = (in + 1) % max;
              n++;
        or (n > 0):
              accept get()
                  treturn buf[out];
              out = (out + 1) % max;
              n--;
        or
              terminate;
        }
}
```

6.2 Limitations of the Terminate Alternative

If it looks like you can get collective termination just by adding a *terminate* alternative to each *select* statement, you are right: in most cases this is all you will need. The *terminate* alternative is a simple technique that satisfies the collective termination needs of most concurrent programs.

However, there are two situations in which a simple *terminate* alternative does not work very well. The first is that this mechanism will not terminate a process until *every* process in the program is finished. For example, suppose that we simulated a multi-table dining philosopher problem. After the philosophers at one table have completed, the forks are no longer needed. However, these forks will continue to exist until the philosophers at *all* of the tables have finished.

The other problem is that the *terminate* alternative does not work well with the *delay* alternative. For example, consider a process that wants to do some low-priority background work if it has not received a request for 30 seconds:

```
for ( ; ; )
    select {
        accept request(...)
            ...
    or
        delay 30.0;
        do background work;
    or
        terminate;          /*this has problems!*/
    }
```

The problem is that if several processes are structured like this, we have a race condition. The processes will collectively terminate only when—and if!—they are all waiting at the same time. There is no guarantee that this will ever happen, so the program might never terminate.

However, *delay* alternatives are not necessarily a problem. For example, consider the printer controller process in Section 5.1. It is safe to add a *terminate* alternative to that process, because the *delay* alternative is only open for a brief time after a request is received. Once the delay is taken, the *delay* alternative is closed until the next request arrives.

6.3 Client Counts

We will conclude our discussion of collective termination by illustrating the "client count" technique for terminating processes. This technique avoids the problems discussed above—but it is more complicated, it can be less efficient, and it requires more thought and more programming effort. In short, if the *terminate* alternative satisfies your needs, use it.

With the client count technique, we divide the processes into "servers" and "clients". A server process accepts transactions from its client processes, and we want a server process to terminate when all of its client processes have terminated. For example, in the dining philosophers program, the `fork` processes are servers, and the `philosopher` processes are their clients. A client process can be a server of its own clients, although in the dining philosophers program they are not.

Each server process maintains a count of the number of clients that are using it. To do that, we add two additional transactions, say `addClient` and `dropClient`, to the specification of each server process. When a client process starts, it calls transaction `addClient` of each server process that it will use. When a client process terminates, it calls `dropClient` for these servers. Each server process uses these calls to keep track of the number of clients, and the server terminates when the count is zero.

To apply this to the dining philosopher's problem, we first revise the specification of the `fork` process:

File: `fork-cnt.h`
```
process spec fork()
{
    trans void pickUp(), putDown();
    trans void addClient(), dropClient();
};
```

We then revise the `fork` process:

File: `fork-cnt.cc`
```
#include "fork-cnt.h"
process body fork()
{
    int nclient = 0;
    accept addClient() nclient++;
    while (nclient > 0)
        select {
            accept pickUp(); accept putDown();
        or
            accept addClient() nclient++;
        or
            accept dropClient() nclient--;
        }
}
```

Notice that the process first waits for an `addClient` call. If it did not, the client count would be zero, and the process would terminate immediately.

The `philosopher` processes have the same specifications as before. The only addition to the `philosopher` process body is to call the client count transactions of the two `fork` processes that are called by the `philosopher` process:

File: `phil-cnt.cc`

```
#include "fork-cnt.h"
#include "phil.h"
#define LIMIT 100000
process body philosopher(id, left, right)
{
    int nmeal;

    left.addClient();
    right.addClient();
    for (nmeal = 0; nmeal < LIMIT; nmeal++) {
        same as before;
    }
    printf("Phil. %d: That's all, folks!\n", id);
    left.dropClient();
    right.dropClient();
}
```

Note that there a potential problem with this solution. Suppose that one of the `philosopher` processes starts, eats all of its meals, tells its forks that they have one less client, and terminates—and does all that *before* any other `philosopher` process gets a chance to execute and tell its `fork` processes that they have a client. This is unlikely, but not impossible. But if that did happen, then the `fork` processes used by the first philosopher would terminate prematurely. We could solve that problem by having the `fork` processes know that they have two clients. In this case we could initialize `nclient` to 2 and eliminate the `addClient` transaction. However, this is not a general solution, because a server process may not know in advance the number of its clients. In the general solution, suppose a process C1 is a client of a server process S. Whenever C1 gives the id of S to another process C2, then C1 must ensure that C2 will call transaction `addClient` of S before C1 calls transaction `dropclient` of S. In the dining philosophers example, this would mean that

1. `main` must become a "client" of each of the `fork` processes by calling their `addClient` transactions,
2. we add an `initialize` transaction to the `philosopher` process,
3. the `philosopher` process must accept the `initialize` transaction

after it calls the `addClient` transactions of its `fork` processes,

4. `main` calls the `initialize` transaction of each `philosopher` after creating it, and

5. before completing, make `main` call transaction `dropClient` of each `fork` process.

7. Transaction Pointers

A transaction pointer refers to a specific transaction associated with a specific process. Transaction pointers are similar to function pointers except that their declarations are prefixed by the keyword `trans`:

> `trans` *type-specifier trans-ptr-declarator*$_1$, ... , *trans-ptr-declarator*$_n$;

trans-ptr-declarator$_i$ are identical to the declarators derived from function pointers. Transaction pointer declarations specify the result type and the parameter types associated with the transaction but are independent of the process type. For example,

```
trans void (*tp)(char);
```

declares `tp` as a pointer to a transaction that takes one `char` parameter and returns no value, and

```
trans int (**ptp)(float, float);
```

declares `ptp` as a pointer to a transaction pointer that takes two `float` parameters and returns an `int` value.

Our syntax does not allow the direct declaration of a pointer to a transaction that returns a transaction pointer. However, this can be done in two steps, using an intermediate *typedef* statement to define the return-value type:

```
typedef trans int (*TpType)(int, int);
trans TpType (*xtp)(int);
```

Provided the parameter and return value types match, an expression of the form $p.t$, where p is a process-valued expression and t is the name of one of p's transactions, can be used wherever a transaction pointer value is expected. For example, the following assignment sets `tp` to point to the `put` transaction of process `b`:

```
tp = b.put;
```

Expression

```
(*tp)('a');
```

calls the transaction to which `tp` points, giving the character `'a'` as an argument. The syntax of a transaction call using a transaction pointer is identical to that used for calling a function with a function pointer.

The value 0 is guaranteed to be an invalid transaction pointer value and it can be assigned to a transaction pointer variable or compared against transaction pointer values.

As an example, consider the function `getline`, which calls a transaction, using a transaction pointer, to read a line into an array:

File: `getline.cc`

```
/* Read from *getp to \n, save chars in a. */
void getline(getp, a)
    trans char (*getp)(); char a[];
{
    int i = 0;   char c;
    do {
        c = (*getp)();
        a[i++] = c;
    } while (c != '\n');
    a[i] = '\0';
}
```

We can call `getline` with a pointer to a transaction of any process, as long as this transaction returns a character. The following `getline` function call reads a line of characters from a `buffer` process:

```
process spec buffer(int max)
    { trans char get(); ... };
process buffer b;
char linebuf[100];
...
getline(b.get, linebuf);
```

If we did not have transaction pointers, we would have had to pass a process id to `getline`. This would work, but it would require us to specify the process type and transaction name within the `getline` function. We will then have to write a separate function for each process type from which we want to get lines. Using a transaction pointer allows us to write one function which will work with any process type. A transaction pointer lets us "factor out" the process type. Because a transaction pointer does not include the process type, a transaction pointer can refer to transactions of different processes types, provided these transactions have the same parameter types and the same return-value type.

8. Asynchronous Transaction Calls

Transaction calls are normally synchronous, in that the caller waits until the called process accepts the call and completes it. However, as an option, a transaction which does not return a value—a void-valued transaction—can be declared as *asynchronous*. With an asynchronous transaction, Concurrent C sends the values of the caller's arguments to the called process, and allows the calling process to continue execution without waiting for the called process to accept the call.

To declare a transaction as asynchronous, use the keyword async instead of void as the base type in the transaction declaration, as in

```
process spec consumer()
{
    trans async send(int c);
}
```

This specification says that for the send transaction, the caller will not wait for the consumer process to accept the call; the caller will send the character and continue. Except for the lack of synchronization, asynchronous transactions are used exactly like void-valued transactions. Thus we could use the body of the consumer process in Section 7 of Chapter 1 with the above process specification.

8.1 When To Use Asynchronous Transactions

While asynchronous transactions have their place, we recommend that you use them with care, and only use them when synchronous transactions are inappropriate. For example, one reason for using an asynchronous transaction would be that the called process cannot accept calls quickly; it is doing a lot of other work, and only rarely executes an *accept* statement for this transaction. Another reason might be that there is a long communication delay for sending a message; this can happen in a loosely-coupled distributed implementation, where the processors are connected by a local area network.

You should *not* use asynchronous transactions just "because they must be faster." They are not necessarily faster. In fact, asynchronous transactions require much more overhead than synchronous transactions.

8.2 Flow Control Problems

A Concurrent C implementation must buffer all pending (outstanding) asynchronous calls in memory. If your program exceeds implementation defined limits on such calls, its performance may suffer, and it might even deadlock. Typically 100 pending calls will be fine, but 100,000 pending calls will not be acceptable.

As a result, when using asynchronous transactions, you must provide some form of flow control: you must provide some upper bound on the number of pending asynchronous transaction calls. For some programs, this happens naturally. But for other programs, you may need to insert extra code to enforce such a limit. Flow control problems are particularly nasty to detect because a program with flow control problems can run perfectly during simple tests, and then fail under heavy load. As an example, consider the unbuffered synchronous producer-consumer program from Chapter 1:

File: pc-sync.h

```
process spec consumer()
{
    trans void send(int c);
};
process spec producer(process consumer cons);
```

File: pc-sync.cc

```
#include <stdio.h>
#include "ctype.h"  /*for islower(), toupper()*/
#include "pc-sync.h"
process body producer(cons)
{
    int c;
    while ((c = getchar()) != EOF)
        cons.send(c);
    cons.send(EOF);
}
process body consumer()
{
    int xc;
    for (;;) {
        accept send(c)
            xc = c;
        if (xc == EOF)
            break;
        if (islower(xc))
            xc = toupper(xc);
        putchar(xc);
    }
}
main()
{
    create producer(create consumer());
}
```

As we discussed in Chapter 1, the producer and consumer must synchronize on every character, and hence cannot run in parallel. Chapter 1

showed how to use an intermediate buffer process to decouple the two processes
and provide more concurrency.

Another way to decouple the processes is to declare send to be an
asynchronous transaction. As shown earlier, we can just replace void by
async in the specification for the consumer process. No other code needs
to be changed. This solution works, but it does not provide any flow control;
the producer process can get thousands of calls ahead of the consumer
process. The resulting program might run slower than the original synchronous
program.

The correct way to use asynchronous transactions for the producer-consumer
problem requires the program to limit the number of pending send
transaction calls. If the producer process gets too far ahead, it must wait
for the consumer process to catch up. One way to do this is to have the
consumer process occasionally send an acknowledgement to the producer
process. We can change the specification of the consumer process to allow
the producer process to supply a transaction pointer as an argument when
calling transaction send:

File: pc-async.h

```
process spec consumer()
{
      /* If acktp != 0, call that transaction */
      /* after accepting this send. */
    trans async send(int c,
                     trans async (*acktp)());
};

process spec producer(process consumer cons)
{
    trans async acknowledge();
};
```

Here is the body of the revised producer process:

```
#include <stdio.h>
#include "pc-async.h"

#define PROD_LEAD 100
process body producer(cons)
{
    int c, n = 0;
    trans void (*acktp)();

    acktp = ((process producer)
                   c_mypid()).acknowledge;
    for (;;) {
        c = getchar();
        cons.send(c, n == 0 ? acktp : 0);
        if (c == EOF)
            break;
        if (++n == PROD_LEAD) {
            accept acknowledge();
            n = 0;
        }
    }
    accept acknowledge();
}
```

The producer process starts by asking the consumer process to send an acknowledgement for the first call (an acknowledgement is requested if the second argument of the send transaction call is not a null transaction pointer). After every 100 calls, the producer process waits for an acknowledgment transaction call from the consumer process. This tells the producer process that the consumer process is at most 100 calls behind. The producer process then requests another acknowledgment and goes off to make another 100 calls. The end result is that the producer process can get at most 200 calls ahead of the consumer process.

Here is the body of the revised consumer process:

File: `cons-async.cc`

```
#include <stdio.h>
#include "ctype.h"  /*for islower(), toupper()*/
#include "pc-async.h"

process body consumer()
{
    int xc;
    trans void (*xacktp)();

    for (;;) {
        accept send(c, acktp) {
            xc = c;  xacktp = acktp;
        }
        if (xacktp != 0)
            (*xacktp)();
        if (xc == EOF)
            break;
        if (islower(xc))
            xc = toupper(xc);
        putchar(xc);
    }
}
```

This solution works, and it can be more efficient than using an intermediate buffer process. However, we also think that this solution is considerably harder to understand and debug than the version with an intermediate buffer process.

9. Examples

9.1 Performing Requests in Parallel

In Section 5.3, we presented a process that managed a disk device, accepted requests from clients, and used the "elevator" algorithm to schedule requests. This process has one limitation, namely that a client process cannot ask the disk controller process to perform several disk operations in parallel. To see why this is a limitation, suppose that a client process wants to read a set of disk blocks that are scattered on the disk. The client would like to tell the scheduler, "Here is a set of requests; do them in the best order." However, the client cannot. Instead, the client must pick an order in which to present these requests to the scheduler process. This order will not necessarily be optimal. As another example, suppose that we have two disks, each with its own scheduler process, and a client process wants to read from both disks. The client would like both requests to be executed in parallel. However, the scheduler process in Section 5.3 does not allow this; the client must issue one request, wait for it to complete, and then issue the other.

This section will present two techniques for structuring a server process, such as our disk scheduler, so that it will allow several requests from one client to be done in parallel.

9.1.1 Laundry-Ticket Solution: The first technique is based on the concept of "laundry tickets." With this technique, a client process calls the scheduler twice for each request. The first call tells the scheduler about the request. The scheduler accepts the call, enters the request in its queue, and returns a ticket. The client then calls the scheduler again, using the ticket as an argument, and the scheduler accepts the second call when it completes that disk request.

First, we must change the specification of the scheduler process:

```
                                            File: disk-ticket.h
process spec diskScheduler()
{
    trans int read( long blkno, char *buf);
    trans int write(long blkno, char *buf);
    trans int done(int ticket);
    trans async interrupt();
};
```

The `interrupt` transaction is called by the Concurrent C run-time system when a disk interrupt occurs; clients do not call it.[2]

To start a request, a client calls either transaction `read` or transaction `write`. These transactions return a ticket value. To wait for a request to complete, the client calls the `done` transaction, giving the ticket returned by a `read` or a `write` transaction call as an argument. For example, here is how a client would start and wait for the completion of a single disk read operation:

```
process diskScheduler ds;
...
status = ds.done(ds.read(blk, buf));
```

The following code fragment shows how a client can start two disk reads, on the same or different disk schedulers, and then wait for them to complete:

---

2. For more details on how interrupts are converted to transactions, see the description of the `c_associate` function in Chapter 3.

```
process diskScheduler ds1, ds2;
int t1, t2;
...
t1 = ds1.read(blk1,buf1);  t2 = ds2.read(blk2,buf2);
status1 = ds1.wait(t1);  status2 = ds2.wait(t2);
```

Here is an outline of the body of the scheduler process:

File: `disk-ticket.cc`

```
#include "disk-ticket.h"
process body diskScheduler()
{
    array of requests:
        each has status indicator, pending or completed;
        pending requests are linked in order;

    for (;;) {
        select {
            accept read(blkno, buf) {
                pick free array element, save args;
                treturn array index as ticket;
            }
            if (request is invalid)
                mark request as completed;
            else
                insert in pending list;
        or
            accept write(blkno, buf)
                same as read;
        or
            accept interrupt();
            mark request as completed;
        or (there are completed requests):
            accept done(ticket)
                    suchthat(ticket is completed)
                treturn status;
            mark array element as free;
        }
        if (disk is idle and there are pending requests)
            start next pending request;
    }
}
```

The scheduler has an array, with one element for each pending request. The
elements can be in one of three states: pending, completed, or free. A ticket

value is an index into that array. To see how this works, suppose that the disk is idle—there are no pending requests—and a client calls the read transaction. The scheduler process accepts this call, saves the information describing the request in the array, and returns the array index. Because the disk was idle, the scheduler tells the disk to start this request, and the scheduler then waits for the next transaction call. The scheduler will not accept the client's done call yet, because the call does not satisfy the suchthat clause.

Eventually the disk completes the operation and generates an interrupt. This causes the Concurrent C run-time system to generate a call to the scheduler's interrupt transaction. The scheduler then accepts this transaction, saves the status indicators from the disk, marks the current request as completed, and tells the disk to start the next request (if any).

At this point, the request is completed, and the client's done call satisfies the suchthat clause, so the scheduler accepts this transaction and returns the completion status of the request.

While the disk is actually executing an operation, the scheduler process is waiting at the *select* statement for the next transaction call. Thus the scheduler can accept read and write requests very quickly. This is typical of how interrupt-driven device driver processes are written in Concurrent C.

Also note that if a disk operation completes before the client issues the done call, then the scheduler just holds the completed request, and accepts the done call when the client finally issues it. If the client never issues the done call, then the scheduler's array of requests will eventually fill up and the scheduler will be unable to accept new requests. The server can protect itself from this problem by periodically scanning the request array and discarding completed requests that have been waiting too long—just as a laundry might throw out an order that has not been picked up after 30 days.

9.1.2 Call-Back Solution: The second technique is similar, in that it also involves two calls. Again, the first call is from the client to the scheduler, to ask the scheduler to enqueue the request. However, when the request completes, the scheduler calls the client, using a transaction pointer that the client provides in the first call. Hence this is the "call-back" solution.

Here is the specification for this version of the scheduler process:

File: `disk-callback.h`

```
typedef trans async (*dstp)(int, int);
process spec diskScheduler()
{
    trans async read(long blkno, char *buf,
                        dstp tp, int val);
    trans async write(long blkno, char *buf,
                        dstp tp, int val);
    trans async interrupt();
};
```

The transaction pointer is of type `dstp` which specifies an asynchronous transaction that takes two integer arguments. The first is a value provided by the client, to identify this request, and the second is the status of the request. Here is how a client process will ask the scheduler to read a single disk block:

```
process spec user(process diskScheduler ds)
{
    trans async ack(int val, int status);
};
process body user(ds)
{
    dstp tp = ((process user)c_mypid()).ack;
    ...
    ds.read(blk, buf, tp, 1);
    accept ack(val, status)
        check status;
    ...
}
```

Here is how another client process would do two disk reads in parallel:

```
process spec user2(process diskScheduler ds)
{
    trans async ack(int val, int status);
};
process body user2(ds)
{
    dstp tp = ((process user)c_mypid()).ack;
    ...
    ds.read(blk1, buf1, tp, 1);
    ds.read(blk2, buf2, tp, 2);
    for (i = 0; i < 2; i++)
        accept ack(val, status)
            if (val == 1) stat1 = status;
            else stat2 = status;
    check stat1 and stat2;
}
```

Here is the body of this version of the scheduler process. The basic outline is the same as that of the other version of the scheduler process; the only difference is that when an operation completes, this scheduler immediately calls the client process:

File: disk-callback.cc

```
#include "disk-callback.h"
process body diskScheduler()
{   array of requests:
            Each has status indicator, pending or completed.
            Pending requests are linked in order.

    for (;;) {
        select {
            accept read(blkno, buf, tp, val) {
                pick free array element, save args;
            }
            if (request is invalid) {
                call client's transaction;
                mark array element as free;
            } else {
                insert in pending list;
            }
        or
            accept write(blkno, buf, tp, val)
                same as read;
        or
            accept interrupt();
            call client's transaction;
            mark array element as free;
        }
        if (disk is idle and there are pending requests)
            start next pending request;
    }
}
```

9.1.3 Comparison: Both techniques work, and they both have their uses. The advantage of the call-back technique is that it can be faster and more efficient. That is, the laundry-ticket approach requires an *accept* statement with a suchthat clause in a *select* statement. Because of the search implied by the suchthat clause, the *select* statement in the laundry-ticket version of the disk scheduler may be slightly less efficient than the simple *accept* statement used in the call-back approach.

The disadvantage of the call-back approach is that the client's code is more complicated, because it involves accepting transaction calls instead of just calling transactions. For example, with the call-back technique, the code to accept the call-back transaction *must* be in the process body (remember that *accept* statements can only appear in process bodies). With the laundry-ticket technique, all of the interactions with the server can be encapsulated in functions.

9.2 Simulating Semaphores

One of the earliest synchronization tools, called the *semaphore*, was invented by E. W. Dijkstra [1968a, 1968b]. A semaphore[3] is a variable that is used to exchange timing signals between concurrent processes by means of the operations p (wait) and v (signal).[4] Here are the semantics of the p and v operations associated with binary semaphores [Brinch Hansen 1973b]:

> p(s)   If semaphore s is 0, then suspend the calling process; otherwise, set s to 0 and let the process continue execution.

> v(s)   If one or more processes are suspended as a result of executing a p operation on semaphore s, then allow one such process to proceed; otherwise set s to 1.

The p and v operations are *atomic*, i.e., indivisible, and are mutually exclusive on the same semaphore. Semaphores are assumed to be 1 initially.

Using semaphores, mutual exclusion is easily implemented by requiring all processes to execute the p operation before accessing the shared data (or using the shared resource) and the v operation after completing access (or use):

    p(s);
    access shared data;
    v(s);

Exclusive access to the shared data is guaranteed if every process sharing the data uses the above paradigm to access the data. A process executing the p operation is delayed if another process is in the midst of accessing the shared

---

3. According to the *Webster's New Collegiate Dictionary*, a *semaphore* is an apparatus for visual signaling. The version of the semaphore discussed in this section is also called the *binary* semaphore, because it can have only one of two values. Another version of the semaphore, called the *integer* semaphore, can be initialized to any non-negative integer value.

4. p and v originally represented the Dutch words *passeren* (pass) and *vrygeven* (release). Later on, p was considered to represent the word *prolagen* formed by combining the two Dutch words *proberen* (try) and *verlagen* (decrease) and v to represent the Dutch word *verhogen* (increase) [Andrews & Schneider 1983].

data. In this case the delayed process will be allowed to continue only after the process accessing the shared data has completed its access and executed a v operation.

Several processes may be waiting as a result of executing the p operation. Which waiting process should be allowed to resume execution when a v operation is performed? Any reasonable scheduling discipline may be used to select this process. For example, an implementation of the v operation may use the FIFO scheduling discipline. Alternatively, a priority scheduling discipline can be used, but this will require modification of the p operation to allow the specification of a resumption priority. The v operation can then be implemented to allow the process with the highest priority to resume execution; if there is more than one process with the highest priority, then the process that has waited the longest could be allowed to resume execution.

As discussed above, semaphores can be used for both mutual exclusion and synchronization. Although semaphores are simple to use, they are a low-level tool and must be used with care. They do not directly express the concepts of concurrent programming, e.g., mutual exclusion, and must be used to the express high-level concepts just as assembly language instructions are used to express high-level programming constructs. Like programs that use *gotos*, programs that use the semaphore are hard to understand, difficult to prove correct and error prone. These problems arise because [DoD 1979]

- it is possible to bypass semaphore operations by jumping around them,

- forgetting to use the p operation before accessing shared data will allow more than one process to update the shared data simultaneously, resulting in data inconsistency; using them in the wrong order also causes similar problems,

- forgetting to use the v operation after accessing the shared data can cause a process to wait forever,

- it is not possible to perform an alternative action if a semaphore is busy,

- it is not possible to wait for more than one semaphore, and

- semaphores are visible to processes that do not need them.

Here is a Concurrent C process that implements a binary semaphore. One such process is created for each semaphore variable, and clients call the process' p and v transactions:

```
process spec semaphore( )
{
    trans void p( ), v( );
};
process body semaphore( )
{
    for( ; ; )
        select {
            accept p( );
            accept v( );
        or
            terminate;
        }
}
```

9.2.1 Integer Semaphores: An integer semaphore can be initialized to any non-negative integer value. The p and v operations are defined as follows:

p(s) If semaphore s is 0, then suspend the calling process until it becomes positive. If s is positive, decrement s by 1 and let the calling process continue execution.

v(s) Increment semaphore s by 1, and if there are processes suspended as a result of executing a p operation on s, then allow one of these processes to proceed.

Again, these operations are executed atomically. Such semaphores are often used for resource management problems. A process that wants to consume a unit of some resource calls p with an integer semaphore that controls this resource as the argument. A process that produces the resource will call operation v with this semaphore. The semantics of the integer semaphore ensure that a consumer will not proceed until something has been produced.

Here is a Concurrent C process that implements an integer semaphore. The process parameter is the initial value for the semaphore:

```
process spec semaphore(int n)
{
    trans void p( ), v( );
};
process body semaphore(n)
{
    for( ; ; )
        select {
            (n > 0):
                accept p( );
                n--;
        or
                accept v( );
                n++;
        or
                terminate;
        }
}
```

9.3 Concurrent Readers and Writers Example

Concurrent C does not forbid processes from referencing global variables, nor does it forbid them from exchanging pointers. However, programmers do so at their own risk; such programs will not work as expected unless they are run on a implementation that supports shared memory. If a program does use shared memory, it is the programmer's responsibility to synchronize the processes when they access the shared data. The following example presents several ways to do this.

Suppose several processes want to access the same shared data. Processes are classified into two categories: readers and writers. Reader processes read the data but do not update it; writer processes update the data. Multiple readers should be able to access the shared data simultaneously, but a writer process must be given exclusive access to avoid inconsistencies.

A database is one example of an application with many concurrent reader and writer processes. Database transactions are either queries (reads) or updates (writes), and many processes can make requests concurrently. There are several strategies for scheduling the readers and writers:

1. *One Reader or Writer*: Only one reader process or one writer process is allowed to access the shared data at any time.

2. *Many Readers, One Writer*: The first strategy is unduly restrictive because it prevents multiple readers from simultaneously accessing the data. Allowing multiple readers increases the concurrency and decreases the average waiting time for accessing the shared data.

3. *Many Readers, Priority for Writers*: In the second strategy, a steady stream of readers can prevent the writer processes from ever accessing the shared data. This problem can be solved by giving the writers priority over the readers. When a writer is waiting to access the shared data, no new readers will be allowed access to the data.

4. *Many Readers, Limited Priority for Writers*: The third strategy is fine as long as there are only a few writers. But if there are a steady stream of writers, the writers can prevent the readers from accessing the shared data. To provide fair access for readers, the fourth strategy allows all pending readers to proceed before a new writer is allowed to access the shared data.

9.3.1 Process Specification and Use: The solutions implementing the above scheduling strategies will all use the same process specification:

```
                                              File: rw.h
process spec rw()
{
    trans void read(), write(), done();
};
```

A reader process uses the following code to gain access:

```
process rw manager;
manager.read();
access data;
manager.done();
```

A writer process is similar, except that it calls `write` instead of `read`.

9.3.2 Solution 1 (One Reader or Writer): Here is the implementation of the first version of the manager process; it accepts only one `read` or `write` request at a time:

File: rw1.cc

```
#include "rw.h"
process body rw()     /* One Reader or Writer */
{
   for (;;)
      select {
         accept read();
         accept done();
      or
         accept write();
         accept done();
      }
}
```

9.3.3 Solution 2 (Many Readers, One Writer): Our second implementation of the manager process allows several readers to simultaneously access the shared data:

File: rw2.cc

```
#include "rw.h"
process body rw() /* Many Readers, One Writer */
{
   int nreaders = 0, nwriters = 0;
   for (;;)
      select {
         (nwriters==0):
            accept read();
            nreaders++;
      or
         (nwriters==0 && nreaders==0):
            accept write();
            nwriters = 1;
      or
            accept done();
            if (nreaders > 0)
               nreaders--;
            else
               nwriters = 0;
      }
}
```

9.3.4 Solution 3 (Many Readers, Priority for Writers): Our third implementation of the manager process gives writers priority over readers. To do this we use the built-in function c_transcount, which returns the number of pending calls for a transaction. The transaction is specified by giving a transaction pointer for the desired process and transaction:

```
                                              File: rw3.cc
#include "rw.h"
process body rw()      /* Priority for Writers */
{
    int nreaders = 0, nwriters = 0;
    trans void (*wtp)()
                 = ((process rw)c_mypid()).write;
    for (;;)
        select {
            (nwriters==0 && c_transcount(wtp)==0):
                accept read();
                nreaders++;
        or
            (nwriters==0 && nreaders==0):
                accept write();
                nwriters = 1;
        or
                accept done();
                if (nreaders > 0)
                    nreaders--;
                else
                    nwriters = 0;
        }
}
```

9.3.5 Solution 4 (Many Readers, Limited Priority for Writers): In the third solution, a steady stream of writers can prevent the readers from ever getting access. Our final implementation of the manager process avoids this problem by accepting all outstanding requests for read access after a writer releases the shared data. The number of such requests is finite because a reader can access the data only once in this phase (no done transaction calls are accepted here). Note the use of nested *select* statements; the inner *select* statement accepts only read access requests:

```
#include "rw.h"
process body rw()    /*limited writer priority*/
{
   int nreaders = 0, nwriters = 0;
   trans void (*wtp)()
               = ((process rw) c_mypid()).write;
   for (;;)
      select {
         (nwriters==0 && c_transcount(wtp)==0):
            accept read();
            nreaders++;
      or
         (nwriters==0 && nreaders==0):
            accept write();
            nwriters = 1;
      or
            accept done();
            if (nreaders > 0)
               nreaders--;
            else {
               nwriters = 0;
               for (;;)
                  select { /*get pending reads*/
                     accept read();
                     nreaders++;
                  or
                     break;
                  }
            }
      }
}
```

9.4 Job-Shop Scheduling

The problem is to write a program to simulate a machine job shop with groups of identical machines that process *jobs* [Kaubisch, Perrot & Hoare 1976; Gehani 1984a]. Jobs arrive at random intervals. Each job consists of a number of *steps*. The steps are done sequentially, and each step requires the exclusive use of one machine from a specific group of machines, for a specified time period. Different jobs can have a different series of steps and processing time in each step. Here is a figure showing how the jobs might flow from one machine group to another:

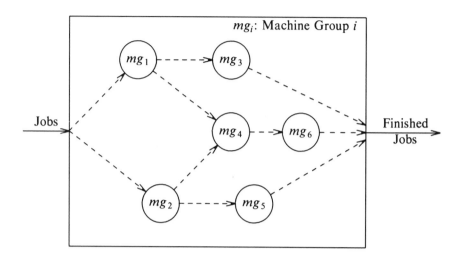

There are a maximum of 10 groups, and a maximum of 20 steps per job. The simulation is described by a stream of data in the following format; the "group size" is the number of machines in the group:

> *num-groups   group-1-size   group-2-size   group-3-size   ...*
> *job_1-arrival-interval $num\text{-}steps_1$ $group_{11}$ $time_{11}$ $group_{12}$ $time_{12}$ ...*
> *job_2-arrival-interval $num\text{-}steps_2$ $group_{21}$ $time_{21}$ $group_{22}$ $time_{22}$ ...*
>
>   ...
>
> *job_n-arrival-interval $num\text{-}steps_n$ $group_{n1}$ $time_{n1}$ $group_{n2}$ $time_{n2}$ ...*

The machines in each group are managed by a process of type `mg` ("machine group"). This process has two transactions, `request`, which allocates a machine from its group, and `release`, which releases a previously allocated machine. The parameter of process `mg` specifies the number of machines in the group.

Each job is represented by a process of type `job`. This process manages the flow of the job through the machine shop by requesting machines for the various steps. The description of the job, and the identifiers of the `mg` processes, are passed as process parameters.

The `main` process controls the simulation. It first creates the processes for managing the machine groups, and then waits for the next job to arrive. When the job arrives, it allocates a process to manage the job and then waits for the next job to arrive; this is repeated until the end of the input.

The header file `job-shop.h` is used by all processes in this program:

File: `job-shop.h`

```
#define MAX_STEPS   20
#define MAX_GROUPS  10

process spec mg(int nmachines)
{
    trans void request(), release();
};
typedef struct {
    int nsteps;
    int gnum[MAX_STEPS];
    double ptime[MAX_STEPS];
} job_t;
typedef struct {
    process mg mgpids[MAX_GROUPS];
} groups_t;
process spec job(groups_t groups, job_t steps);
```

Here is the `main` process:

File: `job-shop.cc`

```
#include "job-shop.h"
main()
{
    groups_t groups; job_t steps;
    int i, n, ngroups; double interval;

    scanf("%d", &ngroups);
    for (i = 0; i < ngroups; i++) {
        scanf("%d", &n);
        groups.mgpids[i] = create mg(n);
    }
    while (scanf("%lf", &interval) == 1) {
        delay interval;
        scanf("%d", &steps.nsteps);
        for (i = 0; i < steps.nsteps; i++)
            scanf("%d %lf",
                    &steps.gnum[i], &steps.ptime[i]);
        create job(groups, steps);
    }
}
```

Here is the body of process `mg`:

File: `mg.cc`

```
#include "job-shop.h"
process body mg(nmachines)
{
    int nused = 0;

    for (;;)
        select {
            (nused < nmachines):
                accept request();
                nused++;
        or
                accept release();
                nused--;
        or
                terminate;
        }
}
```

Here is the body of process `job`:

File: `job.cc`

```
#include "job-shop.h"
process body job(groups, steps)
{
    int i;
    for (i = 0; i < steps.nsteps; i++) {
        groups.mgpids[steps.gnum[i]].request();
        delay steps.ptime[i];
        groups.mgpids[steps.gnum[i]].release();
    }
}
```

Note that this program does not use shared memory. The `main` process passes structures, by value, to the `job` processes to describe the steps in the jobs and the identifiers of the processes that manage the machine groups. Had we declared the `groups_t` structure as a global variable, the program would have worked only in a shared memory implementation of Concurrent C.

Each machine group in this program is controlled by a process. Alternatively, one process could have been used to control all the machine groups in the shop. Although this would require less resources (fewer processes), centralized allocation of machines by one controlling process would unnecessarily make the simulation more sequential. Requests for machines from different groups would then have to be accepted sequentially.

The main purpose of a simulation program is to collect statistics to analyze the problem being simulated. Instructions to collect statistics were omitted from the above program to focus on the dynamic creation of processes; these instructions can be easily added to appropriate parts of the program.

10. Exercises

1. Process `getno`, of the telephone switch program example given in Section 2, uses a special `alarm` process to timeout if the telephone user takes a long time to dial the digits. Why was a *delay* alternative not used in the *select* statement instead of the `alarm` process?

2. The telephone switch program example in Section 2 requires the telephone user to dial all digits of the telephone number within 60 seconds. Suppose we change this requirement to state that each digit must be dialed within 10 seconds. Modify process `getno` to reflect this change and then compare it with the version shown.

3. Suppose Concurrent C did not provide the `suchthat` and `by` clauses. How will you implement the functionality provided by these clauses?

4. Rewrite the lock manager example given in Section 4 without using a `suchthat` clause.

5. Rewrite the disk scheduler process given in Section 4.2 without using a `by` clause.

6. Modify the "elevator algorithm" version of the disk scheduler program given in Section 5.2 so that disk access requests are accepted in the right order by using just the `by` clause (i.e., without using the `suchthat` clause). The *select* statement will not be necessary as this solution does not require use of variable `phase`.

7. Modify the "laundry-ticket" disk scheduler process in Section 9.1 so that it removes completed requests whose tickets have not been presented in 60 seconds.

8. Modify the job-shop problem in Section 9.4 to record and print statistics for the simulation, such as the average number of machines in use per group, and the average transit time of a job.

9. Does our solution of the job-shop problem in Section 9.4 suffer from the *cumulative time drift* discussed in Section 2? If so, then how can this drift be eliminated?

10. Revise the client-count version of the dining philosophers problem to avoid the problem described at the end of Section 6.3.

Chapter 3

Run-time Environment

In this chapter, we will describe the functions that make up the Concurrent C run-time library. Most of these functions are part of the Concurrent C language, and they are provided by all Concurrent C implementations. However, a few of the functions that we will describe here are implementation specific and we will identify them as such.

Declarations of the Concurrent C run-time library functions are contained in the standard header file named `concurrentc.h`. All Concurrent C programs using these functions should include this header file.

We will use the following notation, called a function prototype, to give a summary of the return-value and argument types of a function:

```
int c_changepriority(process anytype pid,int p);
```

This prototype declares `c_changepriority` as a function that has two parameters, of types `process anytype` and `int`, and returns an `int` value.

1. Process Ids

Function `c_mypid` returns the id of the calling process:

```
process anytype c_mypid();
```

Note that the process id is returned as a `process anytype` value. The caller might need to cast the returned value to the type of the calling process.

2. Process States

This section describes the functions that query the state of a process. First recall that at any given time, every Concurrent C process that has not terminated is in one of the following two states:

active   A process becomes *active* upon creation, and remains in this state while executing the statements in its process body.

completed   A process becomes *completed* when it reaches the end of its body, or when it executes a `return` statement in its process body. A completed process is in limbo; it still exists, but it

79

cannot execute.

The following functions test the state of a given process:

```
int c_valid(process anytype pid);
int c_active(process anytype pid);
int c_completed(process anytype pid);
```

These functions all take a process id as their argument, and return a 0 or a 1, depending on the state of the specified process. c_valid returns 1 if the process is active or has completed; otherwise it returns 0. c_active returns 1 if the process is active; otherwise it returns 0. c_completed returns 1 if the process is in the completed state; otherwise it returns 0.

3. Process Abortion

Function c_abort aborts—terminates—the specified process, and all children of this process, and their children, etc.:

```
void c_abort(process anytype pid);
```

Aborting a terminated process has no effect. Process abortion should be used with care. Concurrent C defines several conditions under which it is safe to abort a process. Remember that these conditions apply to *all* the processes being aborted by c_abort:

- It is safe to abort a process when it is not interacting with other processes. That is, it is safe to abort a process when (a) it does not have any pending calls from other processes, (b) it is not calling a transaction of another process, and (c) it is not in the body of an accept statement.

- It is safe to abort a process when it is only interacting with its descendants, and its descendants are interacting only with each other. That is, it is safe to abort a process when all of its interactions are with processes that are being aborted by this c_abort call. c_abort terminates the entire tree of processes, and quietly deletes any pending interactions between processes in that tree.

- It is safe to abort a process when it is calling a transaction of another process, provided that (a) the called process has not yet accepted the call, and (b) the aborted process does not have any pending calls from other processes. In this case, the calls from the aborted process are withdrawn, and are not seen by the called process. For example, it is safe to abort a process that is trying to call a transaction of the process calling c_abort.

- It is safe to abort a process that is waiting at an accept or select statement, provided the process has no pending transaction calls.

All other situations are undefined, and a Concurrent C implementation can do whatever it wants. In particular, the implementation can handle pending calls to the process being aborted however it likes. For example, the implementation might terminate the entire Concurrent C program or it might just abort the processes that made these calls.

As an example of process abortion, consider a process that creates processes to search different databases. Only one database will contain the answer (or an answer from only one database is needed). Once an answer is received, the other processes are aborted because to avoid performing unwanted computations. Other examples of similar situations are

1. In a parallel version of a game playing program, many processes may be created to determine the next move. Once one of these processes returns a "satisfactory" move, then the other processes can be aborted.

2. A parallel Prolog-like logic programming language has been implemented on top of Concurrent C [Woo & Sharma 1987]. This implementation uses two types of Concurrent C processes: and processes for evaluating rules, and or processes for evaluating literals. An and process creates several or processes, and waits for them to evaluate their literals and report success or failure. If one of the or processes reports failure, the and process then aborts the other or processes. This is part of a "backtracking" operation performed by the and process.

4. Process Priority

Process priority can be specified when creating the process, by using the priority clause of the create operator (see Section 5 of Chapter 1). The priority is an integer value. Positive values give the process a higher priority; negative values give it a lower priority. If the priority is omitted, then the new process is assigned priority zero.

Processes with higher priorities are given preference when they are scheduled for execution. Process priorities affect only the execution order of processes on the same processor. If there is only one process on a processor, then the process priority has no effect on the execution of the process.

The process scheduler is free to schedule processes subject to the following rules:

1. If two processes that are ready for execution have different priorities, then the one with the higher priority is given preference for execution.

2. No process should be indefinitely denied execution because of processes with the same or lower priorities.

Priorities should be used to give more execution time to some processes at the expense of others. Priorities should *not* be used for synchronizing processes.

For example, programmers should *not* assume that a higher priority process will immediately preempt all lower priority processes.

The points at which the scheduler is invoked (for processes on the same processor) are left to the implementation. For example, an implementation may use a round-robin scheduling strategy modified to use process priorities.

There are several functions that manipulate process priorities:

```
int c_getpriority(process anytype pid);
int c_setpriority(process anytype pid, int p);
int c_changepriority(process anytype pid, int del);
```

c_getpriority returns the priority of the specified process. c_setpriority sets the priority of the specified process to the given value, and returns the previous priority of the process. c_changepriority changes the process priority by the signed integer value del and returns the previous priority.

5. Number of Pending Transaction Calls

Function c_transcount returns the number of pending calls for a specific transaction:

```
int c_transcount(transaction-pointer);
```

The transaction is specified by a transaction pointer; the return value type of the transaction is ignored. For example, if c_transcount is called by a process of type buffer, which has a transaction named put, then the following c_transcount call returns the number of pending put calls:

```
process buffer me;
...
me = c_mypid();
n = c_transcount(me.put);
```

This could also have been written as one expression, by using a cast:

```
n = c_transcount(((process buffer)c_mypid()).put);
```

The value returned by c_transcount includes pending asynchronous and timed transaction calls. Because timed calls can be withdrawn by the calling process, the returned value is only an approximate indication of the number of pending calls.

To illustrate the use of c_transcount, we will write a process trafficLight that controls a traffic light at the intersection of a main road and a lightly used side road. The traffic light is normally green for the main road and red for the side road. The light changes to red for the main road and green for the side road when

1. a sensor detects that a car has arrived at the intersection on the side road, or

2. a pedestrian, who wants to cross the main road, presses a button provided for the purpose.

Both the sensor and the pedestrian button cause an interrupt. Here is the specification of how the traffic light must operate:

1. Traffic flow on the main road is stopped only after the main road has had the green light for at least 3 minutes.

2. Traffic flow on the main road is stopped for only 30 seconds at a time.

3. Sometimes several interrupts may occur before traffic flow is stopped on the main road. For example, they can occur when cars arrive at both sides of the side road, or when a car arrives at the side road and a pedestrian presses the button, or when a pedestrian presses the button several times. When this happens, only the first interrupt is used; the additional interrupts are discarded.

Here is the specification of process `trafficLight`:

File: `light.h`

```
process spec trafficLight(int ia)
{
    trans async stopMain();
};
```

Parameter `ia` is the hardware address at which the sensor and the pedestrian button generate an interrupt.

Here is the body of process `trafficLight`:

File: `light.cc`

```
#include "concurrentc.h"
#include "light.h"
#define MAIN_MIN    180.0
#define SIDE_OPEN    30.0

void start(), change();

process body trafficLight(ia)
{
    trans async (*sm)() = ((process trafficLight)
                            c_mypid()).stopMain;
    int n;

    c_associate(sm, ia);
    start();
    for (;;) {
        delay MAIN_MIN;
        accept stopMain();
        change();
        delay SIDE_OPEN;
        for (n = c_transcount(sm); n > 0; --n)
            accept stopMain();
        change();
    }
}
```

Process `trafficLight` uses functions `start`, which initializes the traffic light so that the main road has a green light, and `change`, which changes the state of light. Function `c_associate` takes a transaction pointer as an argument, and arranges for that transaction to be called whenever the indicated hardware interrupt occurs.

6. Giving Names to Process Instances

By default, the symbolic name given to a process is the name of its process type; an alternative name can be assigned to any Concurrent C process. The Concurrent C run-time system uses these names in error messages, so they are useful if you have several different processes of the same type. The following functions are used for manipulating process names:

```
void  c_setname(process anytype pid, char *name);
char *c_getname(process anytype pid, char *name);
```

`c_setname` sets the name of the indicated process to the string specified by the `name` parameter. `c_getname` gets the name of the indicated process; it copies the name into the character array `name`, which must have at least `c_NAMELEN` (defined in `concurrentc.h`) characters, and then returns the address of this array.

As an example, we will revise the dining philosophers problem given in Chapter 1, to give a name to each `philosopher` process:

File: `phil-named.cc`

```
#include "concurrentc.h"
#include "fork.h"
#include "phil.h"
#define LIMIT 100000

process body philosopher(id, left, right)
{
    int nmeal;
    static char *names[] =
        { "Plato", "Marx", "Sartre",
          "Hypatia", "Lao Tse" };

    c_setname(c_mypid(), names[id]);
    for (nmeal = 0; nmeal < LIMIT; nmeal++) {
        same as before
    }
}
```

7. Processor Selection on a Multiprocessor

When creating a process, you can optionally specify a processor, as in

```
create buffer() processor(n);
```

n is a integer "processor number" expression identifying the processor to which the newly created process is to be assigned. These processor numbers may be obtained using the following Concurrent C library functions:

```
int c_processorid(process anytype pid);
int c_bestprocessor();
int c_giveprocessors(int max, int procs[]);
```

`c_processorid` returns the number of the processor on which the indicated Concurrent C process is running. If the specified process id is invalid, then `c_processorid` returns -1. For example, the following expression creates a new `buffer` process on the same processor as the creating process:

```
create buffer()
      processor(c_processorid(c_mypid()))
```

`c_bestprocessor` returns the number of a processor which the Concurrent C system considers to be the "best" in some sense. This is up to the implementation, but it could be a processor that is lightly loaded.

`c_giveprocessors` provides the caller with a set of processor numbers. The caller passes in integer array as the second argument, and passes the number of elements in this array as the first argument, as in

```
int nproc, procs[10];
nproc = c_giveprocessors(10, procs);
```

`c_giveprocessors` copies the processor numbers into this array, and returns the number of processors. If there are more processors than will fit in the array, `c_giveprocessors` copies as many as it can.

As an example, we will again revise our dining philosophers program to explicitly assign each `fork` process to a different processor (assuming there are enough), and to place each `philosopher` process on the same processor as its left-hand `fork` process. We only have to change the `main` process:

File: `dining-multi.cc`

```
#include "concurrentc.h"
#include "fork.h"
#include "phil.h"

#define MAX_PROCS 10

main()
{
    process fork f[5];
    int j, n, procs[MAX_PROCS];

    n = c_giveprocessors(MAX_PROCS, procs);
    for (j = 0; j < 5; j++)
        f[j]=create fork() processor(procs[j%n]);
    for (j = 0; j < 5; j++)
        create philosopher(j, f[j], f[(j+1)%5])
                processor(procs[j%n]);
}
```

8. Interrupts and Transactions

Interrupts can be associated with transactions; when an interrupt occurs, Concurrent C generates a call to the associated transaction. The implementation-dependent library function `c_associate` does the association; one of its parameters is a transaction pointer. The other parameters define the interrupt, and are obviously implementation dependent. For the examples in this section, assume that c_associate is declared as

```
void c_associate(trans async (*tp)(), int addr);
```

where tp is a transaction pointer that identifies the transaction to be called when the interrupt associated with the address addr occurs.

8.1 Example: An Automobile Cruise Controller [Gehani 1984a]

Some automobiles have a cruise control mechanism that automatically maintains the automobile at a constant speed selected by the driver. To engage the cruise control mechanism, the driver drives the automobile at the desired speed, and then pushes the cruise control button. To disengage the cruise control, the driver presses either the brake or the gas pedal (the accelerator). The problem is to write a program that monitors and maintains an automobile at a constant speed, i.e., an *automobile cruise controller*.

Before we can write this controller, we need to describe the hardware environment. When the driver pushes the cruise control button, the hardware generates an interrupt at memory location 060. Depressing the brake and gas pedals generate interrupts at locations 062 and 064. The current speed of the automobile, an integer value, can be accessed from memory location 024. To change the speed, the program can write a signed integer value to memory location 026; this causes the automobile to speed up or slow down by that amount. The automobile takes about half a second to respond to the change in speed.

The cruise controller accepts speeds between 25 and 55 miles per hour. Attempts to set a cruising speed outside these limits cause an alarm signal to be sounded (by writing a non-zero value to memory location 022). The alarm is also sounded and the cruise controller is deactivated if the cruise controller cannot maintain the automobile speed to within 2 miles of the specified cruising speed.

The cruise controller algorithm can be abstractly described as

```
for (;;) {
    wait until the driver activates the cruise control;
    check if cruising speed is within the specified limits;
    if not, warn driver but do not activate mechanism;
    for (;;) {
        select {
            if brake pedal is depressed, deactivate mechanism;
        or
            if gas pedal is depressed, deactivate mechanism;
        or
            try and maintain automobile speed at the cruising speed;
                otherwise, deactivate mechanism;
            wait 0.5 seconds for the automobile speed change;
        }
    }
}
```

The specification of the cruise controller process is

```
                                                    File: cruise.h
process spec cruiseControl()
{
    trans async takeOver(), brake(), gasPedal();
};
```

The body of the cruise controller is

File: cruise.cc

```
#include "concurrentc.h"
#include "cruise.h"
#define ABS(x)      (((x)>0)?(x):-(x))
#define BOUND       2
#define LOW         25
#define HIGH        55

process body cruiseControl()
{
    int *alarm = (int*) 022;
    int *spd = (int*) 024;
    int *changeSpd = (int*) 026;
    int curSpd, cruiseSpd;
    process cruiseControl me = c_mypid();

/*associate interrupts with transactions*/
    c_associate(me.takeOver, 060);
    c_associate(me.brake, 062);
    c_associate(me.gasPedal, 064);

    for (;;) {
        accept takeOver(); cruiseSpd = *spd;
        if (cruiseSpd < LOW || cruiseSpd > HIGH)
            *alarm = 1;
        else
            for (;;)
                select {
                    accept brake(); break;
                or
                    accept gasPedal(); break;
                or
                    curSpd = *spd;
                    if (ABS(cruiseSpd-curSpd)>BOUND)
                        {*alarm = 1; break;}
                    else
                        *changeSpd = cruiseSpd-curSpd;
                    delay 0.5;
                }
    }
}
```

9. Process Stack Size

Some implementations put a limit on the maximum size of the stack allocated for each Concurrent C process. Our implementations provide two functions for manipulating this stack size:

```
int c_setstksiz(int);
int c_getstksiz();
```

To understand how the stack size is determined, note that in our implementations, the stack size for a process is determined by the process' parent, when the process is created. Once a process has been created, its stack size cannot be changed. Each process has a "create-stack-size" attribute, which is the stack size used whenever this process creates a child process. Function c_setstksiz is used to specify an alternative create-stack-size value for the calling process (otherwise, the default value is used). Thus c_setstksiz sets the stack size for all processes *subsequently* created by the calling process. c_getstksiz returns the value of the create-stack-size attribute for the calling process. When a process is created, its create-stack-size attribute is set to that of its parent.

Typically c_setstksiz is called in the main process, before it creates any other processes. If this is done, then all processes will have the specified stack size.

The stack size of the main process is specified by defining and appropriately initializing the external int variable c_stksiz.

Again, we must stress that we consider these two functions to be part of our implementation of Concurrent C, not part of the language definition. Other implementations might use different techniques for controlling stack sizes.

10. C and UNIX Functions

10.1 C Library Functions

Concurrent C programs can call standard C library functions. Because many of these functions update global or static variables, the Concurrent C compiler ensures that a process is not interrupted while it is in the middle of executing these functions. Otherwise, the results will not be consistent. However, this guarantee only applies to library functions; it does not apply to functions that the programmer writes and links into a Concurrent C program. The programmer must ensure that if such a function is called by multiple processes, then the function does not update global or static variables.

10.2 UNIX Functions

Some Concurrent C implementations on UNIX systems place restrictions on the UNIX system functions that a Concurrent C program can call. The details depend on the specific implementation, of course, but here are some restrictions from our implementations of Concurrent C:

1. Concurrent C programs cannot call the `alarm` function because it is used by the Concurrent C implementation for time slicing.

2. For the `setjmp` and `longjmp` functions to work properly, `longjmp` must be called by the same Concurrent C process that called `setjmp`.

3. Signals should be used with care. Some signals cannot be used, because the Concurrent C implementation uses them. Other signals can be used, but there is no guarantee as to which Concurrent C process will be interrupted when the signal occurs. Thus you cannot call `longjmp` from a signal handler.

11. Exercises

1. Process `trafficLight` in Section 5 has the following code:

   ```
   delay(SIDE_OPEN);
   for (n = c_transcount(sm); n > 0; --n)
       accept stopMain();
   ```

   Suppose we put the `delay` statement after the loop. How would this change the algorithm that the controller implements?

2. Give examples of situations where it would be appropriate to explicitly specify the processor on which a process should execute (instead of letting the implementation pick the processor).

3. Give an example of a situation in which you may need to change the priority of a process dynamically.

Chapter 4

Large Examples

Up to now, we have shown you several small concurrent programs. We will now show you several large programs. For some examples we will give you the complete code while for other examples we will show you a sketch of the solution.

1. Protocol Simulation

Communication protocols are rules and conventions used by the components of distributed systems and networks to exchange information and synchronize with each other. These protocols must handle a wide range of problems, such as communication errors and variations in message-transfer times. Protocols are simulated for a variety of reasons, e.g., to check their correctness, to check their performance, or to try alternative strategies. Our problem is to write a program to simulate a very simple protocol, the *alternating bit* protocol. This protocol alternatingly assigns 0s and 1s to messages to ensure that they are transmitted in sequence and are delivered reliably over an unreliable communication medium. The protocol assumes that if the message is delivered, it is delivered in an uncorrupted form; the receiver can check whether or not it is corrupted and request message retransmission.

First, here is a figure showing the relationship between the components of the protocol:

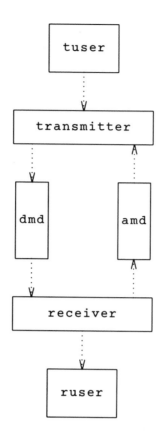

········>   Dotted arrows indicate direction of information flow

Figure 4.1: Protocol Components

`transmitter` receives messages from the transmitting user `tuser` and alternately assigns them sequence bits 0 and 1. It then sends these messages via the data medium `dmd` to the `receiver`. The `transmitter` then waits for an acknowledgment with a matching sequence bit. If it does not receive the acknowledgment within a specified period, it retransmits the message. Each time the `receiver` receives a message, it sends an acknowledgment with the right sequence bit to the `transmitter` via the acknowledgment medium `amd`. The receiving user, `ruser`, gets the messages from the `receiver`. (Note that the data medium and the acknowledgment medium can be the same medium, i.e., the communication medium.)

To simulate the protocol, we will model each protocol component as a separate process. The following figure describes the structure of the Concurrent C program implementing the alternating bit protocol:

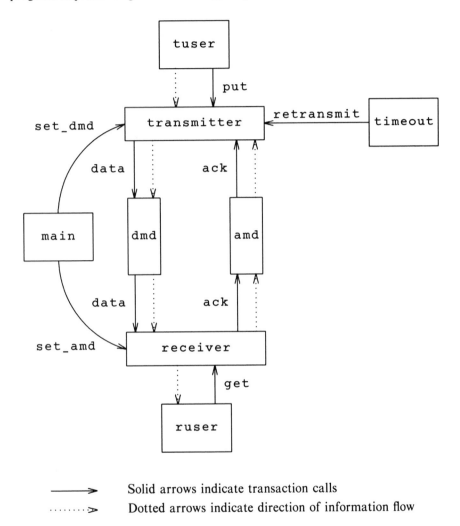

Solid arrows indicate transaction calls
Dotted arrows indicate direction of information flow

Figure 4.2: Structure of the Concurrent C Program

The `main` process creates the processes that model the protocol components. Process `timeout` is created by the `transmitter` process so that it gets a retransmission notification.

Here are the specifications of the `tuser`, `timeout` and `ruser` processes:

File: tuser.h
```
process spec tuser(process transmitter t);
```

File: timeout.h
```
process spec timeout(trans void (*rt)(),float d);
```

File: ruser.h
```
process spec ruser(process receiver r);
```

Here is the specification of the transmitter process:

File: trans.h
```
process spec transmitter()
{
    trans void put(int msg);
    trans void retransmit();
    trans void set_dmd(process dmd dm);
    trans void ack(int bit);
};
```

Transaction set_dmd is called by the main process to give the name of the process modeling the data medium. tuser calls transaction put to transmit a message. Transaction retransmit is called by the timeout process to inform the transmitter process that it is time to retransmit the message. Transaction ack is called by the process modeling the acknowledgment medium to signal the receipt, by receiver, of a message.

Here is the specification of the dmd process:

File: dmd.h
```
process spec dmd(process receiver r)
{
    trans void data(int bit, int msg);
};
```

Transaction data is called by the transmitter process to send messages.

Here is the specification of the receiver process:

File: r e c . h

```
process spec receiver()
{
    trans int get();
    trans void set_amd(process amd am);
    trans void data(int bit, int msg);
};
```

Transaction set_amd is called by the main process to give the name of the process modeling the acknowledgment medium process. ruser calls transaction get to receive messages. Transaction data is called by the data medium process to deliver messages to the receiver.

Here is the specification of the amd process:

File: amd . h

```
process spec amd(process transmitter t)
{
    trans void ack(int bit);
};
```

Transaction ack is called by the receiver process to send an acknowledgment.

Functions lose_data and lose_ack are used to simulate transmission errors; every time the random number generated by rand is divisible by 7, a message or acknowledgment is lost. These functions can be modified to simulate desired kinds of transmission errors. Their definitions are

File: lose . cc

```
int rand();
/*lose data/ack when random number%7 == 0*/
int lose_data()
{
    return (rand()%7 == 0);
}
int lose_ack()
{
    return (rand()%7 == 0);
}
```

Now it is time to show the bodies of the protocol component processes. First, I will show you the bodies of the two user processes, i.e., tuser and ruser. Here is the body of the tuser process:

File: tuser.cc

```
#include <stdio.h>
#include "trans.h"
#include "tuser.h"
process body tuser(t)
{
    int ch;
    while ((ch = getchar()) != EOF)
        t.put(ch);
    t.put(EOF);
}
```

Here is the body of the `ruser` process:

File: ruser.cc

```
#include <ctype.h>
#include <stdio.h>
#include "rec.h"
#include "ruser.h"
process body ruser(r)
{
    int ch;
    while ((ch = r.get()) != EOF)
        putchar(islower(ch)?toupper(ch):ch);
}
```

Now here is the body of the `transmitter` process:

File: trans.cc

```
#include "timeout.h"
#include "dmd.h"
#include "trans.h"
process body transmitter()
{
    process dmd d; process timeout t;
    int tryagain, cur_bit, b, m;
    trans void (*rt)();

    rt = ((process transmitter)
                    c_mypid()).retransmit;
    accept set_dmd(dm) d = dm;
    for (cur_bit = 0;; cur_bit = !cur_bit) {
        select {
            accept put(msg) m = msg;
        or
            terminate;
        }
        for (tryagain = 1; tryagain;) {
            d.data(cur_bit, m);
            t = create timeout(rt, 1.0);
            for (;;)
                select {
                    accept retransmit(); break;
                or
                    accept ack(bit) b = bit;
                    if (b == cur_bit) {
                        tryagain = 0;
                        c_abort(t); break;
                    }
                }
        }
    }
}
```

The `transmitter` process waits for the name of the data medium and then it enters a loop. In this loop, it first enters a *select* statement where it waits for a message (via transaction `put`) for transmission or program termination. The `transmitter` process sends the message (via transaction `data`) to the data medium process. It then creates a `timeout` process and waits for an appropriate acknowledgment or the `retransmit` transaction call which indicates that it is time to retransmit the message. While waiting for the acknowledgment, the `transmitter` process ignores acknowledgments that do not correspond to the value of `cur_bit` (which alternates between 0 and 1). If a correct acknowledgment is received before the `retransmit` transaction call is received from the `timeout` process, the `transmitter` aborts the `timeout` process and goes on to accept the next message to be transmitted. Otherwise, it retransmits the message and repeats the procedure while waiting for an acknowledgment or a retransmission indication. The `transmitter` process alternates forever between sending messages tagged 0 and 1 (the value of `cur_bit`).

The `timeout` process is given a transaction pointer that points to transaction `retransmit` of the `transmitter` process. The `timeout` process calls this transaction upon the expiration of the specified timeout period. We use the `timeout` process to determine the end of the timeout period instead of the *delay* alternative in the `transmitter` process because this allows the `transmitter` process to accept, for example, a sequence 1 acknowledgment when it is interested in a sequence 0 acknowledgment without having its timeout period reset. Note accepting any alternative in a *select* statement causes the *delay* alternative in that *select* statement, if any, to be reset when the *select* is next executed.

Here is the body of the `timeout` process:

File: `timeout.cc`

```
#include "timeout.h"
process body timeout(rt, d)
{
    delay d;
    (*rt)();
}
```

Here is the body of the `dmd` process:

File: `dmd.cc`

```
#include "rec.h"
#include "dmd.h"
process body dmd(r)
{
    int b, m, lose_data();
    for (;;) {
        select {
            accept data(bit, msg) {
                m = msg; b = bit;
            }
            if (!lose_data()) r.data(b, m);
        or
            terminate;
        }
    }
}
```

Here is the body of the `receiver` process:

File: `rec.cc`

```
#include "amd.h"
#include "rec.h"
process body receiver()
{
    process amd a; int b, m, cur_bit;
    accept set_amd(am) a = am;
    for (cur_bit = 0;; cur_bit = !cur_bit) {
        for(;;) {
            select {
                accept data(bit, msg) {
                    b = bit; m = msg;
                }
                if (b==cur_bit) break;else a.ack(b);
            or
                terminate;
            }
        }
        a.ack(cur_bit);
        accept get() treturn m;
    }
}
```

Here is the body of the amd process:

```
                                                        File: amd.cc
#include "amd.h"
#include "trans.h"
process body amd(t)
{
    int b;

    for (;;) {
        select {
            accept ack(bit) b = bit;
            if (!lose_ack())
                t.ack(b);
        or
            terminate;
        }
    }
}
```

Finally, here is the body of the main process:

```
                                                        File: protocol.cc
#include "trans.h"
#include "rec.h"
#include "dmd.h"
#include "amd.h"
#include "tuser.h"
#include "ruser.h"
main()
{
    process transmitter t;
    process receiver r;

    t = create transmitter();
    r = create receiver();
    t.set_dmd(create dmd(r));
    r.set_amd(create amd(t));

    create tuser(t);
    create ruser(r);
}
```

The main process just instantiates the appropriate processes and supplies the transmitter and the receiver processes with the names of the data and acknowledgment medium processes.

2. Robot Controller

The problem is to write a program to control the motion of two-dimensional (Cartesian) robots [Cox & Gehani 1987, 1988]. The XY motion of the robot is provided by two orthogonal stepper motors. The stepper motor controller hardware is supplied with the direction, distance and speed of travel and, upon completing the move, the motor generates an interrupt at the associated interrupt location The program should accept requests to move a robot and then initiate movement of the robot by sending appropriate commands to its two motors which operate concurrently.

We will first write a program to control a single robot and then a program that controls motion of two robots sharing a common work area. Collisions are avoided by using a simple scheme that models the workspace as a resource. The second program makes use of the program components developed for the program to control the single robot. The programs that we will show you were compiled on a SUN workstation and executed on the Concurrent C implementation running on a Motorola 68010 based NRTX system [Kapilow 1985] which communicates with the robot hardware.

The Concurrent C program to control a single robot is structured as

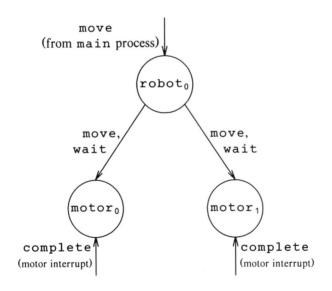

Figure 4.3: Single Robot Controller

First we will show you the `main` process:

```
                                              File: OneRobot.cc
#include <stdio.h>
#include "icma.h"
        /*contains declarations for the      */
        /*hardware functions motor_init()     */
        /*hardware_init(), motor_complete(),*/
        /*move()*/
#include "vec.h"
#include "robot.h"
main()
{
    process robot r;
    vec pos;
    short d = 0;

    hardware_init();
    pos.x = 0; pos.y = 0;
    r = create robot(0, pos);
    r.calibrate();

    printf("type x, y: ");
    while (scanf("%d %d", &pos.x, &pos.y) == 2)
        r.move(pos);
}
```

The `main` process first calls the function `hardware_init` to initialize the hardware. Next, `main` creates the `robot` process and then calls its transaction `calibrate` to initialize the robot. After the initialization, the `main` process repeatedly calls transaction `move` of the `robot` process to move the robot to user-requested positions. Note that a new move request is accepted only after the robot has completed its previous move.

File `vec.h` used in the above program defines type `vec` which is used to specify the x and y components of a position or a velocity:

```
                                              File: vec.h
typedef struct {
    int x, y;
} vec;
```

Here is the specification of the `robot` process:

File: robot.h

```
process spec robot(short rn, vec ip)
{
    trans void calibrate();
    trans void move(vec p);
};
```

The robot process takes as arguments the robot number (starting with 0) and the initial position of the robot. It has two transactions: calibrate, which moves the robot to the initial position, and move, which synchronously moves the robot to the specified position.

The body of the robot process is

File: robot.cc

```
#include "vec.h"
#include "robot.h"
#include "icma.h"
#include "motor.h"
process body robot(rn, ip)
{
    process motor xm, ym;
    vec cur_pos = ip, pos, v, rel_vel();

    xm = create motor(2*rn);
    ym = create motor(2*rn+1);
    for(;;)
        select {
            accept calibrate() {
                v = rel_vel(ip);
                xm.move(ip.x, v.x);
                ym.move(ip.y, v.y);
                xm.wait(); ym.wait();
            }
        or
            accept move(p) {
                pos.x = p.x - cur_pos.x;
                pos.y = p.y - cur_pos.y;
                v = rel_vel(pos);
                xm.move(pos.x, v.x);
                ym.move(pos.y, v.y);
                xm.wait(); ym.wait();
                cur_pos = p;
            }
        }
}
```

Upon instantiation, the robot process immediately creates two motor processes. Note that motors 2*rn and 2*rn+1 are associated with robot numbered `rn`. The `robot` process then enters a loop in which it will accept either a `calibrate` or a `move` transaction.

After accepting a `move` request, the `robot` process first computes the distances to be moved and the x and y velocities (using function `rel_vel`). Then it initiates moves in the x and y directions by calling transaction `move` of the `motor` processes. The `robot` process then waits for the motors to finish moving by calling transaction `wait` of the `motor` processes before updating the robot location.

Function `rel_vel` used in the `robot` process is defined as

File: `rel-vel.cc`

```
#include "vec.h"
#include "icma.h"
vec rel_vel(p)
    vec p;
{
    vec v;
    v.x = v.y = DEFAULT_VEL;
    if((ABS(p.x) < ABS(p.y)) && (p.x != 0))
        v.y = (DEFAULT_VEL * ABS(p.y))/ABS(p.x);
    else if (p.y != 0)
        v.x = (DEFAULT_VEL * ABS(p.x))/ABS(p.y);
    return (v);
}
```

Now here is the specification of the `motor` process:

File: `motor.h`

```
process spec motor(int motor_id)
{
    trans async move(int distance, int vel);
    trans async complete();
    trans void wait();
};
```

The `motor` process has three transactions:

1. `move`: initiate the motor motion asynchronously,
2. `complete`: associated with the motor interrupt indicating that the motor has completed the requested action, and
3. `wait`: called by the process requesting the move to wait until the move has completed.

Here is the body of the motor process:

File: motor.cc

```
#include "icma.h"
#include "motor.h"

process body motor(motor_id)
{
    int dist;
    trans async (*tp)();

    tp = ((process motor) c_mypid()).complete;
    c_associate(tp, IVEC(motor_id));
    init(motor_id);
    accept complete();

    for(;;)
    {
        accept move(distance, vel)
            if ((dist = distance) != 0) {
                motor_move(motor_id, distance, vel);
                accept complete()
                    motor_complete(motor_id);
            }
        accept wait();
    }
}
```

The interesting thing to notice is the use of the function c_associate. It converts interrupts generated by the motor into calls to the transaction complete. The second argument of c_associate identifies the interrupt to be associated with the transaction specified by the first argument. Note that given the motor id, IVEC returns the interrupt address.

After calling c_associate, the motor process initializes the hardware by calling the init function. The motor process then waits for the complete transaction which indicates completion of the initialization sequence.

The motor process then enters a loop in which it first accepts a move transaction; if the distance to be moved is greater than zero, then the function motor_move is called to start the motor. motor then waits for the completion of the motion which is signaled by the arrival of the complete transaction. The motor_complete function call in the body of the complete transaction checks to see if the move was successfully completed; if not, it prints an error message. The motor process then waits to accept transaction `wait` from the `robot` process before going back to the beginning of the loop.

2.1 Two Robots in a Common Workspace

We will now extend the program for controlling one robot to handle two robots moving in a common workspace. The following figure describes the structure of the program:

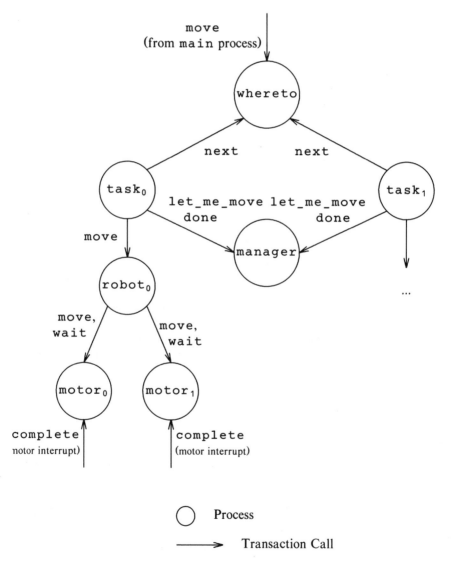

Figure 4.4: Two Robot Controller

For simplicity, we will assume that the robots perform independent tasks and that only collisions are to be avoided. One simple solution for avoiding collisions consists of modeling the workspace as a resource. Before moving, a robot must first request the "resource manager" to allocate the "volume of workspace" needed to perform the move. The resource manager accepts the allocation request only when the robot will be able to move safely. After completing the move, the robot returns the workspace allocated to it by telling the resource manager that it is done moving.

Extending the first example, which controls a single robot, to control two robots is straightforward. Each robot is now controlled by a task process. We could have combined the functionality of the task process into the robot process thus reducing the number of processes by two. However, we decided to use the organization shown to avoid modifying the robot process used in the single robot example. As such, information about a specific robot application can be encapsulated in the task processes leaving the robot process to worry about robot details. Here are the specification and body of the task process:

File: task.h

```
process spec task(short rn, vec ip,
                  process manager mngr,
                  process whereto where);
```

File: task.cc

```
#include "vec.h"
#include "task.h"
#include "robot.h"
#include "manager.h"
#include "whereto.h"
process body task(rn, ip, mngr, where)
{
    vec pos; process robot my_robot;
    my_robot = create robot(rn, ip);
    my_robot.calibrate(); mngr.init(rn, ip);
    for(;;) {
        pos = where.next_position(rn);
        mngr.let_me_move(rn, pos);
        my_robot.move(pos); mngr.done(rn);
    }
}
```

Process task gets the coordinates for the next move from the whereto process. It then requests permission to move from the resource manager process `manager` by calling transaction `let_me_move`. This transaction is accepted if and only if the move will not result in a collision. On receiving permission, the `task` process initiates movement of the robot by calling transaction `move` of the `robot` process. Finally, after the robot has moved, the resource manager is informed that the robot has completed moving by calling transaction `done`.

Now here are specification and body of the resource manager:

File: `manager.h`

```
process spec manager()
{
    trans void init(short rn, vec pos);
    trans void done(short rn);
    trans void let_me_move(short rn, vec pos);
};
```

File: `manager.cc`

```
#include "vec.h"
#include "robot.h"
#include "manager.h"
#include "two.h"

static status r_status[NROBOTS];
static area rarea[NROBOTS];

process body manager()
{
    for (;;)
        select {
            accept init(rn, pos) {
                r_status[rn].moving = 0;
                r_status[rn].cur = pos;
                r_status[rn].prev = pos;
            }
        or
            accept let_me_move(rn, pos)
                    suchthat(!collision(rn, pos)) {
                r_status[rn].prev=r_status[rn].cur;
                r_status[rn].cur = pos;
                r_status[rn].moving = 1;
            }
        or
            accept done(rn)
                r_status[rn].moving = 0;
        }
}
```

The `manager` process executes a loop in which it accepts transaction calls to

1. initialize the robot position,
2. allow a robot to move, and
3. record the fact that a robot has completed the move.

The interesting aspect of this process is the `suchthat` clause. A `task` process calling transaction `let_me_move` to request permission to move to the specified destination `pos` is blocked until it can move without colliding with the other robot. The `suchthat` clause can examine the parameters of a transaction call without accepting it. In this case, this clause ensures that the path to the requested destination is clear by calling the function `collision`. The `suchthat` clause is useful in that it avoids the need for the `robot` process to periodically poll the resource manager. If there are no `init` or `done` requests and no `let_me_move` request satisfying the `suchthat` clause, then execution of the process is suspended. The process is only reactivated when an appropriate request arrives.

The `whereto` process buffers requests to move the robots. Unlike the single robot version, the introduction of the `whereto` process allows new move requests to be accepted even though the specified robot may not have completed its last move. Here is the specification of the `whereto` process:

File: `whereto.h`

```
process spec whereto()
{
    trans void new_move(short rn, vec p);
    trans vec next_position(short rn);
};
```

The body of the `whereto` process is

```
#include  "vec.h"
#include  "whereto.h"
#include  "queue.h"
#include  "two.h"

static queue q[NROBOTS];

process body whereto()
{

    for (;;)
        select {
            accept new_move(rn, p)
                        suchthat(!full(&q[rn]))
                put(&q[rn], p);
            or
                accept next_position(rn)
                        suchthat(!empty(&q[rn]))
                    treturn(get(&q[rn]));
            }
}
```

Moves are accepted as long as there is space to store them. These are given to
the `task` processes controlling the robots. Here are the files containing
declarations and code for the queue manipulation functions:

```
#define MAX_SIZE 64
struct queue {
    vec a[MAX_SIZE];
    int first;
    int last;
    int n;
};
int empty(), full();
vec get();
void put();
```

```
#include <stdio.h>
#include "vec.h"
#include "queue.h"

void fatal(err)
    char *err;
{
   fprintf(stderr, "%s\n", err); exit(1);
}

vec get(q_ptr)
    queue *q_ptr;
{
   vec temp;
   if (empty(q_ptr))
      fatal("queue.add: Error, queue empty");
   q_ptr->n--;
   temp = q_ptr->a[q_ptr->first];
   q_ptr->first = (q_ptr->first+1) % MAX_SIZE;
   return(temp);
}

void put(q_ptr, p)
   queue *q_ptr; vec p;
{
   if (full(q_ptr))
       fatal("queue.add: Error, queue full");
   q_ptr->n++; q_ptr->a[q_ptr->last] = p;
   q_ptr->last = (q_ptr->last+1) % MAX_SIZE;
}

int empty(q_ptr)
   queue *q_ptr;
{
   return (q_ptr->n == 0);
}

int full(q_ptr)
   queue *q_ptr;
{
   return (q_ptr->n == MAX_SIZE);
}
```

Finally, the body of the main process is

File: TwoRobots.cc

```
#include <stdio.h>
#include "icma.h"
#include "vec.h"
#include "manager.h"
#include "whereto.h"
#include "task.h"
main()
{
    process manager mngr;
    process whereto where;
    process task task0, task1;
    short r;
    vec pos;

    pos.x = pos.y = 0;
    hardware_init();
    mngr = create manager();
    where = create whereto();
    task0 = create task(0, pos, mngr, where);
    task1 = create task(1, pos, mngr, where);

    printf("type robot number, x, y: ");
    while(scanf("%hd%d%d",&r,&pos.x,&pos.y)==3)
        where.new_move(r, pos);
}
```

Collision avoidance is done dynamically because it is assumed that the robots'
movements are not known *a priori*. Modeling the workspace as a set of
resources and determining if the resources required for the move are available
is a simple yet elegant collision avoidance scheme. However, it should be noted
that this simple approach does not prevent deadlock. For example, if the two
robots wished to exchange positions, each would be denied permission to move
and would then wait forever. A further level of planning is required to avoid
this, but is not relevant to the discussion.

3. Concurrent Make

make [Feldman 1979] is a tool for automatically constructing a system from
its components; make automatically executes the commands (e.g.,
compilations) needed to construct a system. Concurrent Make (cmake) is a
parallel version of make; cmake speeds up the system construction process by
executing commands in parallel on one or more processors [Cmelik 1986].

make constructs a system by

- using information supplied by the user indicating dependencies between the components (*target files*) to be constructed and the components required for constructing them (*prerequisite files*);

- invoking commands supplied by the user to construct the target files from the prerequisite files.

The user supplies this information via a file named makefile. make executes the commands necessary to construct the target files that are out-of-date, and only these commands. Thus if one file is changed, only the files that depend on it will be reconstructed; the other files will be unchanged. make uses the last-modified times of the files to determine if files are out-of-date.

For example, consider the following makefile:

File: test.mk

```
   test: x.o y.o z.o
          cc x.o y.o z.o -o test
   x.o: x.c comm.h
          cc -c x.c
5  y.o: y.c comm.h
          cc -c y.c
   z.o: z.c comm.h
          cc -c z.c
```

Dependencies are specified in lines 1, 3, 5, and 7. The program to be constructed is called test; it depends upon three object files x.o, y.o, and z.o which in turn depend upon the C files x.c, y.c, and z.c. All of these C files include the header file comm.h, so all three object files depend on that. Commands to construct the target files are given in lines 2, 4, 6, and 8. If a target file does not exist, or if its last-modification time is less than the last-modification time of the files it depends upon (i.e., its prerequisite files), then make executes the command to construct the file. Thus if the user changes y.c, make will execute the commands on lines 6 and 2.

If the user changes comm.h, make will execute the commands on line 4, 6, 8, and 2, one at a time. But note that the commands on lines 4, 6, and 8 are three independent compilations. If three processors are available, we could speed things up by executing these three commands at the same time, on different processors. cmake does this; it executes the commands on lines 4, 6, and 8 in parallel, using the available processors. Then, after these commands have completed, cmake executes the command on line 2. Thus cmake can speed up the system construction process by doing independent compilations in parallel.

The rest of this section gives an outline of how `cmake` is implemented in Concurrent C. The general version of `cmake` is designed for an environment in which the processors do not have a shared file system; `cmake` copies files to and from the processors as needed. We will not describe the details of how this is done. Instead, we will describe a slightly simpler version of `cmake`, and we will assume that the file system is shared by all processors, and that any command can execute on any processor.

3.1 Data Structures

`cmake` uses the following data structures:

```
                                              File: cmake.h

    /* Mach: Data about a processor. */
typedef struct {
    int m_proc;        /* processor number */
    data about load on machine;
} Mach;

    /* Node: information about a target file. */
typedef struct NODE Node;
struct NODE {
    int    n_state;     /* state of node */
    Mach  *n_mach;      /* machine assigned */
    char  *n_cmd;       /* command to make file */
    char  *n_name;      /* file/node name */
    Node  **n_deps;     /* dependents of node */
    other data;
};

    /* State codes: */
#define N_INIT     0  /* initial: unexamined */
#define N_MAKING   1  /* being made */
#define N_MADE     2  /* successfully made */
#define N_FAIL     3  /* unsuccessfully made */

#define is_made(s)   ((s)==N_MADE || (s)==N_FAIL)
```

There is an array of `Mach` structures, one for each processor on which `cmake` can execute commands. Each structure contains information about the commands that `cmake` is currently executing on that processor, and the information needed to execute commands remotely on that machine.

`cmake` creates an instance of a `Node` structure for each target file described in the makefile, and links them together into a tree, based on the dependency rules in the makefile. This tree is created sequentially, before `cmake` executes any commands. The n_state element gives the state of each target file. Files start out in the "initial" state, which means that cmake does not know whether they are up-to-date or not. While a file is being created, it is in the "making" state. When done, it goes into either the "made" or "failed" state.

To see how cmake works, it helps to know how the sequential make works. make starts by creating a similar tree of Node structures. To make a target file, make finds the Node structure for the file, and recursively makes all of its prerequisite files. Then, if the target file is out-of-date with respect to any of its prerequisite files, make executes the command that creates the target file, and waits for it to complete. Thus make does a depth-first walk of the dependency tree, executing commands as it goes.

cmake uses the same basic idea, but instead of having a single process that recursively walks the tree, cmake creates a new Concurrent C process for each file. Thus in our example, cmake creates a process to make test. This process then creates processes to make files x.o, y.o, and z.o, and waits for these processes to complete. Then if test is out-of-date, the process (the one whose task is to make test) executes the command to re-create test, waits for this command to complete, and then marks test as "made".

The three files x.o, y.o, and z.o are compiled in parallel because a separate Concurrent C process makes each file, and these three Concurrent C processes execute in parallel. Thus cmake does not need to analyze the dependency tree to determine what commands can be executed in parallel.

Of course, things are not quite this simple. For example, suppose that comm.h itself depends on another file, and needed to be constructed. Because x.o depends on comm.h, the process that constructs x.o will first create a process to construct comm.h. However, y.o and z.o also depend on comm.h; we do not want to create three separate processes each of which is trying to construct comm.h! Instead we want to create just one process for comm.h. For example, if the process making x.o is the first one to need comm.h, then this process should create a process to make comm.h. When the process making y.o later needs comm.h, it should *not* create a new process. To avoid this problem, we define a "manager" process which is responsible for creating all the new processes. When the process that is making x.o needs comm.h, it asks the manager process to create a process for comm.h. The manager process creates a new process to make comm.h only if one has not already been created. Subsequent sections describe how this works.

3.2 Processes

The Concurrent C program that implements cmake consists of the following processes:

process name	parent process	machine where run	description
`main`		master	Read makefile and command line arguments.
`makerMgr`	`main`	master	Coordinate `maker` processes, each of which makes a single target file.
`maker`	`makerMgr`	master	Make one file.
`rmtsh`	`maker`	any	Run a command on a remote machine.

The master processor is the processor where the `cmake` command is invoked, i.e., the processor running the `main` process.

The `main` process reads the makefile and creates the tree of `Node` structures. This is done sequentially. `main` then creates the `makerMgr` process. Then for each target file specified on the command line, `main` asks `makerMgr` to create a `maker` process to construct this target file.

A `maker` process constructs one target file. A `maker` process first asks `makerMgr` to create a `maker` process for each of the target's prerequisite files, and then waits for all of them to complete. Then if the target file is out-of-date, the `maker` process executes the command to reconstruct the target file. A `maker` process will be created for every file that is examined, although these processes are not necessarily created simultaneously.

There is only one `makerMgr` process, and it ensures that only one `maker` process is created per file. On the first request to create a `maker` process for a target file, `makerMgr` creates the process, and changes the `n_state` field in the file's `Node` structure to indicate that a `maker` process has been created. When given a subsequent request to create a `maker` process for this file, `makerMgr` does not create a new process.

`makerMgr` also assigns commands to processors, and enforces the limits on how many commands can be active simultaneously. The `maker` processes call transactions of the `makerMgr` process to ask it to create new `maker` processes for dependents, to request a processor on which to execute a command, and to inform `makerMgr` that a file is now up-to-date.

The `main`, `maker`, and `makerMgr` processes all access the same tree of `Node` structures, and hence must share memory. Therefore these processes all execute on the same processor. As we will see, the mutual exclusion is handled implicitly: once the tree has been created, only `makerMgr` can update elements of the tree, and `maker` processes can only examine elements when given permission by `makerMgr`.

When we need to execute a command on a processor, we create an instance of the rmtsh process on this processor.

3.3 MakerMgr Process

Here is the specification of the makerMgr process:

```
                                              File: makerMgr.h
process spec makerMgr()
{
    trans void make(Node *n);
    trans int  wait(Node *n);
    trans void run(Node *n);
    trans void made(Node *n, int okay);
};
```

Each transaction takes a pointer to a Node structure for a target file. The make transaction creates a maker process to make this file, if one has not already been created. The wait transaction waits until the file has been made. Thus the following code requests the parallel creation of updated versions of two files and waits for both to be created:

```
process makerMgr mgr;
Node *n1, *n2;

mgr.make(n1); mgr.make(n2);
mgr.wait(n1); mgr.wait(n2);
```

A maker process calls the run transaction of makerMgr when it wants to execute a command to construct a file. This transaction assigns a processor and saves the assignment in the Node structure.

A maker process calls transaction made of the makerMgr process to indicate that a target file has been constructed successfully (or unsuccessfully).

Here is the body of the makerMgr process:

File: `makerMgr.cc`

```
process body makerMgr()
{
    int proc = c_processorid(c_mypid());

    for (;;)
        select {
            accept make(n)
                if (n->n_state == N_INIT) {
                    n->n_state = N_MAKING;
                    create maker(n) processor(proc);
                }
        or
            accept run(n) suchthat(pickmach(n)>=0)
                assignmach(n);
        or
            accept made(n, okay) {
                n->n_state = okay ? N_MADE : N_FAIL;
                relsmach(n);
            }
        or
            accept wait(n)
                    suchthat(is_made(n->n_state))
                treturn n->n_state != N_MADE;
        or
            terminate;
        }
}
```

Process `makerMgr` maintains the state `n_state`; it is the only process that is allowed to read the state or update it. This is how we control concurrent access to this shared data structure. `makerMgr` accepts transactions from the `maker` processes, or from the `main` process, until the *terminate* alternative is taken. This happens when the `main` process has completed, and when all `maker` processes have terminated.

If the file has not yet been examined, transaction `make` creates a new `maker` process for it. Otherwise, transaction `make` does nothing. This ensures that only one `maker` process is created for each file.

Transaction `wait` is not accepted (thus blocking the caller) until the desired file has been made, or failed to be made. It returns the file's status to the caller. Note that if a file has already been made, then transactions `make` and `wait` are accepted immediately.

Transaction `run` is accepted whenever the `pickmach` function can find a machine on which to execute the command to create this file. This function examines the array of `Mach` structures to determine the load on the processor. It returns a processor number, or -1 if it cannot find a processor. However, `pickmach` does not update any data. Function `assignmach` actually assigns the file to the machine: it calls `pickmach`, records the assignment in the `Node` structure, and updates the load estimates in the assigned machine's `Mach` structure. When the transaction returns, the `maker` process executes the command on the selected machine.

A `maker` process calls transaction `made` when it has finished making a file. `makerMgr` then marks the file as having been made or having failed to be made. `makerMgr` calls the function `relsmach`; if a processor had been assigned to construct this file, `relsmach` removes the load estimates recorded by `assignmach`.

Notice the careful use of shared memory: multiple `maker` processes examine data items in the `Node` structures, but only the `makerMgr` process updates the `Node` structures.

3.4 Maker Process

A `maker` process is responsible for making a single file. It arranges for the file's prerequisites (if any) to be made, and then, if necessary, it executes the command to (re-)construct the file. The specification for the `maker` process is

File: `maker.h`
```
process spec maker(Node *n);
```

Here is the body of the `maker` process:

```
                                              File: maker.cc
process body maker(n)
{
    extern process makerMgr Mgr;
    int   failed = 0, needcmd = 0;
    for (each prerequisite, nn)
        Mgr.make(nn);
    for (each prerequisite, nn) {
        if (Mgr.wait(nn))
            failed = 1;
        else if (n is out-of-date with respect to nn)
            needcmd = 1;
    }
    if (!failed && needcmd) {
        Mgr.run(n);
        if (rmtrun(n->n_mach, n->n_cmd) != 0)
            failed = 1;
    }
    Mgr.made(n, !failed);
}
```

The `maker` process starts by asking the `makerMgr` process to create `maker` processes for all the prerequisite files needed by it to construct the target file assigned to it, and then calls transaction `wait` to wait for each of these files to be made. Note that the `maker` calls `make` for all prerequisite files before calling `wait` for any of them. This allows the prerequisite files to be constructed in parallel, if feasible. Then if the target file is out-of-date, the `maker` process asks `makerMgr` to assign a processor, and then calls `rmtrun`. Function `rmtrun` creates a `rmtsh` process on that processor, which then executes the appropriate command. `rmtsh` returns 0 if the command succeeds, and non-zero if it fails.

3.5 Rmtsh Process

To execute a remote command, a `rmtsh` process is created with the command to be executed as its argument. The specification of the `rmtsh` process is

File: `rmtsh.h`

```
typedef struct {
    char buf[NBUF];
} Buf;

process spec rmtsh(Buf cmd)
{
    trans int exit();
};
```

The command to be executed is encapsulated in a structure which is passed by value to the remote process.[1] Process `rmtsh` executes this command, waits for it to finish, and then accepts the `exit` transaction and returns the exit status of the command (zero if successful; otherwise, non-zero). Process `rmtsh` then terminates. The process that created `rmtsh` calls transaction `exit` to wait for the command to finish and to get its exit status.

The `maker` process calls the function `rmtrun` to execute a command on another processor. `rmtrun` creates an `rmtsh` process and returns the status of the command:

File: `rmtrun.cc`

```
int rmtrun(mach, cmd)
    Mach *mach;
    char *cmd;
{
    Buf b;
    rmtsh x;

    strcpy(b.buf, cmd);
    x = create rmtsh(b) processor(mach->m_proc);
    return x.exit();
}
```

Here is a skeleton of the body of the `rmtsh` process. We have omitted the code necessary to ask the underlying operating system to execute the command, redirect its input and output back to the user, wait for it to complete, etc:

---

1. Note that pointers are not passed across processors because the processors do not share memory.

```
                                                    File: rmtsh.cc
process body rmtsh(cmd)
{
    int status;

    spawn operating system process to run command;
    wait for that process to finish;
    status = exit status of command;

    accept exit()
        treturn status;
}
```

4. Window Manager

When several processes simultaneously write to the same terminal, their output
will be intermingled on a line-by-line basis at best, and at worst on a
character-by-character basis. For example, here is the output produced by a
version of the dining philosophers program in which all the philosopher
processes write to the same terminal:

```
philosopher 0: pick up right fork
philosopher 1: pick up right fork
philosopher 2: pick up right fork
philosopher 0: pick up left fork
philosopher 0: good food -- thanks!
philosopher 0: put down left fork
philosopher 3: pick up right fork
philosopher 0: put down right fork
philosopher 4: pick up right fork
philosopher 1: pick up left fork
philosopher 1: good food -- thanks!
philosopher 1: put down left fork
philosopher 0: pick up right fork
philosopher 1: put down right fork
```

Fortunately, the above output can be read because it is intermingled on a line-
by-line basis. However, even though each line is labeled with the philosopher
number, it is difficult to trace the actions of a single philosopher. The problem
gets worse when several processes simultaneously attempt to read from the
same terminal, because we do not know which input characters should be given
to which process.

One way of solving the problem of simultaneous input/output by multiple
processes from the same terminal is to partition the terminal into several logical

terminals, traditionally called windows, and assign one window to each process. Each process writes to its own window and reads the input entered at its window. Keyboard and/or mouse commands allow the user to control interaction with the windows. For example, these commands let the user specify the window that should receive characters typed on the keyboard.

One Concurrent C tool for partitioning a terminal into multiple windows is the Concurrent C window manager [Smith-Thomas 1984]. This allows a user to interact with a number of independent and cooperating Concurrent C processes. The Concurrent C window manager simulates windows on any character-oriented display terminal, using the `curses` screen manipulation package that is available on the UNIX operating system. The terminal does not need to have hardware graphics or windowing capabilities.

The Concurrent C window manager is written in Concurrent C, and is implemented as a user process. Client processes interact with the window manager by calling a set of interface functions. We will first describe these interface functions, and then describe how the window manager process is implemented in Concurrent C.

4.1 Use

User processes interact with the window manager by calling the functions `wopen`, `wgetchar`, `wputchar`, `wprintf`, and `wclose`. These functions mimic the corresponding C functions with similar names and call appropriate transactions of the window manager process. Before using the window manager, one client process (usually the `main` process) must call function `wcreate` to start the window manager. Opening a window yields a window number which is used to identify the window where input is to be read from or where output is to be sent. Windows are open for both reading and writing.

Windows are manipulated by means of commands entered using the keyboard. We shall not discuss this aspect of the window manager.

Here is a version of the dining philosophers program that uses the Concurrent C window manager. Each philosopher creates her own window, and sends all of its output to this window:

```
process body philosopher(i, left, right)
{
    int nmeal;
    int wn = wopen();
    void think();

    for (nmeal = 0; nmeal < LIMIT; nmeal++) {
        think(wn);

        right.pickUp();
        wprintf(wn, "\tpick up right fork\n");
        left.pickUp();
        wprintf(wn, "\tpick up left fork\n");

      /*eat*/
        wprintf(wn, "good food -- thanks!\n");

        left.putDown();
        wprintf(wn, "\tput down left fork\n");
        right.putDown();
        wprintf(wn, "\tput down right fork\n");
    }
    wprintf(wn, "That's all, folks!\n");
}
main()
{
    process fork f[5];
    int j;

    wcreate();
    for (j = 0; j < 5; j++)
        f[j] = create fork();
    for (j = 0; j < 5; j++)
        create philosopher(j, f[j], f[(j+1)%5]);
}
```

Function `think` simulates "thinking" by calling the UNIX command `fortune`. It returns a random "fortune-cookie" saying, which `think` prints on the window passed as an argument:

```
#include <stdio.h>
void think(wn)
    int wn;
{
    int n = 0;
    FILE *f, *popen();
    char buf[80];
/* Repeat until we get a "short" fortune. */
    while (1) {
        f = popen("fortune -s", "r");
        if (f == NULL) {
            break;
        } else {
            n = fread(buf, 1, sizeof(buf)-1, f);
            pclose(f);
            if ((n > 0) && (buf[n-1] == '\n'))
                break;
        }
    }
    buf[n] = '\0';
    wprintf(wn, "%s", buf);
}
```

Finally, here is an example of the screen output from one execution of this version of the dining philosophers program. The five lines at the top of the screen give a summary of the state of several of the Concurrent C processes. The window manager continually updates these summary lines.

```
!fork2     !fork3     !fork4     !          !          !Hypatia  !Lao Tse
!w_@ accpt!w_@ accpt!w_@ accpt!          !          !w_f trans!w_f trans
!          !          !          !          !          !v win # 3!v win # 4
!          !          !          !          !          !          !
!proc#  6 !proc#  7 !proc#  8 !          !          !proc# 11 !proc# 12
====+ vir win no   4 +===================+ vir win no   1 +==============
!     put down left fork               !     pick up left fork
!     put down right fork              !good food -- thanks!
!Behold the warranty...the bold       !     put down left fork
!print giveth and the fine print      !     put down right fork
!taketh away.                         !That's all, folks!
!     pick up right fork              !
!                                     !
====+ vir win no   2 +===================+ vir win no   3 +==============
!     pick up left fork               !     put down right fork
!good food -- thanks!                 !Sex is not the answer.  Sex is the
!     put down left fork              !question.  "Yes" is the answer.
!     put down right fork             !     pick up right fork
!That's all, folks!                   !     pick up left fork
!                                     !good food -- thanks!
!                                     !
======================================================================
input -> C !>Processes frozen; control commands enabled; <esc> resumes.
           !>
```

4.2 Implementation

Here is the specification of the window manager process:

File: windows.h

```
process spec windows()
{
    trans int   open();
    trans int   write(int wn, char *buf, int n);
    trans int   readchar(int wn);
    trans void  close(int wn);
    trans void  inputReady(char ch);
};
```

Transaction open creates a new window, and returns its window number. Transaction close closes a window. Transaction readchar reads one character from a window. If no characters are available, it waits for the user to type a character. Transaction write writes an array of characters to the window. For simplicity, transaction write assumes that all processes share memory, so that we can pass pointers between processes. Because client processes call the interface functions instead of calling transactions of the window manager, clients do not know about this simplifying assumption about shared memory. In fact, it is possible to change the transactions of the window manager process to avoid this assumption; this will change the implementations of the interface functions, but it will not change the interface presented to the client processes (this modification is left as an exercise for the reader).

Transaction `inputReady` is called by another process, to give the window manager a character that the user has typed on the keyboard. We will describe this process later.

Here are the interface functions for the window manager. These hide the existence of the window manager process and its transactions from the client process:

File: `wm-interface.cc`

```
#include "windows.h"

process windows WindowPid;

int wopen()
{
    return WindowPid.open();
}
int wgetchar(wn)
    int wn;
{
    return WindowPid.readchar(wn);
}
void wclose(wn)
    int wn;
{
    WindowPid.close(wn);
}
void wprintf(wn, fmt, a1, a2, a3, a4, a5)
    int wn, a1, a2, a3, a4, a5;
{
    char buf[500];
    sprintf(buf, fmt, a1, a2, a3, a4, a5);
    WindowPid.write(wn, buf, sizeof(buf));
}
void wcreate()
{
    WindowPid = create windows();
}
```

Here is an abstract skeleton of the body of the window manager process:

```
#include "windows.h"

process body windows()
{   ...
    for (;;) {
        select {
            accept open()
                if (window can be allocated)  {
                    allocate window;
                    treturn window number;
                } else treturn -1;
            if (screen space is available)
                display newly allocated window;
        or accept close(wn)
                if (wn is valid)  {
                    release window structure;
                    display another window;
                }
        or accept readchar(wn)
                    suchthat(wn has input or EOF, or is bad)
                if (wn is valid and has input)
                    treturn next character;
                else treturn -1;
        or accept write(wn, buf, n)
                if (wn is valid)  {
                    copy parameters into local variables;
                    treturn number of bytes copied;
                } else treturn -1;
            write data into window
        or accept inputReady(ch)
                put character in buffer for current input window;
        or delay 5;
        or terminate;
        }
        update process status area;
    }
}
```

In addition to the windows, the window manager also displays, at the top of the screen, the status of several Concurrent C processes. The window manager process updates these after every few requests. To allow the window manager to update the process status information even when it has not received a request, the window manager uses a *delay* alternative to wake up every few seconds.

The window manager also wants to wake up whenever the user types a character on the terminal's keyboard. Function getchar reads a character from the keyboard. If no characters are available, getchar waits until some become available. If the window manager process called getchar directly, it would wait until the user types something, and would ignore any input or output requests from other processes. This is not acceptable. Instead, we want keyboard input to arrive via a call to one of the window manager's transactions, so that the window manager process can accept keyboard input as another alternative of the *select* statement. To do this, the window manager creates another process, reader, whose sole purpose in life is to call getchar and then call transaction inputReady of the window manager:

```
process spec reader(process windows win);

process body reader(win)
{
    int ch;

    while ((ch = getchar()) != EOF)
        win.inputReady(ch);
    win.inputReady(EOF);
}
```

4.3 Observations

In the window manager, we have used two techniques that are commonly used for structuring concurrent programs. The first is to provide a function interface that hides the transaction interface of a process. Client processes call these interface functions, not the transactions of the underlying process. Although the interface functions are called by client processes, they are considered to be part of the window manager package. This allows us to change the transaction interface to the process *without* changing the interface to the client processes. One of the exercises illustrates the advantages of this structuring technique.

The other structuring technique is use to the additional process, reader in this example, that turns an event from the outside world into a transaction (for the window manager). This technique allows the window manager to treat such an outside event, i.e., the arrival of a character, as a transaction call, which it can accept whenever it wants.

5. Exercises

1. Suppose Concurrent C did not have asynchronous transactions; this means that transactions move and complete of the motor process

in the robot program will have to be synchronous transactions. Modify the `motor` process to make transaction `move` be effectively asynchronous so that the `robot` process is not forced to wait for one `motor` process to complete moving before it can instruct the other `motor` process to move.

2. Modify the window manager process in Section 4 to eliminate the assumptions about shared memory. This will require changing its specification. Modify the interface functions as needed. Do this *without* changing the arguments of the interface functions. This way the change will be transparent to the clients of the window manager.

3. Implement other input operations for the window manager in Section 4, including a function to read a signed integer, and a function to read a string of characters separated by "white space" (blanks, tabs, new-lines, etc.). Hint: you may need to add a new transaction to the window manager process to "put back" an unwanted character.

Chapter 5

Concurrent C + +

Although data abstraction facilities are important for writing concurrent programs, we did not provide them in Concurrent C because we did not want to duplicate the work of Stroustrup [1986] in designing C++, a superset of C with data abstraction facilities. Instead, we decided that we would eventually integrate C++ and Concurrent C to produce a language with both data abstraction and parallel programming facilities: Concurrent C++. Having gained experience with Concurrent C, we decided to merge these two languages to produce Concurrent C++ [Gehani & Roome 1988b]. In this chapter, we will give a brief introduction to C++ and then present two examples of how classes, the data abstraction facility of C++, can be valuable for writing concurrent programs.

1. Brief Summary of C + +

The C++ data abstraction facility is called the *class*. Class declarations consist of two parts: a specification and a body. The class specification represents the class "user interface". It contains all the information necessary for the user of a class. The class specification also contains information necessary for the compiler to allocate class objects. The class body consists of the bodies of the functions declared in the class specification but whose bodies were not given there. In the rest of this section, we will give a brief overview of the C++ class facility. For a detailed explanation, see *The C++ Programming Language* [Stroustrup 1986].

Class specifications have the form

```
class name {
    private components
public:
    public components
};
```

The private components of a class are data items and functions that implement class objects. These represent internal details of the class and cannot be accessed by the user of a class.

The public class components can be data items, constructors, destructors, member functions (and operators), and friend functions (and operators). The public components represent the class user interface. These are the components that the user of a class can use or call. Constructors are functions that are called automatically to construct a class value. Destructors are functions that are called automatically when the scope of a class object is left; they can perform "clean up" actions. Member and friend functions can manipulate class objects.[1] In C++, functions and operators can be "overloaded."

As an example of the C++ data abstraction facilities, consider the class `complex`:

	File: `complex.h`

```
      class complex {
        double re, im;
      public:
        complex(double  r,  double  i);
  5     complex(double  r);
        complex();

        double  real();
        double  imag();
 10
             // Overload  common  operators:
        friend  complex  operator+(complex,  complex);
        friend  complex  operator-(complex,  complex);
        friend  complex  operator-(complex);
 15     friend  complex  operator*(complex,  complex);
        friend  complex  operator/(complex,  complex);
        friend  int  operator==(complex,  complex);
        friend  int  operator!=(complex,  complex);
      };
```

Lines 4-6 of the `complex` class are constructor declarations. An appropriate constructor, selected according to the initialization values supplied, is automatically called when `complex` variables are defined. Lines 8 and 9 are the declarations of member functions (`real` and `imag`) and the remaining lines declare friend operators.

---

1. In this chapter, we shall not distinguish between member and friend functions except to say that their syntax is slightly different.

In C++, all characters from // to the end of the line are taken as comments, and are ignored. You can also use C-style comments (/ * * /) in C++.

Here are some examples illustrating uses of the complex class:

```
complex a=complex(5.0,6.0), b=complex(1.0,1.0);
complex c;
double x;
...
x = a.real();
c = a + b;
```

Note that for illustration purposes, variables a and b have been initialized explicitly, and variable c has not been initialized explicitly. For variables a and b, the first constructor (line 4 of complex.h) is automatically invoked to construct the initial values, while the third constructor (line 6) is invoked for variable c. The constructor invoked depends upon the initial arguments supplied (or not supplied) when defining a class variable.

Note that in the case of member function calls, the class object specified in the call is passed as an implicit argument. Unqualified component names used in the body of a member function refer to the components of this class object.

We will now show you the implementation of the complex class by showing you the definitions of one constructor function, one member function and one friend operator:

```
#include "complex.h"
complex::complex(double r, double i)
{
    re = r; im = i;
}
double complex::real()
{
    return re;
}
complex operator+(complex a, complex b)
{
    return complex(a.re+b.re, a.im+b.im);
}
```

2. Data Abstraction and Concurrent Programming

All the advantages of using data abstraction facilities in sequential programming also apply to concurrent programming. Specifically, with regard to concurrent programming, data abstraction facilities can provide a better, higher-level and more robust interface for the services provided by one or more processes. Classes can be used to ensure that the protocol for interacting with a process is properly observed and that the implementation details are hidden from the user. For example, the user does not need to know whether a service is provided by one process, by multiple processes, or by sequential code.

We shall illustrate advantages of using classes for concurrent programs by means of two examples. These examples illustrate the use of classes to conveniently provide better user interfaces: ones with greater functionality and more robustness.

2.1 User-Interface Example: A Disk Driver

Consider the following specification of a disk driver process:

```
                                            File: diskDriver.h
process spec diskDriver()
{
    trans int request(int op, long blk,
                      char *buf);
    trans int wait(int ticket);
    trans async diskdone();
              /* disk-completion interrupt */
};

#define READ  1   /* op code for read */
#define WRITE 2   /* op code for write */
```

Performing a disk operation takes two transactions. First the client process calls the disk driver's request transaction. Upon accepting request, the disk driver examines it for validity. If invalid (e.g., a bad disk block address), the disk driver returns an error code, thus ending the request. Otherwise, the disk driver saves the request in a pending request queue, and returns a "laundry ticket." The disk driver process then performs the requested operation at some later time. The client process then calls the wait transaction, with the laundry ticket, to wait for the completion of the operation. When a disk operation completes, the disk driver accepts the corresponding wait transaction. If the operation is successful, transaction wait returns zero; otherwise, it returns an error code.

Here is an outline of the body of the diskDriver process:

File: `diskDriver.cc`

```
#include "diskDriver.h"
process body diskDriver()
{
    diskDriver me = c_mypid();
    pending-request & completed-request queue declarations;

       ...
    c_associate(me.diskdone, interrupt address);
    for(;;) {
        select {
          (there is space in the queues):
              accept request(op, blk, buff) {
                  if (invalid request)
                      treturn error-code;
                  else {
                      add to pending-request queue;
                      treturn request-index;
                  }
              }
        or
            accept diskdone();
            move completed request from pending-request queue to
                completed-request queue;

        or  (completed-request queue is not empty):
            accept wait(t)
                    suchthat(t is in completed-request queue)
                treturn completion-status;
            remove request from completed-request queue;
        }

        if (disk is idle and there are pending requests)
            start first request on pending-request queue;
    }
}
```

In Concurrent C++, a process name can be used by itself as a type. Thus we do not need the keyword `process` in the declaration of the local variable `me`.

One problem with the specification of the `diskDriver` process is that transaction `diskdone`, which is called by the run-time system when the disk sends an interrupt signaling completion of a requested operation, is visible to client processes. Transaction `diskdone` is associated with the disk interrupt and is not to be called by client processes. Concurrent C does not provide a mechanism for specifying selective visibility of transactions.

When interacting with the disk driver, a process must use the protocol mentioned above. For example, the following code reads block 27 into `mybuf`:

```
process diskDriver dd;

t = dd.request(READ, 27, mybuf);
if (t < 0)
        invalid request —print error message
else if (dd.wait(t) != 0)
        device error —print error message
```

There are two problems with this code: writing it for every disk access is tedious, and there is no way of ensuring that this protocol is followed correctly. Providing an interface function for encapsulating this protocol can eliminate the tedium of writing the code, but it will not guarantee that all client processes will use this function. For example, a programmer who needs a different error message style would be tempted to bypass the interface function.

Finally, suppose a programmer wants to send multiple requests to the disk driver, i.e., "pipeline" several requests, and then wait for all of them to complete. Pipelining multiple requests will not only avoid unnecessary blocking of the client process, but it will also allow the disk process to select the disk requests in an optimal order. To do this, the client process must first save the tickets returned by the disk driver for each request, and then call transaction `wait` using each of these tickets. We would like to hide this "ticket management" from the client process and make it part of the "disk access" service. We could do this by having the disk driver process manage the tickets, but that is not appropriate. Putting ticket management in the disk driver process will increase its work, and the disk driver process could become a bottleneck. Ticket management should be offloaded to the client process.

We can solve these problems, and provide an easy method for handling concurrent disk requests, by declaring an appropriate interface class, say `disk`, which encapsulates the `diskDriver` process. All disk interactions then take place via the member functions of this class. The `disk` class provides two types of interfaces: one for single block reads and writes, and the other for multiple block reads and writes. Error messages are printed by a virtual function which allows for customization of error message handling by using the notion of derived classes (more on this later).

Here is the specification of the disk interface class `disk`:

File: `diskClass.h`

```
class disk
{
    static const int MaxPending = 20;
    diskDriver dd;
    int nwaiting, nbadreq;
    int tickets[MaxPending], ops[MaxPending];
    long blkaddrs[MaxPending];
    char *bufs[MaxPending];
public:
    disk();   //constructor
    ~disk();  //destructor
// single-block request functions:
    int readblk(long blk, char *buf);
    int wrtblk(long blk, char *buf);
// multiple-block request functions:
    void startread(long blk, char *buf);
    void startwrt(long blk, char *buf);
    int wait();
// overrideable error message handler:
    virtual void prterr(int badreq, int ecode,
                        int op, long blk, char *buf);
};
```

The constructor function `disk` obtains the identifier for the disk driver process by calling a "name manager" function (which may itself be an interface for a process), and then initializes the class variables to indicate that no disk operations are in progress:

File: `disk::disk.cc`

```
#include "diskClass.h"

disk::disk()
{
    extern process anytype namemngr(char*);

    dd = (process diskDriver)
                    namemngr("diskDriver");
    nbadreq = nwaiting = 0;
}
```

Single blocks are updated as illustrated by the following program segment that updates block 27:

```
disk d; char buf[1024];
...
if (d.readblk(27, buf) == 0) {
    update buf;
    d.wrtblk(27, buf);
}
```

Single blocks are read by calling `readblk` which starts the read operation, waits for it to complete, and returns 1 if successful, 0 otherwise:

```
#include "diskClass.h"
#include "diskDriver.h"

int disk::readblk(long blk, char *buf)
{
    int t = dd.request(READ, blk, buf);
    if (t < 0) {
        prterr(1, t, READ, blk, buf);
        return 0;
    } else if ((t = dd.wait(t)) != 0) {
        prterr(0, t, READ, blk, buf);
        return 0;
    } else
        return 1;
}
```

Function `wrtblk` is similar.

Functions `startread`, `startwrt`, and `wait` allow a client to do several operations "in parallel." Functions `startread` and `startwrt` add another read or write request to the queue of pending operations. They return immediately, before the operation is completed. Thus the disk scheduler can do these operations in the optimal order. The `wait` function waits for them to complete. That is, `wait` waits for the completion of all `startread` and `startwrt` requests which have been issued through the same instance of the `disk` class. If all operations succeed, `wait` returns 0; otherwise, `wait` calls `prterr` for each failed operation, and returns the number of operations that failed. As an example, the following program fragment reads blocks 27 and 321, updates the copies it read, and then writes them back:

```
disk d; char buf1[1024], buf2[1024];
...
d.startread(27, buf1);
d.startread(321, buf2);
if (d.wait() == 0) {
    update buf1 and buf2;
    d.startwrt(27, buf1);
    d.startwrt(321, buf2);
    d.wait();
}
```

The ticket management is done by the functions of class disk. Note that it is the programmer's responsibility to call wait before using the results of the startread operations or before updating the buffers specified in the startwrt operations; this is the only way to ensure that the requested operations have completed.

Function startread starts a read operation. It saves the ticket that it gets, along with other information about the request, in private arrays within the instance of the disk class:

File: disk::startread.cc

```
#include "diskClass.h"
#include "diskDriver.h"
void disk::startread(long blk, char *buf)
{
    int t;

    if (nwaiting >= MaxPending) {
                        // too many pending ops
        prterr(1, 0, READ, blk, buf);
        nbadreq++;
    } else if ((t=dd.request(READ, blk, buf))<0){
                        // invalid request
        prterr(1, t, READ, blk, buf);
        nbadreq++;
    } else {
        tickets[nwaiting] = t;
        ops[nwaiting] = READ;
        blkaddrs[nwaiting] = blk;
        bufs[nwaiting] = buf;
        nwaiting++;
    }
}
```

Function `startwrt` is similar to function `startread`. Function `wait` waits for the requests to complete, and returns the number of requests with errors (either invalid parameters or device errors):

File: `disk::wait.cc`

```
#include "diskClass.h"
#include "diskDriver.h"

int disk::wait()
{
    int i, t, nerr = nbadreq;

    for (i = 0; i < nwaiting; i++)
        if ((t = dd.wait(tickets[i])) != 0) {
            prterr(0,t,ops[i],blkaddrs[i],bufs[i]);
            nerr++;
        }
    nbadreq = nwaiting = 0;
    return nerr;
}
```

When an instance of the `disk` class is deallocated, the destructor function `~disk` waits for the completion of any operations started through this instance. This makes it less likely that the disk driver process will be left with outstanding tickets:

File: `disk::~disk.cc`

```
#include "diskClass.h"

disk::~disk()
{
    wait();
}
```

Whenever an error occurs, the `disk` member functions call `prterr` with arguments to describe the offending request. The default version of `prterr` prints this information in a standard format:

File: `disk::prterr.cc`

```
#include "diskClass.h"
#include "diskDriver.h"

void disk::prterr(int badreq, int ecode,
                  int op, long blk, char *buf)
{
    if (badreq)
        printf("Bad disk request: ");
    else
        printf("Disk error %d: ", ecode);
    printf("on %s of blk %ld into buf %lx\n",
           op == READ ? "READ" : "WRITE",
           blk, (long) buf);
}
```

Note the `prterr` is declared as a virtual function. Virtual functions can be replaced by alternative functions. A disk user can supply an alternative error printing function by deriving a new class interface, say `myDisk`, from `disk`:

File: `myDisk.h`

```
#include "diskClass.h"

class myDisk: disk
{
public:
    ...
    void prterr(int badreq, int ecode,
                int op, long blk, char *buf);
};
```

The derived class `myDisk` specifies its own `prterr` function. Except for this function, it inherits all the other operations of the `disk` class. Clients can use class `myDisk` just as they use class `disk`. The new version of `prterr` is defined as

```
#include "myDisk.h"
#include <stdio.h>

void myDisk::prterr(int badreq, int ecode,
                    int op, long blk, char *buf)
{
    fprintf(stderr, "Disk error!!");
    exit(0);
}
```

2.2 The Concurrent C Window Manager

Let us now take a second look at the Concurrent C window manager described in Chapter 4. It partitions the screen of an ordinary display terminal into windows, i.e., virtual terminals. Concurrent C processes can read from and write to these windows. Windows are identified by numbers. We will first briefly describe the Concurrent C interface to the window manager. We will then describe the limitations of this interface, and show how to make this interface more robust by rewriting it in Concurrent C++ using classes.

The window manager consists of a process and a set of interface functions. Client processes call these interface functions, which then call the window manager process' transactions; the interface functions hide the existence of this process. Here are some of the interface functions:

function	explanation
`wopen()`	Open a new window and return the window number.
`wclose(int wnum)`	Close the specified window.
`wprintf(int wnum, char *fmt, ...)`	Write formatted output to a window; the formatting options are the same as the C library function `printf`.

This interface has several limitations:

1. A process can terminate without closing a window created by it; this results in a "dangling window", i.e., a window that cannot be reused.

2. We cannot ensure that a process is using a valid window number (i.e., a number returned by `wopen` which refers to a currently open window).

3. The `wprintf` function suffers from the same problems as the `printf` function [Stroustrup 1986]: if the argument types do not match the format specification, then the program will print garbage or it will crash with a memory fault.

Using Concurrent C++, we can provide a robust interface which avoids these problems. We will write a class, `window`, which acts as the new client interface. This class hides the existence of the window manager process, which becomes an implementation detail.

The dangling window problem is solved with a destructor that automatically deallocates the window. The invalid window problem is solved by putting a flag in each instance of the `window` class, to indicate whether or not the instance is currently associated with a window. A window is allocated when the first operation is performed. Finally, as in [Stroustrup 1986], we solve the "`printf` problems" by overloading the `<<` operator.

An instance of the `window` class refers to a specific window on the display screen. When a `window` variable is defined, it is *unbound;* that is, it does not refer to a screen window. The first operation on an unbound `window` variable automatically creates a new window and binds this window to the `window` variable.

Here is the specification of the class `window`:

```
                                                File: window.h
class window
{
    windowProc wm;       //window manager pid
    int wnum;            //window number, if != -1
    void openw();        //private function to
                         //allocate new window
public:
 // Constructors, destructor, etc:
    window();
    window(window &);
    ~window();
    window& operator=(window &);

 // Output operations:
    window& operator<<(long);    //output integer
    window& operator<<(double);  //output double
    window& operator<<(char *);  //output string

 // Input operations:
    window& operator>>(long&);   //input integer
    window& operator>>(double&); //input double
    window& operator>>(char *);  //input string
};
```

A new window is opened by just declaring a `window` variable and using the

<< operator to write to the window. As an example illustrating the use of the class `window`, consider the following process body:

```
process body foo( )
{
    window w;  int x;
    ...
    w << "The value of x is:  " << x << "\n";
    ...
}
```

The first input or output operation using the `window` variable w automatically creates a screen window for w; all subsequent operations on w will use this window. This window will be closed automatically when process `foo` terminates (because of the destructor `~window`). If several instances of this process type are created, each process gets a different window. Note that a screen window is created only when necessary, i.e., at the time of the first operation. Thus if the process declares a `window` variable but never uses it, a screen window will never be created for it.

If a process declares several `window` variables, then a separate window will be allocated for each `window` variable. However, if one window variable is assigned to another, both `window` variables will refer to the same window. Passing a `window` variable as an argument has a similar effect—the argument and the parameter will refer to the same window. Any number of `window` variables can refer to the same window; they are *aliases* for that window. These aliases can be in different processes, so that several processes can use the same window.[2]

A window exists as long as some `window` variable refers to it; unreferenced windows are automatically deallocated. E.g., if w is the only reference to a window x, then assigning another `window` variable to w closes x.

To implement the automatic creation and deallocation of windows, the following strategy is used:

1. When a `window` variable is defined, its member wnum is set to -1 indicating that the variable does not as yet refer to a window.

---

2. Several processes could also share a screen window by using references (or pointers) to one common `window` variable. However, that requires the `window` variable to be in some memory that is shared by all processors; we do not want to limit our window manager to shared-memory implementations of Concurrent C.

2. When an input or output operation is performed on a `window` variable, a window is allocated for this variable, if one has not already been allocated, and the reference count for the window is set to one.

3. If one `window` variable is assigned to another, say w2 is assigned to w1, then the reference count for w1's window is decremented by one and the reference count for w2's window incremented by one. If w1's reference count becomes zero when decrementing it, the window is closed.

4. Whenever a `window` variable is passed as an argument, the reference count for the window associated with the variable is increased by one.

5. Whenever a `window` variable is deallocated, we check to see if it refers to a window. If so, the reference count for this window is decremented by one. If the count becomes zero, the window is closed.

Window management is done by a window manger process of type `windowProc`, whose transactions are called by the functions of class `window`. This process differs from the original Concurrent C window manager process in that it has been modified to keep track of reference counts. Here is its specification:[3]

File: `windowProc.h`

```
process spec windowProc()
{
    trans int open();
    trans int write(int wnum, char *buf, int n);
    trans int readchar(int wnum);
    trans int unread(int wnum, char c);
    trans void close(int wnum);
    trans void addRef(int wnum);
    trans void dropRef(int wnum);
    ...
};
```

Transaction `open` creates a new window and returns its number, `close` forcibly closes an open window, and `write` writes n characters to window number wnum.[4] `readchar` reads and returns one character from a window

---

3. The structure of the window manager process is similar to that presented in Chapter 4.

4. Note that this is a "shared memory" interface: the `write` transaction takes a pointer as an argument. However, remember that the process interface is hidden within the implementation of the `window` class. Thus we can remove the shared memory dependency from the process interface without affecting clients of the `window` class; we would only have to change the member `window` functions. For example, we could replace the pointer argument with a 32-byte by-value structure, and change the `window` functions to call `write` as many times as necessary.

provided the user has typed characters in the window. If not, it waits until the user types a character. Transaction unread "puts back" a character that had just been read; the next readchar call will return this character. The window manager process maintains a reference count for each window, i.e., the number of window variables (aliases) that refer to the window. Transactions addRef and dropRef are used to increment or decrement, respectively, the reference count for a window. The window manager process sets the reference count to one when it opens a new window and automatically deallocates a window when its reference count goes to zero.

Now let us go back to discussing class window. Constructor window() is called whenever a new window variable is created; the destructor ~window() is called whenever a window variable is deallocated. The constructor gets the identifier of the window manager process by calling a "name manager" utility. Here are their bodies of the constructor window() and the destructor ~window():

```
#include "window.h"
#include "windowProc.h"

window::window()
{
    extern process anytype namemngr(char *);
    wm = (process windowProc)
                 namemngr("windowProc");
    wnum = -1;
}
window::~window()
{
    if (wnum != -1)
        wm.dropRef(wnum);
}
```

Constructor window(window&) is called whenever a window variable is passed by value:

```
#include "window.h"
#include "windowProc.h"

window::window(window &src)
{
    if (src.wnum == -1)
        src.openw();
    wnum = src.wnum;
    wm = src.wm;
    wm.addRef(wnum);
}
```

Function `openw`, which is private to the `window` class, opens a new window and saves its window number:

```
#include "window.h"
#include "windowProc.h"

void window::openw()
{
    wnum = wm.open();
}
```

The assignment operator is defined as

```
#include "window.h"
#include "windowProc.h"

window &window::operator=(window &src)
{
    if (src.wnum == -1)     //if src is not bound to
        src.openw();        //a window, then bind it
    wm.addRef(src.wnum);
    if (wnum != -1)
        wm.dropRef(wnum);
    wnum = src.wnum;        //copy src window number
    return *this;
}
```

You may be wondering why the assignment operator and the `window(window&)` constructor assign a window to a source or an argument `window` variable if it is unbound. To see why, consider the following code fragment:

```
window w1, w2;
w2 = w1;
w1 << "Hi";
w2 << "There";
```

Clearly, we want w1 and w2 to be aliases for the same window. Suppose that a window is not bound to w1 before it is assigned to w2. Then after the above assignment, both w1 and w2 will be unbound. The first output operation will allocate one window to w1, and the second will allocate a *different* window to w2. Variables w1 and w2 will not be aliases for the same window!

To avoid the printf format mismatch problems mentioned earlier, the << operator is overloaded to allow different types of arguments to be output to windows. Here is the definition of << that outputs an integer value; the other overloaded definitions are similar:

```
#include "window.h"
#include "windowProc.h"

window &window::operator<<(long v)
{
    char buf[20];

    if (wnum == -1)
        openw();
    sprintf(buf, "%ld", v);
    (void) wm.write(wnum, buf, strlen(buf));
    return *this;
}
```

The input functions call transaction readchar to read characters. Here is the input operator that reads a white-space separated character string. Note how readchar reads until it gets a space character, which it tells the window manager process to put back onto the input queue:

```
#include "window.h"
#include "windowProc.h"
#include "ctype.h"

window &window::operator>>(char *p)
{
    int c;

    if (wnum == -1)
        openw();

//skip any space characters
    while ((c = wm.readchar(wnum)) != -1
                && isspace(c))
        ;

//read until get space, then put it back
    if (c != -1)
        for (*p++ = c; 1; *p++ = c)
            if ((c = wm.readchar(wnum)) == -1
                    || isspace(c))
                break;
    if (c != -1)
        wm.unread(wnum, c);
    *p = '\0';
    return *this;
}
```

3. Summary

As seen in our examples, data abstraction facilities are just as useful for parallel programming languages as they are for sequential programming languages. In particular, the concept of an "interface class" for a process is very powerful. A service, such as a disk driver or a window manager, can be structured as a package that consists of one or more processes, plus a class that acts as an interface to these processes. The member functions of the interface class are called by client processes. This can be done in Concurrent C, by using ordinary C functions, but the class mechanism of C++ makes this easier to do.

Class facilities such as constructor and destructor functions can be used to automate initialization, internal accounting (e.g., keeping track of the number of window references as shown in the window manager example), and cleanup. Without the constructor and destructor functions, the provider of the interface would have to rely on the client programmer to do this correctly.

4. Exercises

1. Implement the rest of the input and output operations (i.e., the overloaded definitions of < < and > >) specified in class `window`.

2. Implement the window manager process.

3. The input functions of the `window` class "unget" a character by sending it back to the window manager process. Why could not the functions just "unget" a character by saving it in an instance variable in the `window` class?

4. Suppose we have several processes, each with its own instance of a `window` class, and all of these instances refer to the same screen window. The user types a series of strings, representing commands, into this screen window. Each process reads a command from the window, and executes the command. Thus we have a pool of server processes, and when a server is free, it reads the next command from a common queue of commands typed by the user. We want each process to get a full command. What actually happens is that each process might get part of a command. For example, if the user types "shift make," we want one process to read "shift", and another process to read "make." In reality, one process might read "sft", another might read "him," and a third might read "ake." Modify the input operator so that once it starts to read a string, it will read a contiguous stream of characters, regardless of how many other processes attempt to read from the same screen window. Hint: you might need to add a transaction to the window manager process.

Chapter 6

Concurrent Programming Models

Over the years, several parallel programming models have been proposed. These models can be classified into two fundamental categories: the *shared memory* and the *message passing* models. In the shared memory models, processes communicate with each other by updating and reading common memory. In the message passing models, processes communicate with each other by sending and receiving messages. Message sending can be *synchronous* (blocking) or *asynchronous* (non-blocking).

Processes in a concurrent program must interact with each other because they are all working towards a common goal. Processes interact for several reasons:

1. *Exchanging Information*: Each process may be responsible for a portion of the computation. Consequently, processes interact to exchange information.

2. *Synchronizing Activities*: Processes execute in parallel with independent speeds, i.e., asynchronously. They must therefore synchronize to coordinate their activities.

3. *Sharing Resources*: A process may require exclusive use of a shared resource, such as a line printer or a portion of a database. To get exclusive access to a resource, processes must coordinate with each other by establishing a protocol for using a resource and then always adhering to the protocol. This coordination may be direct or indirect via an intermediate process managing the resource.

We will first give you the rationale for the Concurrent C concurrent programming model and then review and illustrate other concurrent programming models.

1. Concurrent C Concurrent Programming Model

In Concurrent C, programmers define processes that interact via synchronous ("blocking send" and "blocking receive") and asynchronous ("nonblocking send") message passing facilities. Synchronous message passing primitives combine process synchronization with information transfer. Two processes interact first by synchronizing, then by transferring information, and finally by continuing their individual activities. This synchronization is called a

153

rendezvous.

In a *simple* rendezvous, the exchange of information is unidirectional—from the message sender to the receiver. However, many process interactions, such as a client process requesting service from a server process, require bidirectional information transfer, and hence require two simple rendezvous. In the first rendezvous, the client gives a description of the request to the server. The server performs the request, and then, if necessary, does a second rendezvous with the client to give it the results of executing the request.

We adopted the *extended rendezvous* or *transaction* concept for Concurrent C. An extended rendezvous allows bidirectional information transfer using only one rendezvous [DoD 1979]. After the rendezvous is established, information is copied from the process requesting service, i.e., the client, to the server. The client process is then forced to wait while the server process performs the requested service. Upon completion of the service, the results, if any, are returned to the client, which is then free to resume execution. From the viewpoint of a client process, an extended rendezvous is just like a function call.

Concurrent C also allows asynchronous transactions which can be used only for unidirectional information transfer: from the caller to the called process.

1.1 Why This Model?

Initially, we considered several concurrent programming models:

1. Shared memory models.
2. Asynchronous message passing models.
3. Synchronous message passing models.
4. Hybrid models based on a combination of message passing and shared memory.

We rejected the shared-memory models, because we wanted Concurrent C programs to run efficiently on non-shared memory multicomputers, such as a network of workstations connected by a local area network. By doing this we did not intend to rule out shared memory multiprocessors; we merely wished to avoid being tied to them exclusively.

This left us with asynchronous and synchronous message passing models. In one sense, these two models are equivalent, in that primitives of one model can be implemented in terms of the other. We initially selected a synchronous model for the following reasons:

• Most inter-process interactions are synchronous: the client requests a service, and waits for it. This matches the synchronous model perfectly. Thus, while the asynchronous model is more flexible, we believed that few people would actually use this extra flexibility.

* A synchronous model can be implemented more efficiently than an asynchronous model. For example, an asynchronous model requires buffer allocation (and freeing), and the message must always be copied into a buffer. In the synchronous model, no buffer allocation is required and data can be copied directly from the client process to the server, without going through an intermediate buffer, and the server's reply can be copied directly to the client. Thus the synchronous model saves space and saves time [Gehani 1988a].

Despite the equivalence of the synchronous and asynchronous message passing models, many users and potential users of Concurrent C complained about the lack of asynchronous message passing facilities. We investigated the issue of synchronous versus asynchronous message passing [Gehani 1988a] and came to the conclusion that a language should have both synchronous and asynchronous message passing facilities (see Chapter 7 for a detailed discussion). We then extended Concurrent C with asynchronous message passing.

1.2 Shared Memory

Some final comments about shared memory are in order. First and foremost, we wanted Concurrent C to allow (and encourage!) programmers to write portable programs that will run efficiently on multiprocessors with or without shared memory. This is why we choose a message passing model, and that is why we have not added any language constructs for dealing with shared memory or for simulating shared variables in a non-shared-memory environment.

On the other hand, we did not want to forbid programmers from using shared memory altogether, as long as they accepted the resulting limitations on portability. Therefore Concurrent C does not forbid processes from referencing global variables, nor does Concurrent C forbid processes from exchanging pointers. However, programmers do so at their own risk; such programs will not work as expected unless they are run on a uniprocessor or on a shared memory multiprocessor.

2. The Producer-Consumer Example

To illustrate the different models, we will show you the solution of the producer-consumer example (discussed in Chapter 1), in each of the models. We will use a C-like notation for each model; remember that only the Concurrent C example can be executed with the Concurrent C compiler.

First, we will show you a sequential version of this problem written in C:

File: pc.c

```
#include <stdio.h>
#include <ctype.h>

main()
{
    int c;
    while ((c = getchar()) != EOF) {
        if (islower(c))
            c = toupper(c);
        putchar(c);
    }
}
```

The disadvantage of the sequential program is that reading the data, processing the data and writing the output cannot proceed in parallel. Also, a new data value cannot be read until the previous value has been printed.

Now we will show you parallel versions of the producer-consumer example. We must warn you that this is a trivial "concurrent" problem because it has little concurrency in that reading, processing and writing the data and writing require little time. But if these actions were time consuming, then the example would have a high degree of concurrency.

The parallel version will be modeled as follows: one process, called the "producer", reads the data from the terminal and sends it to another process, called the "consumer".

There are several interesting issues to look for in the different parallel versions of the producer-consumer example:

- Are the facilities provided convenient for expressing the solution? If not, programmers will not use them.
- Will incorrect use of the facilities be detected automatically by the compiler? If not, programmers will spend a lot of time debugging.
- Is it necessary for the underlying hardware to have shared memory? If shared memory is required, then the resulting program will have limited portability.
- Can the producer process go ahead of the consumer process by sending it more characters than it has processed, i.e., is there "buffering" between the producer and consumer processes? If yes, then how is the "buffering" implemented?
- Does process interaction require repeated checking to see if an event has occurred, i.e., does the process *poll*? Polling is generally, but not always, undesirable because it wastes system resources.

3. Concurrent C

We reproduce the Concurrent C version of the producer-consumer example here for your convenience:

File: `pc-sync.h`

```
process spec consumer()
{
    trans void send(int c);
};
process spec producer(process consumer cons);
```

File: `pc-sync.cc`

```
#include <stdio.h>
#include "ctype.h"  /*for islower(), toupper()*/
#include "pc-sync.h"
process body producer(cons)
{
    int c;
    while ((c = getchar()) != EOF)
        cons.send(c);
    cons.send(EOF);
}
process body consumer()
{
    int xc;
    for (;;) {
        accept send(c)
            xc = c;
        if (xc == EOF)
            break;
        if (islower(xc))
            xc = toupper(xc);
        putchar(xc);
    }
}
main()
{
    create producer(create consumer());
}
```

3.1 Comments

The facilities are reasonably straightforward to use. There is no need for shared memory because processes communicate by sending messages. In the above example, there is no buffering between the producer and consumer processes. However, buffering can be easily provided by declaring transaction send to be asynchronous (and using flow control to avoid flooding) or by explicitly inserting an intermediate "buffer" process between the producer and the consumer processes.

4. Semaphores

We discussed semaphores in detail in Section 9.2 of Chapter 2. Here is the producer-consumer example written using binary semaphores:

File: pc.sem

```
semaphore sEmpty = 1, sFull = 0; int b;
void put(c)
    int c;
{
    p(sEmpty); b = c; v(sFull);
}
int get()
{   int c;
    p(sFull); c = b; v(sEmpty); return c;
}
process body producer()
{   int c;
    while ((c = getchar()) != EOF)
        put(c);
    put(EOF);
}
process body consumer()
{   int c;
    while ((c = get()) != EOF) {
        if (islower(c))
            c = toupper(c);
        putchar(c);
    }
}
main process
```

Semaphores sFull and sEmpty are used for signaling: the producer uses sFull to signal the consumer that a character is available, and the consumer uses sEmpty to signal the producer that it can put a character in the buffer. Unlike transactions, semaphores are not associated with specific processes; instead they are global variables.

4.1 Comments

Semaphores are typically used with shared memory. Buffering between the two processes can be increased to n by using a pair of integer semaphores and a buffer of size n.

Semaphores are a versatile but low-level process synchronization tool; their use is error prone as discussed in Section 9.2 of Chapter 2. Semaphores do not allow easy expression of several concurrent programming paradigms, e.g.,

- an alternative action cannot be performed if a semaphore is busy (i.e., true), and
- it is not possible to simultaneously wait for multiple semaphores.

5. Critical Regions

A *critical region* statement [Brinch Hansen 1972, 1973b] is a higher-level facility (compared to semaphores) for implementing critical regions; it aims to eliminate some of the problems with semaphores such as the inadvertent omission of the semaphore operations p and v or their use in the wrong order. Critical regions are used to coordinate access to shared memory. The *critical region* statement has the form

    region *sv-list* do *s*

Statement *s*, when executed, is guaranteed to have exclusive access to the shared variables specified in the shared variable list *sv-list*. Execution of *s* is delayed if another process is executing a *critical region* statement that contains one or more of the shared variables specified in *sv-list*.

The *critical region* statement does not allow the specification of synchronization conditions such as "wait until the buffer is not full." An extension of the critical region statement, the *conditional critical region* statement [Brinch Hansen 1972], allows specification of such synchronization conditions. The *conditional critical region* statement has the form

    region *sv-list* when *e* do *s*

Execution of statement *s* is delayed until the synchronization condition *e* becomes true and exclusive access to the shared variables specified in *sv-list* can be guaranteed. Synchronization is implemented by polling: the value of *e* is repeatedly evaluated until it yields true.

Here is the producer-consumer example written using the *conditional critical region* statement:

```
                                                    File: pc.crit
shared int b;    /*used in the region statement*/
int full = 0;

process body producer()
{
    int c;
    while ((c = getchar()) != EOF)
        region b when !full {b=c; full=1;}
    region b when !full {b=EOF; full=1;}
}
process body consumer()
{
    int c;
    for (;;) {
        region b when full {c=b; full=0;}
        if (c == EOF)
            break;
        if (islower(c))
            c = toupper(c);
        putchar(c);
    }
}
main process
```

5.1 Comments

With conditional critical regions, the producer-consumer problem can be written naturally. Critical regions and conditional critical regions solve the mutual exclusion problem elegantly. Critical regions avoid many of the errors that can occur with semaphores; e.g., a compiler can check that shared variables are accessed only from within critical regions. As with semaphores, buffering between the producer and consumer processes can be easily implemented by using a shared queue. The conditional critical region also solves the synchronization problem; however, its implementation requires polling [Brinch Hansen 1972].

6. Monitors

A *monitor* is a mechanism for encapsulating shared variables and specifying functions which must be used to access the shared variables. The monitor serializes concurrent requests to execute these functions by allowing only one process to execute a monitor function at any given time.

A monitor has the form

```
monitor name {
     shared variables & monitor functions f₁, f₂, ..., fₙ
}
```

The shared data can be accessed only by calling the monitor functions f_1, f_2, ..., f_n. Simultaneous calls to monitor operations are serialized and executed in some unspecified order. Monitors must be complemented by a synchronization mechanism such as the semaphore-like "queue of processes" with which are associated two operations: delay and release. A process waits for some condition to become true by executing the delay operation which inserts it in the specified process queue. Another process is then allowed to enter the monitor. A process can resume execution of a process waiting in one of the queues by executing the associated release operation.

Here is the monitor version of the producer-consumer example:

File: pc.mon

```
monitor buffer {
    queue qprod, qcons; int b, full = 0;
    void put(c)
        int c;
    {
        if (full) delay(qprod);
        b = c; full = 1; release(qcons);
    }
    int get()
    {
        int c;
        if (!full) delay(qcons);
        c = b; full = 0; release(qprod); return c;
    }
}
process body producer()
{
    int c;
    while ((c = getchar()) != EOF) buffer.put(c);
    put(EOF);
}
process body consumer()
{
    int c;
    while ((c = buffer.get()) != EOF) {
        if (islower(c)) c = toupper(c);
        putchar(c);
    }
}
main process
```

6.1 Comments

Like semaphores and critical regions, monitors are used with shared memory. Buffering between the producer and consumer processes can be easily implemented by using a shared circular buffer instead of the single variable b. The high-level monitor eliminates most of the problems associated with semaphores and critical regions. Unfortunately, the use of monitors can be quite complex because of the necessity of using the semaphore-like process queues. As a result of the process queues, the monitor suffers from many of the same problems associated with semaphores.

7. Communicating Sequential Processes

The rendezvous unifies the concepts of synchronization and communication. It was proposed by Hoare [1978] as the basis of process interaction in his concurrent programming model called "Communicating Sequential Processes" (CSP). CSP processes synchronize and communicate by means of *input* and *output* statements which are used to establish a rendezvous. A rendezvous is established when one process is ready to execute an *input* statement and the second process is ready to execute the corresponding *output* statement. If either process is not ready, then the other process is forced to wait. Specification of process synchronization conditions is straightforward, because *input* statements can be prefixed with synchronization conditions.

The CSP *input* statement has the form

$$p?id(x_1, x_2, ..., x_n);$$

which specifies that values are to be received from process p and assigned to variables $x_1, x_2, ..., x_n$. Identifier *id* specifies the communication type.

The CSP *output* statement has the form

$$p!id(e_1, e_2, ..., e_n);$$

which specifies that expressions $e_1, e_2, ..., e_n$ are to be output to process p. As in case of the input operations, identifier *id* specifies the communication type.

Here is the CSP version of the producer-consumer example:

```
process producer()
{
    int c;
    while ((c = getchar()) != EOF)
        consumer!send(c);
    consumer!send(EOF);
}
process consumer()
{
    int c;
    for (;;) {
        producer?send(c);
        if (c == EOF)
            break;
        if (islower(c))
            c = toupper(c);
        putchar(c);
    }
}
```

main process

7.1 Comments

The CSP version of the producer-consumer problem is like the Concurrent C version. This is not surprising because Concurrent C facilities are based upon the CSP concurrent programming model. However, there are some important differences:

1. Information transfer is unidirectional in the CSP rendezvous but bidirectional in the Concurrent C extended rendezvous.

2. A CSP rendezvous allows only argument to parameter copying (done automatically), while in the Concurrent C extended rendezvous, the called process can execute statements and return results to the calling process. The calling process is suspended for this period.

3. CSP requires that process names be specified in both *input* and *output* statements. Consequently, general purpose server processes cannot be implemented.

CSP interactions are synchronous and buffering must be implemented by interposing a buffer process.

8. Distributed Processes

In the "distributed processes" (DP) concurrent programming model proposed by Brinch Hansen [1978a], processes communicate and synchronize with other processes by calling procedures associated with processes. Such procedure calls are called *external requests*. Each process interleaves execution of external requests with a background process called the *initial* statement. A process begins by executing its initial statement. Execution of an external request or the initial statement continues until it terminates or until further execution is not immediately possible because of an unsatisfied synchronizing condition.

A DP process has the form

```
process name
{
    variables
    functions f₁, f₂, ..., fₙ
    initial statement;
}
```

Here is the DP version of the producer-consumer problem:

File: pc.dp

```
process body producer()
{
   int c;
   while ((c = getchar()) != EOF)
      consumer.put(c);
   put(EOF);
}
process body consumer()
{
   int c; int full = 0;
   void put(xc)
      int xc;
   {
      when (!full): {c = xc; full = 1;}
   }
   for (;;) {
      when (full): {
         if (c == EOF) break;
         if (islower(c)) c = toupper(c);
         putchar(c); full = 0;
      }
   }
}
main process
```

8.1 Comments

The DP version is much like the Concurrent C version except for the semantics of communication. Buffering can be implemented by modifying put so that it writes into a circular buffer instead of into a single variable.

9. Ada

Ada [DoD 1983] is based on CSP and DP; in fact, Concurrent C borrowed its basic model from Ada. Here is the Ada version:

File: pc.ada

```
with TEXT_IO; use TEXT_IO;
with ISLOWER, TOUPPER;
procedure MAIN is
   task PRODUCER;
   task CONSUMER is
      entry SEND(C: in CHARACTER);
   end CONSUMER;

   task body PRODUCER is
      C: CHARACTER;
   begin
      while not END_OF_FILE(STANDARD_INPUT) loop
         GET(C); CONSUMER.SEND(C);
      end loop;
      CONSUMER.SEND(ASCII.EOT);
   end PRODUCER;

   task body CONSUMER is
      X: CHARACTER;
   begin
      loop
        accept SEND(C: in CHARACTER) do
           X := C;
        end SEND;
        if X = ASCII.EOT then exit; end if;
        if ISLOWER(X) then X=TOUPPER(X); end if;
        PUT(X);
      end loop;
   end CONSUMER;
begin    --PRODUCER and CONSUMER become active
   null; --subprogram body must have a statement
end MAIN;
```

9.1 Comments

The Ada version is similar to the Concurrent C version except that interaction between the PRODUCER and CONSUMER processes cannot be decoupled by declaring the transaction (entry in Ada terminology) to be asynchronous.

10. Final Comments

The semaphore, critical region, and monitor solutions are all based on the existence of shared memory. The Concurrent C, CSP, DP, and Ada solutions are based on the concept of message passing.

Concurrent C, DP, and Ada use the bidirectional message passing model which is often also called the remote procedure call model. The remote procedure call model used in Concurrent C and Ada are similar to each other but different from the DP model. In Concurrent C and Ada, remote procedure calls are not accepted until the called process is ready to accept them, i.e., until the synchronizing conditions are satisfied. Once a call is accepted it is executed to completion. On the other hand, in DP, a remote procedure call is accepted immediately and execution started as soon as the specified process is free; execution of the remote call is suspended only if the synchronizing conditions within the procedure body are not satisfied. Execution of new or other remote procedure calls is then initiated or resumed. Execution of a remote procedure call may be suspended or resumed several times before it completes.

11. Exercises

1. How would you implement the semaphore operations on your computer (in terms of assembler operations)?

2. Describe how to implement monitors using semaphores.

3. Describe how to implement CSP using semaphores.

4. Describe how to implement Concurrent C using semaphores.

Chapter 7

Concurrent Programming Issues

In this chapter, we will discuss some concurrent programming issues: message passing, deadlock, maximizing concurrency, and polling.

1. Message Passing

Synchronous and asynchronous message passing facilities are equivalent in that one can be implemented in terms of the other. Most concurrent programming languages support either synchronous or asynchronous message passing but not both. For example, CSP [Hoare 1978] and Ada [DoD 1983] have synchronous message passing facilities and PLITS [Feldman 1979] has asynchronous message passing facilities. Two concurrent programming languages that have both asynchronous and synchronous message passing facilities are Concurrent C and SR [Andrews & Olsson 1985]. Note that operating systems typically provide asynchronous message passing facilities for interaction between operating system processes.

We initially selected the synchronous message passing model for Concurrent C in preference to the asynchronous message passing model because we felt that it was simpler to understand and implement. We felt that a language should have either synchronous or asynchronous message passing facilities but that both kinds of facilities were not necessary.

Despite the theoretical equivalence of the asynchronous and synchronous message passing models, some users and some potential users of Concurrent C indicated that they preferred asynchronous message passing because asynchronous communication maximizes concurrency. The debate over synchronous and asynchronous message passing has been the subject of much controversy [Tanenbaum & Renesse 1985]. Preference for synchronous or asynchronous passing can be so strong as to even become a "religious" issue. Reacting to this preference we decided to take another look at asynchronous message passing. Eventually, we came to the conclusion that asynchronous message passing can indeed be beneficial in many situations. Consequently, we extended Concurrent C to provide asynchronous message passing [Gehani 1988a].

In this chapter, we will explain this decision by taking a detailed look at both synchronous and asynchronous message passing. We will discuss the

167

advantages of each, compare an example written using synchronous facilities with one written using asynchronous facilities, discuss some details about implementing synchronous and asynchronous message passing facilities, and examine the costs involved in using these facilities.

1.1 Synchronous and Asynchronous Message Passing

Message passing primitives are used in concurrent programs for inter-process communication and synchronization. These primitives can be classified into two categories: synchronous (blocking) and asynchronous (non blocking). In case of a synchronous message send, the sender waits (blocks) until the receiver has accepted the message. On the other hand, in case of an asynchronous message send, the sender continues execution after sending the message without waiting for the receiver to accept the message. The difference between synchronous and asynchronous message receives is similar.

Synchronous and asynchronous message passing facilities allow only unidirectional inter-process communication. The "extended rendezvous" [DoD 1983] or "transaction" (in Concurrent C terminology) model, which is an extension of the synchronous message passing model, allows bidirectional communication between interacting processes. As in the case of ordinary synchronous message passing, arguments are used for transmitting information from the caller to the sender; in addition, information can be returned by the called process by means of parameters and the transaction result.

Transactions are like remote procedure calls with one difference: the receiving process can schedule the acceptance of the calls. The caller of a transaction waits until the specified process accepts the message and executes the code associated with the transaction. To maximize concurrency, the code associated with a transaction should be as fast as possible so that the sending process is not blocked longer than necessary.

1.2 Programming Ease

Because of the blocking associated with synchronous message passing, richer semantics can be and usually are associated with synchronous message passing (e.g., bidirectional message passing and timeouts). When comparing synchronous and asynchronous message passing, we will therefore include the richer blocking semantics in the comparison. Specifically, unless explicitly specified, we shall use the term synchronous message passing to refer to facilities for both unidirectional and bidirectional communication.

We will first discuss the advantages of synchronous message passing and then those of asynchronous message passing.

1.2.1 Advantages of Synchronous Message Passing

Bidirectional Information Transfer: Many process interactions, such as a client process requesting service from a server process, require bidirectional information transfer [Andrews & Schneider 1983]. With transactions, this requires only one interaction between the client and server processes. With asynchronous message passing, bidirectional information transfer requires two interactions: one message is sent by each of the two processes involved. In the first message, the client gives a description of the request to the server. The server performs the request, and then sends a message containing the results to the client. Using transactions is more efficient for bidirectional information transfer than sending two asynchronous messages primarily because it avoids the extra context switches and because it avoids the buffer management overhead associated with asynchronous messages (discussed later). Moreover, transactions are a higher-level abstraction than asynchronous messages.

Understandability: Synchronous message passing is easier to understand than asynchronous message passing because when the process sending a message resumes execution, it knows that the message has been delivered. In case of transactions, the process also knows from the return response what the receiver did. None of this can be taken for granted in case of asynchronous messages. Unlike asynchronous message sends, synchronous message sends, especially transactions, behave like function (procedure) calls. For example, as in case of function calls, a process making a transaction call is "suspended" until the call has been executed and a result returned.

Asynchronous message passing provides maximum flexibility because processes can compute and perform message sends and receives in parallel in any way they want. However, few people actually use this extra flexibility. Asynchronous message passing facilities make programming tricky and difficult because they lead to programs whose behavior is hard to reproduce due to timing dependencies [Tanenbaum & Renesse 1985]. For example, a process can send an asynchronous message and then go ahead and modify a shared buffer. The timing of this modification can depend upon the system load and scheduling policy. Nevertheless, it is important to mention that asynchronous messages can be used safely and their use is entirely appropriate in many important cases, e.g., in sending acknowledgment messages in protocols [Andrews & Schneider 1983].

Semantics: Unlike asynchronous message passing, the semantics of synchronous message passing does not depend upon the system resources. Synchronous message passing is always synchronous, but asynchronous message passing is not always asynchronous. For example, the semantics of asynchronous message passing depends upon whether or not space is available for allocating message buffers to store the message being sent. When no free space is available, the process sending the message is blocked until space becomes available and it cannot continue with other activities immediately after sending the message. Asynchronous message passing in effect becomes synchronous message passing.

Error Indication: Error responses can be easily associated with synchronous message passing, especially transactions. This is because the process sending the message waits for an acknowledgment indicating that the message was received and, in case of transactions, for the answer (which implicitly contains the acknowledgment). For example, if a disk write request results in an error, then an appropriate status value can be returned to the requesting process. In case of asynchronous message sends, if a status value is to be returned to the process requesting the disk write, then this process must explicitly perform a message receive to get the status value after making the request. Moreover, in case of multiple disk requests, it is the programmer's responsibility to correctly match the disk write status values with the corresponding disk write requests.

With synchronous message passing, it is straightforward to indicate to the sending process that the receiving process terminated before accepting the message. This information can be given to the calling process as an operation status value or as an exception. Similarly, in case of transactions, termination of the process while it is in the middle of accepting the transaction (i.e., executing the code associated with it) can also be indicated easily to the transaction caller. In case of asynchronous messages, once the sender has sent the message, it may not be possible to indicate failure of the receiving process to the sender.

Synchronization And Polling: With synchronous message sends and receives, the message passing primitives can themselves be used for process synchronization. There is no need for an explicit synchronizing mechanism. With asynchronous message passing, an explicit synchronizing mechanism would be needed if *both* message send and receive primitives are asynchronous. In the absence of synchronization mechanisms, processes will poll for events (which is wasteful of resources). Note that polling can also be avoided by means of interrupts (and waiting) but the addition of interrupts will further complicate the semantics of the language. It is also not possible to implement mutual exclusion easily or efficiently [Andrews & Schneider 1983; DoD 1978].

As an example of polling, consider a process that uses asynchronous message receives to receive messages of two types:

```
for (;;) {
    select {
        accept message of type M1 { ... }
    otherwise
        ;
    }
    select {
        accept message of type M2 { ... }
    otherwise
        ;
    }
}
```

The above program fragment repeatedly checks to see if a message of type M1 or M2 has arrived.

To avoid polling (and the mutual exclusion problem), most systems that provide an asynchronous message send facility typically provide a synchronous message receive facility; many systems also provide an asynchronous message receive facility [Andrews & Schneider 1983]. For example, with synchronous message receives, the above program fragment can be written as the following non-polling program:

```
select {
    accept message of type M1 { ... }
or
    accept message of type M2 { ... }
}
```

If no message of type M1 or M2 is available, then the program blocks waiting for such a message to arrive.

Timeouts: Timeouts can be associated with synchronous message sends and receives (because the process doing the send or receive is waiting for the message to be delivered or to arrive). For example, if a service request message is not accepted within the specified period then the request can be withdrawn and the service requested from another process. Such semantics cannot be associated with asynchronous message sends because the requested message is sent immediately. Of course, the programmer can write the program in a manner that incorporates a timeout protocol. For example, the sender can cancel a request by sending a special message requesting that an earlier message be canceled if it has not already been processed. The receiving process must give such messages a higher priority than that accorded to other messages; the code to do this must be explicitly written by the programmer.

Concurrent Programming Errors: With synchronous message passing, problems such as deadlock usually can be discovered more easily, and are often discovered in simple test cases. In case of programs with asynchronous message passing, it may be hard to detect these problems because they may show up only when the system is under "stress" (for example, when the run-time system runs out of storage for buffering asynchronous messages).

1.2.2 Advantages of Asynchronous Message Passing

Flexibility: The main advantage of asynchronous message passing is that it gives the maximum flexibility to the programmer to maximize concurrency. Processes are not blocked waiting for other processes; instead, they can compute and perform message sends and receives in parallel in any way they want. The process sending a message does not have to wait for the destination process to accept the message before continuing other activities. This is particularly valuable when the process sending the message is not expecting an answer.

Expressiveness: Let us first consider unidirectional synchronous message passing. Suppose a client process requests service and then waits for an answer from the server process. After performing the service, the server sends an answering message. If the client is not waiting for the answer, then the server will block; this is unacceptable for a server with multiple clients. This problem does not happen with asynchronous message passing.

The server-waiting problem does not arise when transactions are used because the client waits for the answer. But this can lead to a different problem. Consider a server S that discovers that a resource needed for its current activity, say accepting a transaction from a client C, is momentarily unavailable. S should be able to temporarily set aside this activity and turn its attention to requests from other clients. Implementing this strategy requires the use of two transactions: one transaction to request the service and another to get the results. The server accepts the first transaction with a high priority and gives the client a ticket. The client is then free to do what it wants, but it must eventually make another transaction call, using its ticket, to get the results of the service. This technique is called the "early reply" technique; the first transaction is essentially used to simulate asynchronous message passing. Giving this example, Liskov, Herlihy & Gilbert [1986] argue that synchronous communication in a language with a static process structure (in which a process can handle only one request at a time) is computationally complete but it is not sufficiently expressive. As they point out, in some cases splitting a transaction into two parts can be avoided by providing a facility that ensures a transaction is accepted only when it can be satisfied immediately (e.g., guards in SR [Andrews 1982] or the `suchthat` clause in Concurrent C). Note that the client process will be forced to wait until the service is provided.

Pipelining and Throughput: Unlike synchronous message passing, asynchronous message passing reduces the time required for sending multiple messages because message transmission can be "pipelined", i.e., overlapped with the next operation. Also a smart implementation can pack multiple asynchronous messages, destined for the same processor, in a single buffer and send them as one inter-processor message. As an example, consider a process that sends a series of messages to a window process **w** [Liskov, et al 1987]:

```
w.display(string₁);
w.display(string₂);
w.change_color(red);
w.display(string₃);
```

With synchronous message passing, there may be considerable delay in sending these messages especially if the message sending time is substantial (as may be the case for inter-processor communication in some distributed implementations, e.g., the LAN multiprocessor implementation of Concurrent C [Cmelik, Gehani & Roome 1988b]).

Asynchronous message passing, in addition to maximizing throughput of the sending process, also allows the receiving process to select messages in an optimal order. For example, if a process makes the following asynchronous requests to a disk scheduler process

```
tptr = ((process user) c_mypid()).ack;
disk.request(blk_no₁, WRITE, buf₁, tptr);
disk.request(blk_no₂, WRITE, buf₂, tptr);
disk.request(blk_no₃, WRITE, buf₃, tptr);
wait for 3 ack messages
```

then the above requests will be pipelined, and they will all be available to the disk scheduler. Using the **by** clause, the disk scheduler process can accept these requests in an order that minimizes the movement of the disk head.

With unidirectional synchronous messages, it is not possible to pipeline multiple requests from one process, nor is it possible for the disk process to handle the requests from one process in an optimal order. Moreover, sending completion acknowledgments by the disk process can cause problems if the client process is not waiting to receive the acknowledgments, because it will block the disk process. Note that this problem does not arise with transactions because the client process is forced to wait for the acknowledgement.

Simulating Synchronous and Asynchronous Message Passing: Using asynchronous primitives, synchronous message passing can be simulated trivially: send the message asynchronously, and then immediately wait for an answering message from the other process acknowledging that the message had been received.

However, simulating asynchronous facilities with synchronous facilities is not as simple. It can be done by introducing an intermediate "buffer" process whose sole purpose is to take the message from the sender and deliver it to the receiver. The buffer process is (almost) always ready to receive the message from the sender, which gives the sender the effect of an asynchronous message send. Instead of using an intermediate buffer process, asynchronous messages can also be simulated by creating agent processes. For each message to be sent asynchronously, an agent process is created and given the message to be sent which it accepts immediately. The agent process sends the message to the specified process; it does the waiting instead of the process that created it [Habermann & Perry 1983].

Simulating asynchronous messages with synchronous messages complicates the program structure, and it can be inefficient (the latter depends upon the cost of context switches and the cost of allocating and freeing buffers; see Section 1.5 for details).

Deadlock: If process A sends a synchronous message to process B just as B sends a synchronous message to A, then the two processes will deadlock. However, if these processes send asynchronous messages, then they will not deadlock.

Miscellaneous: Finally, asynchronous message passing primitives match the underlying message passing facilities in distributed systems which are normally asynchronous, especially at the lower levels.

1.3 Implementation And Efficiency

Even though synchronous message passing in multiprocessor systems is built by using asynchronous message passing provided by the underlying hardware, one argument against providing asynchronous message passing at the user level is that it requires automatic buffering. Automatic buffering is not a primitive hardware operation in conventional bus-based multiprocessors; therefore, it should not be required by a programming language because buffering can be done at the destination process or by interposing an intermediate buffer process. On the other hand, Kieburtz & Silberschatz [1979] argue that software buffering complicates the program structure. With VLSI hardware technology, buffered communication can be provided in hardware and that such communication may actually be preferred.

Implementing synchronous message passing is simpler than implementing asynchronous message passing. Synchronous message passing does not require the buffer allocation and management required for asynchronous message passing [DoD 1978; Gentleman 1981]. In the synchronous model, only a fixed amount of message space (one message buffer) is required per process whereas in the asynchronous case the message storage space required is potentially unbounded; as a result, an arbitrary limit is normally imposed.

Synchronous message passing is also generally more efficient than asynchronous message passing primarily because there is no need to allocate and free buffers to hold the messages. Of course if the message transmission time is large, as may be the case with multiprocessors, then asynchronous messages can speed up program execution despite the time required to allocate and free buffers.

Storing unaccepted asynchronous messages can require a sizeable amount of storage if the sending process is much faster than the receiving process. With each asynchronous message that is stored, other information such as the sender name, pointer to the next message, etc., must also be stored. If the storage used for asynchronous messages is very large, then this can have an impact on program execution time because, for example, this may lead to more paging or larger program swap time. Asynchronous message passing can lead to deadlock if the message buffers are allocated not from a global pool, but from local pools associated with individual processes. Deadlock may occur if some of the local pools are exhausted even though storage may be available elsewhere in the system.

Finally, sending a synchronous message is usually considered to be a scheduling point because the caller cannot proceed further until the message has been received. In case of asynchronous messages, sending a message is not a natural scheduling point. Forcing a scheduling decision may be inefficient while not doing it may result in the sender generating a large number of unaccepted messages.

1.4 Cost of Sending Messages

To give you an idea of the parameters involved in sending messages, we will discuss the cost of sending messages in the context of two implementations of Concurrent C: the uniprocessor implementation and a LAN multiprocessor implementation [Cmelik, Gehani & Roome 1988b].

In the uniprocessor implementation, the processes share a common address space, and the implementation exploits this information and passes pointers to messages, whenever appropriate, instead of copying messages. When a synchronous transaction call is made, the transaction parameters are put on the calling process' stack, and the address of the parameter list is given to the called process. The called process accesses the transaction arguments by using this address, and it puts the transaction result on the called process' stack. For an asynchronous transaction call, the parameters are copied from the calling process' stack to a specially allocated buffer, and the address of this buffer is given to the called process. This buffer is freed after the transaction call is accepted.

In the multiprocessor implementation, when a process makes a remote transaction call, the parameters are taken from its stack and written over the inter-processor communication network. On each processor there is a message handler process that reads network messages. It copies each message into a buffer whose address is then given to the called process. The transaction result is returned in a similar fashion.

Based on these two implementations, the cost of sending a message from one process to another (including receipt of the message by the destination process) can be measured in terms of the time required for the following activities:

1. Copying a message (cp): This is the time required for copying the message from one place to another, for example, copying the arguments to the process stack, from a process stack to a buffer, or from one buffer to another. We assume that a message consists of a set of expressions whose values are to be transmitted from one process to another. Calling a function with these expressions as arguments automatically results in the expression values being put on the stack.

    For large messages, an implementer may be tempted to put a pointer to the message on the stack. In a uniprocessor implementation (with shared memory between processes) and with synchronous message passing, the receiving process can use the pointer to access the message. But in case of asynchronous message passing, the message, and not just a pointer to the message, must be copied into the buffer. Otherwise, any changes made to the message before or during transmission to the receiver, or before the receiver has finished accessing the message will put the program in jeopardy [Tanenbaum & Renesse 1985].

2. Allocating and freeing buffers (buf): In the uniprocessor implementation, a message buffer must be allocated to store the asynchronous message. In the multiprocessor implementation, one message buffer must be allocated on the remote processor to store, for the receiver, any message (synchronous or asynchronous). After the message has been received, the buffer must be freed.

3. Context switch (cxt): After a process has sent a message, the receiving process must eventually get a chance to execute. Assuming there is more than one process per processor, this involves determining the next process to execute, saving the registers of the currently executing process and then restoring the registers of the process that is to execute next.

    Of course, the process that has been sent the message may not get to execute immediately—other processes may get to execute first. We will assume, for our analysis, that the scheduling algorithm selects the process we are interested in to execute next.

4. Interprocessor transmission time (tr): Interprocessor message transmission includes anything that has to be done to get the message from one processor to another, e.g., writing on the output port, reading

from the input port, and the actual transmission. This will most likely involve freeing and allocating additional buffers and doing additional message copies.

5. Writing an inter-processor message (*write*): This is really a component of *tr*, but we need this component for one of the cases discussed below.

The time computations given below do not take into account the time it takes the receiving process to actually get around to accepting a message; the latter is application dependent.

1.4.1 Unidirectional Information Transfer: We will now determine the cost of sending *n* messages from process A to process B:

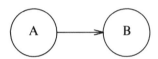

1.4.1.1 Uniprocessor: Sending messages synchronously does not require copying the message to an intermediate buffer. The message is put on the stack of the sending process and is accessed directly from there by the receiving process. With synchronous message passing, process A will be forced to operate in "lock-step" with process B, i.e., A will not be able to continue its execution until B has accepted the message. This means that every time A sends a message, B must get a chance to execute and then, for A to send another message, A must get a chance to execute. The total cost of sending *n* messages is $n \times (2cxt + cp) - cxt$.

With asynchronous messages, the processes do not need to operate in lockstep. Every time A sends a message, a buffer must be allocated and after B receives the message, the buffer must be freed. The message is first copied to the process stack and from there to the buffer. It is not necessary to do a context switch after sending each message. In fact, it is possible that a context switch to B will occur after A has sent all the *n* messages to B. The cost of sending *n* messages will be between $n \times (buf + 2cp) + cxt$ and $n \times (buf + 2cp + 2cxt) - cxt$.

The time required for sending the messages synchronously is clearly less than the upper bound for sending the messages asynchronously. Whether or not it is less than the lower bound depends upon the times for scheduling the next process, the buffer allocation and freeing times and the context switch time.

1.4.1.2 Multiprocessor: Assume that processes A and B are on different processors. Sending a synchronous message from A to B involves writing the message from A's stack onto the inter-processor communication channel, receipt of the message by the message handler on B's processor, and copying of the message into a buffer which is then given to B. Upon acceptance of the message by B, it must send an acknowledgment to the message handler on A which can then itself change A's state to ready. The cost of sending n messages (from A's perspective) is $n \times (2tr + cp + 4cxt)$. (Note that cxt is more in our multiprocessor implementation than in our uniprocessor implementation because there are simply more processes such as message handlers, and the scheduler also looks to see if messages have arrived from other processes.) Depending upon the multiprocessor, the inter-processor transmission time may be so large that other times such as those for context switching and copying messages may be insignificant in comparison. Note that two context switches are required on each processor: one each for the two message handlers, and one each for processes A and B. Also buffer allocation, copy, and freeing will have to be done on the processor where B is executing.

Please note that the inter-processor message transmission time can dominate the other components. For example, on our VAX 8650 LAN implementation, tr is about 8 ms, and cxt is 53 μs (a function call is 4.2 μs).

Sending an asynchronous message is similar except that no return acknowledgment is necessary. The cost of sending n messages (from A's perspective) is $n \times write$.

Clearly, because a synchronous message requires two inter-processor communications, an asynchronous message will be faster.

1.4.2 Bidirectional Information Transfer: The cost of sending n messages from process A to process B followed by n responses from B to A can be computed in a manner similar to that shown for the case of unidirectional information transfer.

1.5 Experimental Observations

To get a better feel for the time required to transmit characters, we ran variations of the producer-consumer programs on a VAX 8650 for the uniprocessor versions and on a pair of VAX 8650s connected by Ethernet for the multiprocessor versions. The programs used for determining character transmission times were essentially the same as the different versions of the producer-consumer example shown in Chapters 1 and 2 with the following changes: the input characters were generated internally; reading from standard input, conversion of lower-case characters to upper case, and writing to standard output were eliminated. This was done to get a more accurate measurement of the time required to send a message. Note that no flow control was used in the asynchronous version; this version was the same as the synchronous version except that transaction `send` was declared to be asynchronous.

The times given are the average times for transmitting a single character (a very small message). In case of the uniprocessor synchronous version, 10000 characters were transmitted while in case of the asynchronous and the multiprocessor versions 1000 characters were transmitted. Fewer characters were sent in the last two cases for the following reasons:

1. In the Concurrent C implementations, we do not consider sending an asynchronous message to be a scheduling point. Consequently, a process can keep generating asynchronous messages until it is descheduled, say by a timer interrupt. And in our test program, all that the producer process does is send asynchronous messages. Transmission of a much larger number of characters, say 10000, slowed down program execution significantly which we initially thought was due to the fact that the buffer space used for storing the asynchronous messages increased the process size substantially (more on this later). In practice, we do not expect a process to generate so many unaccepted asynchronous messages.

2. Interprocessor messages are an order of magnitude slower than intra-processor messages.

The programs were timed with the UNIX `time` command [UNIX 1983a-b]. Note that several other users were using the computers on which the timings were performed. Two times are given for each message transmission: real time and cpu time. The real time includes the transmission time and the cpu time given is only for the processor from where the message was sent.

1.5.1 Unidirectional Information Transfer

message transmission mode	uniprocessor times in μs		multiprocessor times in μs	
	real	**cpu**	**real**	**cpu**
synchronous	95	43	10760	2320
asynchronous (no flow control)	1160	600	3300	430
simulated asynchronous via buffer process	200	121	11180	2570

1.5.1.1 Uniprocessor: Notice that asynchronous message transfers take much longer than both synchronous message transfers and the buffered simulation of asynchronous message transfers. In fact, the time per message transmission increased quite rapidly as we increased the number of asynchronous messages being transmitted. We first thought that this was primarily due to the fact that allocation and freeing of buffers used for storing asynchronous messages was much more expensive than the extra context switches required in the synchronous case, and that this time outweighed even the time required for the extra context switches and extra message transfers required in the buffered case. On a closer examination of the implementation, we discovered what was another example of asynchronous implementations breaking under stress. A new message is appended to the incoming message queue (implemented as a list). In our implementation, finding the end of the list was done by sequentially traversing through the list and not by keeping a pointer to the end of the list. If the list size is small, as we expect it to be normally, then this search time is not significant. But when the list gets very large, then this time becomes significant. The solution is to keep a marker to the end of the list. A change in the implementation reduced the message transmission time to $210\mu s$ (real time) and 160 μs (cpu time). Note that these times could be reduced further by implementing a customized version of the default C storage allocator malloc which is used by our implementation to reduce the number of storage allocations.

1.5.1.2 Multiprocessor: The asynchronous implementation is the clear winner because of the high inter-processor transmission time in our multiprocessor implementation.

1.5.2 Bidirectional Information Transfer: To measure the time required for bidirectional flow of information, we ran another set of variations of the producer-consumer example. Here are the experimentally observed times:

message transmission mode	uniprocessor times in μs		multiprocessor times in μs	
	real	**cpu**	**real**	**cpu**
synchronous (transactions)	88	46	9600	2010
asynchronous (no flow control)	610	260	11980	2150
simulated asynchronous via buffer processes	401	240	18580	4160

The above times are as expected: compared to transactions, asynchronous message passing does not give you any advantage if it is used to implement bidirectional communication. However, asynchronous message passing can be useful if other work can be done between sending and receiving messages.

Please note that in the time measurements performed by us, we did two things that are unfair to asynchronous message passing:

- In our experiment, the receiving process is always ready to accept the message; this is generally not going to be the case. Because the time taken by the receiving process to get around to accepting a message (which is application dependent) has not been taken into account, the time required for unidirectional synchronous message passing will in general be (possibly much) higher.

- In the bidirectional case, even though the time required for asynchronous message passing is higher compared to the time required for a transaction call, with asynchronous message passing the process does not have to wait for the reply; it could do useful work before waiting for the reply.

1.6 Conclusions

It is important in language design to provide facilities that lead to a natural programming style and that can be implemented efficiently. At the same time, it is important to keep the language as small as possible for various obvious reasons such as ease of learning, ease of understanding, ease of implementation, and so forth. We initially did not provide facilities for asynchronous process message passing in Concurrent C because we wanted to keep the language as small as possible and because we felt that they were redundant in the presence of the synchronous message passing facilities that we had provided.

As we have seen, asynchronous message passing facilities can simplify programming and decrease program execution time. Depending upon the situation, it may be more appropriate to use asynchronous message passing instead of synchronous message passing or vice versa. We therefore extended Concurrent C with asynchronous message passing facilities.

2. Deadlock

Deadlock occurs when one or more processes in a program are blocked forever because of requirements that cannot be satisfied. Deadlock can be resolved in some cases by making some of the involved processes give up some resources, or by aborting them.

Deadlock caused by processes competing for shared resources, such as record locks, will occur if the following four conditions are satisfied [Calingaert 1982; Coffman, Elphick & Shoshani 1971]:

1. *Mutual Exclusion*: A process requires exclusive access to a resource.

2. *Incremental Resource Allocation*: A process can acquire its resources incrementally.

3. *Nonpreemptive Scheduling*: Resources allocated to a process cannot be taken back from it until after the process has released them.

4. *Circular Waiting*: There exists a circular wait among the competing processes for the resources held by the other processes.

Deadlocks occur because of errors in program design or the occurrence of unanticipated events; they are often discovered only after the system has been in use for a long time. However, deadlock can be avoided by ensuring that the four conditions necessary for deadlock are not satisfied simultaneously. Satisfaction of the first condition necessary for deadlock, that of *mutual exclusion*, may be unavoidable in the case of some resources. However, it is possible to ensure that the remaining three conditions are not satisfied simultaneously by using one of the following strategies [Havender 1968; Coffman, Elphick & Shoshani 1971]:

1. *Avoid Incremental Resource Allocation:* Each process must specify all the resources needed by it when requesting resources; its execution will be delayed until all the requested resources are available.

2. *Use Preemption:* If a process holding some resources requests additional resources, then it must release all the resources held by it and then issue a request for the original resources plus the additional ones needed by it.

3. *Avoid Circular Waiting:* All resources in the system are linearly ordered; the order of resource requests must conform to this ordering.

The best way to avoid deadlock is to avoid circular waiting. Complete resource allocation can be costly because resources may not be used for a long time. Preemption is appropriate only for resources whose state can be easily saved and restored later, e.g., a CPU.

2.1 Examples of Deadlock

Consider a program with two processes X and Y executing on a system with two disk drives. Each process needs both disk drives, say to copy a file from one disk to the other. Deadlock will occur if each process is granted permission to use one disk drive but is waiting for permission to use the other drive and neither process is willing to give up the permission granted to it, even temporarily.

Another example of deadlock is two processes p1 and p2, both of type player, each of which calls the synchronous transaction move of the other process before accepting the other's transaction call:

```
process spec player()
{
    trans void opponent(process player name);
    trans void move(...);
    ...
};
process body player()
{
    process player op;
    ...
    accept opponent(name)
        op = name;
    for (;;) {
        ...
        op.move(...);
        accept move(...);
        ...
    }
}
main()
{
    process player p1, p2;
    ...
    p1 = create player();
    p2 = create player();
    p1.opponent(p2);
    p2.opponent(p1);
}
```

The deadlock problem must be eliminated by modifying the program.

2.2 Effective Deadlock

A process is said to be in *effective deadlock* if for all practical purposes the
process is blocked even though there is a small probability that it will be able
to resume execution. As an example, consider the following process:

```
process spec service(...)
{
    trans void request(int urgency, ...);
};
process body service(...)
{
    ...
    for (;;) {
        accept request(urgency, ...) by(urgency) {
            ...
        }
        ...
    }
}
```

A process d calling transaction request will be effectively deadlocked if an unending stream of processes call transaction request with a higher value for parameter urgency than that used by d.

As another example, consider a process client that repeatedly calls transaction query of another process server to get some information:

File: client.cc

```
process spec client(process server s);
process body client(s)
{
    ...
    int done = 0;
    for (;;) {
        for (;;) {
            done = within 0.1 ? s.query(...) : 0;
            if (!done)
                perform secondary activity;
        }
        ...
    }
}
```

If transaction query is not accepted within a specified period, then the client process times out and performs some secondary activity, so that it does not waste too much time waiting for the transaction call to be accepted; the call is tried again later. This activity is repeated until the query transaction call is accepted. Effective deadlock will occur if every time the client process calls the server process, it is forced to timeout because the `server` process is momentarily busy doing something else.

The potential for effective deadlock can be resolved in this example by modifying the `client` process to make it wait for the call to be accepted (i.e., an ordinary transaction call) and moving the code for the secondary activity to another process where it can be executed in parallel with the `client` process.

3. Maximizing Concurrency

A process, like a C++ class [Stroustrup 1986], is a data encapsulation mechanism. The data encapsulated by a process is accessed by means of transaction calls, whereas the data encapsulated in a class is accessed via functions declared in the public part of a class specification. A class has no flow of control of its own; execution of a class member function uses the caller's flow of control. On the other hand, a process has its own flow of control, i.e., it executes in parallel with the other processes. Implementing an object as a process can increase the concurrency in the program. For example, the body of the *accept* statement is kept as small as possible; internal bookkeeping by the called process can and should be done in parallel with the calling process.

Suppose we have to implement a set of integers with operations to insert and delete elements and to check set membership. Should the set be implemented as a class or as a process? If multiple processes are going to access the set, then it would be advantageous to implement it as a process, because mutual exclusion is automatically provided by a process. Even if only one process is going to access the set, then this will increase concurrency, especially in case of multiprocessors. But this must be weighed against the fact that processes have a larger overhead than classes (e.g., the process implementing a set will have to be scheduled).

Here is an implementation of a set using a process:

File: set.h

```
process spec set()
{
    trans void insert(int x), delete(int x);
    trans int in(int x);
};
```

```
#include <stdio.h>
#include "set.h"

typedef struct node {int v; node *n;} node;
process body set()
{
    int e; node *hd=NULL, *p;
    for (;;)
        select {
            accept insert(x) e = x;
            for (p=hd; p!=NULL && p->v!=e; p=p->n)
                ;
            if (p == NULL) {
                p = (node *) malloc(sizeof(node));
                if (p != NULL)
                    {p->v = e; p->n = hd; hd = p;}
                else {
                    fprintf(stderr,"No storage!\n");
                    exit(1);
                }
            }
        or
            accept delete(x) e = x;
            if ((p = hd) != NULL)
                if (p->v == e)
                    hd = hd->n;
                else for (; p->n != NULL; p = p->n)
                    if (p->n->v == e)
                        {p->n = p->n->n; break;}
        or
            accept in(x) {
                for (p = hd; p != NULL; p = p->n)
                    if (p->v == e)
                        treturn 1;
                treturn 0;
            }
        or
            terminate;
        }
}
```

Note that the processes calling transactions of process set are delayed only as long as necessary. The actual insertion and deletion of the element are carried on in parallel with the execution of the calling process.

4. Polling

Polling is characterized by a process actively and repeatedly checking for the occurrence of an event that originates outside the process. Polling is generally, but not always, undesirable, because it wastes system resources, e.g., it burns CPU cycles or it may generate unnecessary traffic on the network connecting the processors [Gehani & Cargill 1984].

Polling can be classified into two categories: *rendezvous* and *information*. Process A *rendezvous polls* process B with respect to a transaction T if the rendezvous can be preceded by an unbounded number of attempts by A to rendezvous. An attempt may be an unsuccessful transaction call or a failure to select the *accept* alternative in a *select* statement. Process A *information polls* process B with respect to a transaction T if A calls B an unbounded number of times before it gets the desired information from B.

Consider the program segment of a process A that wants to access some resource managed by a resource manager process rm:

```
free = 0;
while (!free)
    rm.request(&free);
```

Process A calls transaction request of process rm repeatedly until free is set to 1 to indicate that A can go ahead and use the resource. The polling performed by process A is of the second kind, i.e., information polling.

Of course, polling in a program may be a combination of rendezvous and information polling. Between polling, a process may or may not do useful work—leading to the notion of *busy waiting*. A polling process *busy waits* if between (attempted) transaction calls no useful action is performed, i.e., there is no computational progress.

4.1 Example of a Desirable Polling Program

Polling programs may be desirable or even necessary in some cases. For example, in case of device drivers, polling may be necessary when the hardware does not provide interrupts or the device is to be polled to get continuous readings.

The following example illustrates a polling program that is more desirable than a non-polling program simply because it is more efficient. The problem is to display the position of a moving point on a screen (e.g., an airplane on a radar screen) based on the coordinates supplied or by using computations based on the most recent coordinates and velocity available [Kieburtz & Silberschatz 1979]. The point position is to be displayed *as fast as possible* so that it is tracked accurately. If an updated position of the point is not available, then a new position should be computed before displaying the point:

```
process spec airplane(position ip, velocity iv)
{
    trans void update(position p, velocity v);
};

process body airplane(ip, iv)
{
    ...
    for (;;) {
        select {
            accept update(p, v) {
                record position p and velocity v;
            }
        or
            compute new position using old coordinates and velocity;
        }
        display plane position on screen;
    }
}
```

5. Exercises

1. Consider a concurrent program that has the potential of deadlock. Running this program with the same input data sometimes causes deadlock, but not always. Can you explain this phenomena?

2. Suggest modifications for process `service` (given in Section

Chapter 8

Discrete Event Simulation

In "discrete event" simulation, events in the simulated system happen at discrete times, and these are the only times at which the system changes state. For example when simulating a queue of customers waiting for service at a bank, the events include a new customer arriving, a customer reaching the head of a line and being served by a teller, a customer leaving, etc. The key points are the times at which these events happen; as far as the simulation is concerned, nothing happens between the events. Discrete event simulation differs from "continuous time" simulation, which is used to simulate continuous systems like water flowing over a dam.

Concurrent programming can simplify the task of writing a discrete event simulation program; the resulting program is easy to understand and modify. In particular,

- The simulation program is easy to write: for each entity type, a simple sequential process that describes the steps performed by entity is written. These processes communicate when the entities they are simulating need to communicate or synchronize. This is called the "process-interaction model" of simulation.

- It is easy to reuse entity processes from previous simulations or to create a library of processes for standard entities.

- Even if entity processes from previous simulations cannot be reused as is, they can be used templates which can be customized for new simulations.

- It is easy to capture statistics for each entity: just record them in local variables in each entity process (e.g., a running average). If there are several instances of the same entity, each process automatically gets its own versions of these variables.

- The processes can be automatically distributed over the processors in a multiprocessor system. This can speed up a computationally-intensive simulation program (i.e., one in which the entity processes are compute-bound between process interactions).

We will illustrate these points by showing how to write a Concurrent C program that models a multi-stage, multi-server queueing network. Each queue and each server is modeled by a Concurrent C process. This is a natural way to simulate a queueing network: each process runs independently, as do the queues and servers in the real network, and they interact when necessary, for example, when a server takes a job from its input queue. We present several general processes that can be used in other simulation programs; these include an event scheduler process and a queue manager process.

For additional discussions of queueing networks and how to use concurrent programming for simulation, see Bruno [1984], Franta [1977], and Kleinrock [1975].

1. The Process-Interaction Model of Simulation

1.1 A Simple Example

Consider the following queueing system.

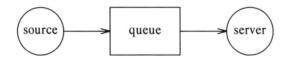

Its simulation uses three process: one for the source, one for the queue, and one for the server. The source process generates items ("jobs"). The inter-arrival time—the time between item arrivals—is a random variable. The body of the source process consists of a simple loop that calculates the next inter-arrival time, waits for that many time units, generates a new item, and then places the new item on the queue:

```
while ( 1 ) {
    delay for random inter-arrival time;
    generate item;
    call queue process to put item in queue;
}
```

Similarly, the server process repeatedly takes the next item from the queue, processes it for the appropriate service time, and finally discards the item. The queue accepts items from the source, and gives them to the server. The queue process is similar to the buffer process presented in Chapter 1.

1.2 General Method

The first step in the process-interaction model is to determine the sequential, independent entities in the system being simulated. The entities in a queueing network include sources, queues, and servers. Each entity performs a well-defined series of operations. Some of these operations may require interaction with another entity; one example is a server taking an item from a queue. Other than that, each entity is independent of the other entities.

The next step is to identify the types of interactions between the entities. Each such interaction becomes a transaction call. It is convenient to divide entities into two categories: *active* entities, such as servers, and *passive* entities, such as queues. In general, passive entities wait for requests, and usually represent "resources" that are used by the active entities. The process that implements a passive entity has one transaction for each type of request. For example, a queue process will have a "put" transaction to put an item into the queue, and a "take" transaction to remove the next item from the queue. The process for an active entity, such as the server, is not called by the other processes, and thus does not have transactions. This is not an absolute rule; for example, while handling a request, a passive process might actively request service from another passive process. But it is often a useful paradigm for structuring the processes in a simulation program.

For each distinct type of entity, we then write the specification and body for the Concurrent C process that simulates it. If the simulation needs several entities of the same type, we can create an instance of the corresponding process type for each entity. The process for simulating an active entity is a simple sequential program that performs the entity's operations. The process for simulating a passive entity consists of a loop that repeatedly executes a `select` statement with alternatives for all of its transactions. In general, each process keeps statistics, such as the mean-time-in-system, and prints them at the end of the simulation.

The final step is to write a `main` process which creates all the entity processes, and connects these processes appropriately.

1.3 Scheduler Process

Delays in simulated time—such as the service time delay—are handled by a scheduler process.[1] This scheduler process maintains the current simulated time, and advances it appropriately. You can think of the scheduler as maintaining a clock that gives the current simulated time. For each delay request from a process, the scheduler determines the simulated time at which the process is to be reactivated, and saves this request in an activation request list. When all processes are waiting for delays to expire, the scheduler searches this list for the entry with the lowest activation time. The scheduler then advances the simulated clock to this time, removes this entry from the list, and re-activates the selected process. If several processes are waiting to be re-activated at the same simulated time, the scheduler awakens all of them

---

1. Simulated time is different from actual time, so we cannot use the Concurrent C `delay` statement to simulate service or arrival delays.

simultaneously. Any computation done by a process takes place in zero *simulated* time.

A complication is that a process can be waiting for an event other than an explicit delay request. For example, suppose that a server process tries to take an item from an empty queue. The server process waits for the queue process, which is waiting for a source process to put an item into the queue. The source process is waiting for a delay to expire, at which point it will place a new item in the queue. Thus the scheduler advances the simulated time when every process is either waiting for a delay request to expire *or* is waiting for some event that will be generated by a process that is waiting for a delay request to expire.

Before showing how the scheduler process can determine when this has happened, we need to introduce some formalism. At any given time, each entity process is in one of three states:

waiting: Waiting for an explicit delay request from the scheduler.
active: Computing in zero simulated time.
passive: Waiting for something other than a delay request.

As an example, consider a source process that waits for a random inter-arrival delay and then places a job on a queue. The source process starts in the active state. It enters the waiting state when it delays for the inter-arrival time; it becomes active again when the scheduler re-activates it. If the queue is not full, the source process stays active while it places the job in the queue. However, if the queue is full, the source process enters the passive state, and remains passive until some server process creates space by removing a job from the queue.

Thus the scheduler accepts delay requests until there are no active entity processes, at which time the scheduler advances the simulated clock and re-activates the appropriate process(es). The scheduler knows the number of processes waiting for the delay requests, so all it needs to know is the number of passive processes. To give the scheduler this information, we will call a scheduler transaction whenever a process changes state from active to passive or vice versa.

2. A Two-Stage Queueing Network

We will develop a simulation program for the following queueing network:

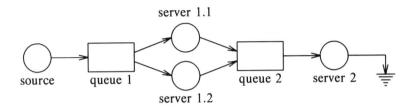

In this network, jobs enter queue 1 from a Poisson source (exponential inter-arrival times). The arrows indicate the direction in which jobs flow. The first stage has two servers (servers 1.1 and 1.2), each of which takes the next available job from a common queue. The second stage has one server; it takes jobs from the second queue, and discards them when done. The queues are FIFO (first-in-first-out), and can hold at most 100 jobs. If a queue is full, the server or source putting an item into this queue is blocked until space is available. Similarly, if a queue is empty, the server taking an item from the queue is blocked until an item is available (if more items are expected) or an "end-of-file" is indicated to the server. The service times are exponentially distributed, and are determined when a job enters the system. Servers 1.1 and 1.2 run at half the speed of server 2; that is, if server 2 takes x time units to process a job, server 1.1 takes $2x$ units.

3. Structure of The Simulation Program

In this section, we present the interfaces to the processes in the simulation program for the queueing network described in Section 2; the next section describes how these processes are implemented. This simulation program uses four types of processes:

> `sched`: Simulated-time scheduler process.
> `queue`: Finite-capacity FIFO queue.
> `source`: Source of arriving jobs.
> `server`: Single input, single output server.

The `main` process creates these processes and connects them appropriately.

The simulation program terminates after simulating the specified number of jobs. The source process terminates after generating these jobs. Before terminating, the source process informs its output queue that no more jobs will arrive. When the queue is empty (and no more jobs are expected), the queue process informs the servers that no more jobs will arrive. Each server then prints its statistics, tells its output queue that it is done, and terminates. In this way, the queues are drained automatically and all processes eventually terminate.

Strictly speaking, this causes our statistics to be distorted by the "edge effects" of filling up the queues at the beginning of the simulation, and draining them at the end. However, we will simulate enough jobs to mitigate this distortion.

3.1 Scheduler Process Interface

The scheduler process manages simulated time. The time units are arbitrary. We will refer to the processes that call the scheduler's transactions as the "clients" of the scheduler. Here is the specification of the scheduler process:

```
                                       File: sim-sched.h
process spec sched() {
    trans long now();     /*return simulated time*/
    trans long reqDelay(long del);
                          /*request delay*/
    trans long wait(long x); /*wait for delay*/
    trans void addUser();   /*add client*/
    trans void dropUser();  /*drop client*/
    trans void passive();   /*client is passive*/
    trans void active();    /*client is active*/
};
```

A delay request requires calling the transactions `reqDelay` and `wait`. The client process first calls `reqDelay`, giving the number of time units to delay, and then calls `wait`, giving the value returned by `reqDelay`. The `wait` transaction returns the simulated time as of the end of the delay. Thus if `s` is the scheduler process, the following statement delays the calling process for 10 time units, and saves the time at the end of the delay in `ts`:

```
    ts = s.wait( s.reqDelay(10) );
```

The scheduler accepts `reqDelay` calls until it has received a request from every active client process. Then the scheduler accepts the `wait` call from the process with the smallest delay request.

For this to work, the scheduler must know the number of its client processes, and must know how many of them are in the passive state. Each client process calls transaction `addUser` when it starts, and calls transaction `dropUser` before it terminates, so that the scheduler can maintain a client count. Whenever an active client process becomes passive, the scheduler is informed by calling transaction `passive`. This call is made by the server process that forces a client to wait. Whenever a passive process becomes active, the process that makes it active calls the scheduler's `active` transaction. Thus the scheduler can determine the number of passive processes.

3.2 Source Process Interface

The source process has the following specification:

```
                                          File: sim-source.h
process spec source(
    process sched s,       /*scheduler*/
    process queue outQ,  /*output queue*/
    long meanIat,          /*mean inter-arrival time*/
    long meanServt,      /*mean service time*/
    long nGen,             /*number to generate*/
    name_t name );        /*symbolic name*/
```

Arrivals are Poisson, and service times are exponentially distributed. The process parameters define the output queue, the mean values for the distributions, etc.

The name parameter is a symbolic name, such as "source1", which the source process uses to identify itself when printing statistics (a simulation program could have several different source processes). The type name_t is a structure containing a character string:

```
typedef struct {char str[20];} name_t;
```

This structure is passed by-value to the source process. A simpler alternative would be to declare the parameter as a character pointer. However, if we did that, our simulation program will only work when run on an implementation that provides shared memory. Passing a structure by-value, on the other hand, will work on any Concurrent C implementation.

3.3 Server Process Interface

The server process has the following specification:

```
                                          File: sim-server.h
process spec server(
        process sched s,       /*scheduler*/
        process queue inQ,   /*input queue*/
        process queue outQ,/*output queue*/
        double speed,          /*speed of server*/
        name_t name );        /*symbolic name*/
```

If the output queue parameter outQ is c_nullpid, then the server discards each job after processing it. The speed parameter is the relative speed of this server; this server takes x/speed time units to process a job whose service time is x.

3.4 Queue Process Interface

Each job in a queue is represented by a structure of type `qItem`:

```
                                              File: sim-qItem.h
typedef struct {
        /*Public:*/
    long servt;       /*service time for job*/
    long arrive;      /*time job arrived*/

        /*Private to queue process:*/
    long qEnter;      /*time entered queue*/
    int  ticket;      /*ticket from takeReq*/
    int  gotItem;     /*!=0 iff item was taken*/
} qItem;
```

We save the job arrival time in this structure so that we can calculate statistics
for the time spent by jobs in the system.

The `queue` process simulates a FIFO queue:

```
                                              File: sim-queue.h
process spec queue(
        process sched s,        /*scheduler*/
        int maxSize,            /*max queue size*/
        name_t name)            /*symbolic name*/
{
    trans int  itemCnt();       /*return queue size*/
    trans void addProd();       /*add producer*/
    trans void dropProd();      /*drop producer*/
    trans void addCons();       /*add consumer*/
    trans void dropCons();      /*drop consumer*/

            /*start and finish put request:*/
    trans int  putReq(qItem);
    trans void putWait(int, qItem);

            /*start and finish take request:*/
    trans qItem takeReq();
    trans qItem takeWait(int);
};
```

A queue process can have several clients. Clients are either consumers
("takers") or else producers ("putters"). A `source` process is a producer; a
`server` process is a consumer for its input queue and a producer for its
output queue. Each producer process calls transaction `addProd` when it
starts, and calls transaction `dropProd` before it terminates. Similarly, each

consumer process calls transactions `addCons` and `dropCons`. This allows the queue process to keep track of the number of producer and consumer clients. When the queue is empty and the last producer has terminated, all subsequent "take" requests return an "end-of-file" indication. The `queue` process terminates when it has no more producers or consumers.

Transactions `putReq` and `putWait` put an item onto the queue, and transactions `takeReq` and `takeWait` take the next item from the queue. However, client processes do not call these transactions directly. Instead, these processes call functions `qPut` and `qTake`, which perform the "put" and "take" operations. Both functions wait until the operation can be performed. If an operation cannot be completed immediately, the `queue` process informs the scheduler process of the client's change of state (active to passive or passive to active). Function `qTake` returns 1 if it is able to take (get) an item, or 0 on "end-of-file". `qPut` and `qTake` are the interface functions for the `queue` process; they hide a complicated transaction interface.

As an example, the following code fragment takes jobs from the queue `qFrom` and places them on the queue `qTo`, and continues until `qFrom` is empty and all of its producers have terminated:

```
qItem item;
process queue qFrom, qTo;

while (qTake(qFrom, &item))
    qPut(qTo, item);
```

The implementations of the `qPut` and `qTake` functions, and the body of the `queue` process, will be described later.

3.5 Statistical Functions

We will use a simple statistical package that calculates the mean and standard deviation of a set of values:

```
                                              File: sim-stats.h
typedef struct {
    long    nv;        /*number of values*/
    long    maxv;      /*max value*/
    double  sumv;      /*sum of values*/
    double  sumsq;     /*sum of squares*/
} stats;

void    stInit();      /*initialize structure*/
void    stVal();       /*add new value*/
double  stMean();      /*return mean value*/
double  stSdev();      /*return standard deviation*/
long    erand();       /*exponential random number*/
```

The statistics are kept in a structure of type `stats`. Each of the functions declared above takes a pointer to such a structure as its first argument. Function `stInit` initializes the structure. Function `stVal` updates the statistics to reflect a new value. Functions `stMean` and `stDev` return the mean and standard deviation of these values. The random number generator `erand(m)` returns an exponentially distributed integer value whose mean is the integer value m.[2]

For example, the follow code fragment generates 1000 random numbers, and prints their average:

```
        stats mystats;
        int   i;

        stInit(&mystats);
        for (i = 1; i <= 10000; i++)
            stVal(&mystats, erand(100));
        printf("Mean is %lf\n", stMean(&mystats));
```

4. Process Implementations

4.1 Main Process

The `main` process creates the processes that simulate the entities and connects them together:

---

2. Strictly speaking, `erand` cannot be exponential because it returns integer values instead of floating point values. However, we will use large mean values so that the roundoff effect will be insignificant.

File: `sim-main.cc`

```
name_t makeName(name) char *name;
{  name_t ret;
   strcpy(ret.str, name);
   return ret;
}

main()
{   process sched s;
    process queue q1, q2;
    long nGen=100000;   /*number of jobs*/
    long servt=500;     /*mean service time*/
    long iat=1000;      /*mean inter-arrival*/
/*Create virtual time scheduler.*/
    s = create sched();   s.addUser();

/*Create queues and servers.*/
    q1 = create queue(s, 100, makeName("Q1"));
    q2 = create queue(s, 100, makeName("Q2"));
    create source(s, q1, iat, servt, nGen,
                        makeName("Src"));
    create server(s, q1, q2, 0.5,
                        makeName("Serv1.1"));
    create server(s, q1, q2, 0.5,
                        makeName("Serv1.2"));
    create server(s, q2, c_nullpid, 1.0,
                        makeName("Serv2"));

/*Wait for all processes to start.*/
    delay 2.0;   s.dropUser();
}
```

Function `makeName` creates and returns a structure of type `name_t` that contains the string passed as an argument.

The structure of the queueing network—the number of stages, the number of servers per stage, etc.—is determined by `main`, and can easily be changed. For example, we can add a third server to the first stage by just replicating the line that creates server 1.2, but with a different symbolic name.

Notice that `main` sleeps for a few seconds before terminating. This delay allows other processes to call the transaction `addUser` of the scheduler and to make their initial delay request (if any). The scheduler will not allow any other process to proceed until `main` calls transaction `dropUser`. Delaying `main` is necessary to allow other processes enough time to register with the scheduler. Otherwise, the scheduler will terminate immediately after `main` calls transaction `dropUser`.

We have assumed that all processes will be dispatched and will perform their initialization within two seconds. To avoid this assumption, we could modify `main` to call an initialization transaction belonging to each of the processes that it creates; this initialization transaction would call transaction `addUser` of the scheduler.

4.2 Source and Server Processes

Here is the body of the source process:

File: `sim-source.cc`

```
process body source(s, outQ, meanIat,
                        meanServt, nGen, name)
{   stats iat, servt;
    qItem item;
    long  i, t;
/*Initialization phase.*/
    s.addUser();
    outQ.addProd();
    stInit(&iat);   stInit(&servt);

/*Main processing phase: generate jobs.*/
    for (i = 1; i <= nGen; i++) {
        t = erand(meanIat);
        stVal(&iat, t);
        item.arrive = s.wait(s.reqDelay(t));
        item.servt = erand(meanServt);
        stVal(&servt, item.servt);
        qPut(outQ, item);
    }
/*Termination phase: print stats, etc.*/
    print statistics;
    outQ.dropProd();   s.dropUser();
}
```

First, the source process initializes the statistics counters, and tells the scheduler and queue processes that they have one more client. Then the source process repeatedly calculates an inter-arrival time, delays for this amount, generates a service time, and places a job in the output queue. Finally the source process prints its statistics, and then tells the scheduler and the output queue that they have one less client. This pattern—initialization, main processing, and termination—is common in our processes.

Here is the body of the server process:

File: `sim-server.cc`

```
process body server(s, inQ, outQ, speed, name)
{   stats sysTime;   /*time-in-system*/
    qItem item;
    long  ts;

    s.addUser();   stInit(&sysTime);
    inQ.addCons();
    if (outQ != c_nullpid)
       outQ.addProd();

    while (qTake(inQ, &item)) {
       ts = s.wait(s.reqDelay(item.servt/speed));
       stVal(&sysTime, ts - item.arrive);
       if (outQ != c_nullpid)
          qPut(outQ, item);
    }
    print statistics;
    if (outQ != c_nullpid)
       outQ.dropProd();
    inQ.addCons();   s.dropUser();
}
```

It starts by telling the scheduler, the input queue, and the output queue to increment their client, consumer, and producer counts, respectively. The server process then repeatedly takes a job from its input queue, delays for the job's service time, and places the job on its output queue. Finally the server process prints statistics on the time that jobs spent in the system. The server process also tells its input and output queues, and the scheduler, to decrement their client counts.

4.3 Queue Process

We will first present the source for the interface functions for the `queue` process:

File: `sim-qPut.cc`

```
/*Put item onto queue; wait if full.*/
void qPut(q, item)
    process queue q;   qItem item;
{   int ticket = q.putReq(item);
    if (ticket >= 0)
        q.putWait(ticket, item);
}

/*Set *itemp to next item; wait if empty.*/
/*Return 1 if item was taken, 0 on EOF.*/
int qTake(q, itemp)
    process queue q;   qItem *itemp;
{
    *itemp = q.takeReq();
    if (itemp->ticket >= 0)
        *itemp = q.takeWait(itemp->ticket);
    return itemp->gotItem;
}
```

A put or take request that can be done immediately requires one transaction call; otherwise two calls are required. As mentioned earlier, functions qPut and qTake, which are called by the clients of a queue process, implement the necessary protocol for interacting with the queue process. To put an item, qPut first calls putReq. If the queue is not full, putReq puts the item and returns −1. If the queue is full, putReq returns a non-negative "ticket" value. In this case, qPut calls the queue's putWait transaction, giving the ticket returned by putReq. When space becomes available in the queue, the queue process accepts transaction putWait and puts the item on the queue.

Function qTake is similar; the only difference is that the takeReq transaction returns a structure which contains either the item taken or else the ticket value.

The body of the queue process uses several auxiliary functions to manipulate the data structures that maintain the queue's state. All the information necessary to define a queue is collected in a structure of type qInfo. The queue process passes a pointer to this structure to the auxiliary functions:

```
                                        ┌─────────────────────────┐
                                        │ File: sim-qInfo.h       │
┌───────────────────────────────────────┴─────────────────────────┴─┐
│ /*tInfo: Describe outstanding tickets.*/                           │
│ typedef struct {                                                   │
│     int acc;    /*next ticket to accept*/                          │
│     int give;   /*next ticket to give out*/                        │
│     int nPass;  /*pending passive clients*/                        │
│ } tInfo;                                                           │
│                                                                    │
│ /*qInfo: Describe one queue.*/                                     │
│ typedef struct {                                                   │
│     process sched s;   /*scheduler process*/                       │
│     int     max;       /*max queue size*/                          │
│     int     nProd;     /*number of producers*/                     │
│     int     nCons;     /*number of consumers*/                     │
│     name_t name;       /*name of queue*/                           │
│     stats   qTime;     /*time-in-queue stats*/                     │
│     stats   qSize;     /*for queue size stats*/                    │
│     int     nElem;     /*items in queue*/                          │
│     int     head;      /*index of head of queue*/                  │
│     int     tail;      /*index of tail of queue*/                  │
│     qItem   *items;    /*alloc'd array of items*/                  │
│                                                                    │
│   /*Describe pending put, take requests:*/                         │
│     tInfo   pPut, pTake;                                           │
│ } qInfo;                                                           │
└────────────────────────────────────────────────────────────────────┘
```

Member `items` of the structure type `qInfo` points to a circular buffer of `qItem` structures. The integer `head` is the index of the next item which can be taken from the queue, and `tail` is the index of the next slot into which an item can be put. We keep statistics on "time in queue" and "number-in-queue." The latter is sampled when a job is placed in a queue.

Ticket numbers returned by `putReq` and `takeReq` are assigned circularly from 0 and 9999. Put and take tickets are assigned independently. Structure `tInfo` contains information about pending tickets. We need one instance of this structure for pending puts, and another for pending takes.

Here is the body of the `queue` process:

File: `sim-queue.cc`

```
process body queue(s, maxSize, name)
{ qInfo q;  qItem x;
  initialize qInfo structure;
  accept addProd() { q.nProd++; }

  while (q.nProd+q.nCons > 0) {
    select {
    (q.nElem<q.max && q.pPut.acc==q.pPut.give):
      accept putReq(item)
        { putItem(&q, &item);  treturn -1; }
    or (q.nElem==q.max):
      accept putReq(item)
        { s.passive();  q.pPut.nPass++;
          treturn incTick(&q.pPut.give); }
    or (q.nElem<q.max):
      accept putWait(qt, item)
          suchthat (qt == q.pPut.acc)
        { putItem(&q, &item);
          incTick(&q.pPut.acc); }

    or (q.nElem>0 && q.pTake.acc==q.pTake.give):
      accept takeReq()
        { treturn takeItem(&q); }
    or (q.nElem==0):
      accept takeReq()
        { x.ticket = incTick(&q.pTake.give);
          s.passive();  q.pTake.nPass++;
          treturn x; }
    or (q.nElem>0):
      accept takeWait(qt)
          suchthat (qt == q.pTake.acc)
        { incTick(&q.pTake.acc);
          treturn takeItem(&q); }
    or (q.nProd==0 && q.nElem==0):
      accept takeWait(qt)
        { x.gotItem = 0;  treturn x; }
    or accept itemCnt()  { treturn q.nElem; }
    or accept addCons() { q.nCons++; }
    or accept addProd() { q.nProd++; }
    or accept dropCons() { q.nCons--; }
    or accept dropProd() { q.nProd--; }
    }
  /*On EOF, make pending takers active.*/
    if (q.nProd==0 && q.nElem==0)
      for (; q.pTake.nPass > 0; q.pTake.nPass--)
        s.active();
  }
  print statistics;
}
```

The `queue` process starts by initializing the `qInfo` structure, and then waits for the first producer's `addProd` request. The queue process then accepts requests as long as it has any clients. Before terminating, the `queue` process prints the statistics that it has recorded.

We will now analyze handling of the "take" requests by the `queue` process in detail. There are two alternatives for `takeReq`, with mutually exclusive guards. The first of these alternatives accepts requests whenever there are items in the queue *and* when there are no pending `takeWait` requests (i.e., no pending take tickets). This alternative calls `takeItem`, which removes an item from the buffer, updates the statistics, and sets the `ticket` and `gotItem` fields to indicate that an item was taken immediately. Also, if another client is blocked on a put request, `takeItem` tells the scheduler that the process is now active. This ensures that the scheduler will not honor another delay request until the process that is blocked on the put request is able to execute its pending `putWait` transaction. This `takeReq` alternative returns the item selected by `takeItem` to the client process.

The second `takeReq` alternative accepts requests whenever the queue is empty. It assigns a ticket, updates the ticket data, tells the scheduler that an active client has just become passive, and returns the ticket to the client.

There are two alternatives for `takeWait`. When there are items in the queue, the first alternative accepts the request with the oldest pending ticket. This alternative takes an item from the buffer and returns it to the client. When end-of-file has occurred (when there are no producers and the queue is empty), the second `takeWait` alternative accepts any remaining `takeWait` calls. This alternative returns an end-of-file indicator to the client.

The put requests are handled similarly. Transactions `addCons`, `dropCons`, `addProd`, and `dropProd` just update the consumer and producer counts.

Here are the auxiliary functions called from the body of the `queue` process:

File: `sim-qAux.cc`

```
/*Increment ticket, return prev value.*/
int incTick(tp)
    int *tp;
{   int t = *tp;
    *tp = (t+1)%10000;
    return t;
}

/*Remove and return the next item in queue.*/
qItem takeItem(qp)
    qInfo *qp;
{

    qItem item;
    item = qp->items[qp->head];
    item.ticket = -1;
    item.gotItem = 1;
    stVal(&qp->qTime, qp->s.now() - item.qEnter);
    qp->nElem--;
    qp->head = (qp->head+1) % qp->max;
    if (qp->pPut.nPass > 0)
        { qp->s.active(); qp->pPut.nPass--; }
    return item;
}

/*Add item *itemp to queue.*/
void putItem(qp, itemp)
    qInfo *qp; qItem *itemp;
{

    qp->items[qp->tail] = *itemp;
    qp->items[qp->tail].qEnter = qp->s.now();
    stVal(&qp->qSize, qp->nElem);
    qp->nElem++;
    qp->tail = (qp->tail+1) % qp->max;
    if (qp->pTake.nPass > 0)
        { qp->s.active(); qp->pTake.nPass--; }
}
```

4.4 Scheduler Process

The scheduler keeps a list of pending delay requests, ordered by the time at which the client is to be reactivated. List entries are pairs (t, n) where t is the simulated time and n is the number of processes to be awakened at that time. Here is an outline of the body of the scheduler process `sched`:

File: `sim-sched.cc`

```
process body sched()
{   int    nUser, nAct, i;
    long curTime= 0;      /*current simulated time*/
    ordered list of pending delay requests;

    initialize pending delay list data structures;
    accept addUser() { nUser = nAct = 1; }
    while (nUser > 0) {
        select {
            accept addUser() { ++nUser; ++nAct; }
        or accept dropUser(){ --nUser; --nAct; }
        or accept active()  { ++nAct; }
        or accept passive() { --nAct; }
        or accept now()  { treturn curTime; }
        or accept reqDelay(x)
            { add request for curTime+x to pending delay list;
              nAct--;   treturn request-index; }
        }
        if (nAct == 0 && pending delay list is not empty) {
            curTime = time of request at head of list;
            nAct = number of processes waiting for that time;
            for (i = 1; i <= nAct; i++)
                accept wait(x)
                    suchthat (x == index-of-head-request)
                        { treturn curTime; }
            discard request at head of pending delay list;
        }
    }
}
```

After initialization, the scheduler process repeatedly accepts requests until all clients become passive. For each delay request, the scheduler calculates the absolute time at which the requesting process should be re-activated, and adds an appropriate entry to the list of pending delay requests. The list is ordered by increasing re-activation times. List entries are allocated from an array; the reqDelay transaction uses the array index as a "ticket" value. When all client processes are passive, the scheduler takes the next request from the list, advances the simulated time, and accepts wait requests from all the clients waiting for the new simulated time.

The suchthat clause performs a linear search through the pending requests; this will be inefficient if there are hundreds or thousands of pending delay requests. However, for small simulations the simplicity of the scheduler makes up for the inefficiency that may result from this linear search. If this search proves to be expensive in large simulations, we can eliminate the `suchthat` clause by making the client process supply a transaction pointer with which the scheduler will call the client when it is ready to accept the client's delay request.

5. A Feedback Queueing Network

Consider the following feedback queueing network:

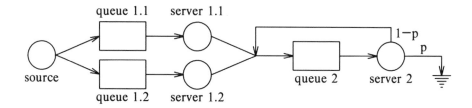

Figure 8.1: A Feedback Queueing Network.

This network differs from the previous network in two ways:

- Each server in the first stage has its own queue. When a job arrives, the source places the job in the *shorter* of the two queues.

- With probability *p,* the second stage server discards a completed job; with probability 1−*p,* it returns the job to queue 2 for further processing.

To simulate this network, we can reuse the server, queue and scheduler processes. We will need two new process types: a source process that puts the job in the smaller of two queues, and another server process that discards a job with some probability.

The new source process will be similar to the original source process, except that it has two output-queue parameters, `outQ1` and `outQ2`. After generating a job, the new source process puts the job on the smaller of the two output queues, which it can do with the following code fragment:

```
if (outQ1.itemCnt() < outQ2.itemCnt())
    qPut(outQ1, item);
else
    qPut(outQ2, item);
```

The new server process is similar to the original server process, except that it has a new parameter `probDone`, which is the probability of discarding a job after processing it. Because this new server is a feedback server, it does *not* tell the output queue that it is a consumer process.[3]

6. Extensions and Modifications

We will now discuss some ways of extending our simulation program to model other queueing problems.

6.1 Other Queue Disciplines

Our `queue` process can be easily modified to use a last-in-first-out (LIFO) discipline, or a more complicated queue discipline, such as shortest-service-time-first. This would require simple changes to the `putItem` and `takeItem` functions, but the basic structure of the queue process would remain unchanged.

6.2 Servers With Multiple Output Queues

Modeling a more general queueing network in which servers output to multiple queues is straightforward. For example, the server could be given an array of output queue process identifiers, and the server could randomly select the output queue for each job. Alternatively, the server could send each job to *all* of its output queues.

6.3 More General Networks

The structure of the queueing network is determined by how the `main` process creates the source, server, and queue processes, and how it connects them together. This is easy to extend; we could even write a `main` process that reads a network description at run time.

6.4 Statistics

In general, we want to measure the steady-state performance of a queueing system. Our processes do not; instead, they measure the entire simulation run, including the initialization phase (starting with an empty queue) and the termination phase (draining the queues after the source stops). We compensate for this by simulating many jobs, so that the initialization and termination phases are small compared to the steady state period.

A better technique is to monitor the statistics during the simulation, and terminate the simulation when the statistics have been stable for a long time.

---

3. If it does this, the simulation would never terminate. That is, the server will not terminate until its input queue indicates end-of-file. This will not happen until all of the input queue's producers have terminated. If the server process were one of these producers, it would never terminate.

We can accomplish this by adding a `giveStats` transaction to each entity process. This transaction will return the current statistics of the process to which it belongs. After starting all the processes, `main` would repeatedly delay for an interval and then call all the `giveStats` transactions. `main` would repeat this cycle until it decided that the simulation had a reached steady state. Thus `main` would look something like:

```
main( )
{
    create all processes
    while ( 1 ) {
        s.wait( s.reqDelay( 10000 ) );
        for each entity process  p
            entity-stats = p.giveStats( );
        if ( statistics have been stable for long enough )
            break;
    }
    print final statistics
    for all processes  p
        c_abort( p );
}
```

Transaction `giveStats` is easy to add to the queue process; it is just another alternative in the central `select` statement. For the source and server processes, the central loop would be modified to conditionally accept a `giveStats` transaction (i.e., accept a call if one is available, but continue if no call is pending).

Appendix A
Concurrent C Reference Manual

We will describe only the concurrent programming facilities that Concurrent C adds to the C programming language. We assume that the reader is familiar with C. Appendix D gives a brief, informal review of the C programming language; for a more complete description of C, please refer to Kernighan and Ritchie [1978], Ritchie [1980], and Harbison & Steele [1984].

Concurrent C++ adds the same concurrent programming facilities to the C++ programming language, so this appendix also serves as a reference manual for Concurrent C++. Users interested in a description of C++ should refer to Stroustrup [1986]. The concurrent programming extensions of Concurrent C also apply to ANSI C, the ANSI standard version of the C programming language [ANSI 1988a; Gehani 1988c].

The Concurrent C grammar given here uses and adds to the C grammar given in *The C Programming Language—Reference Manual* [Ritchie 1980].

1. Keywords

Concurrent C adds the following keywords to the list of C keywords:

accept	delay	select	treturn
async	or	spec	within
body	priority	suchthat	
by	process	terminate	
create	processor	trans	

2. Processes and Process Interaction

First, some terminology. A *process definition* consists of two parts: a *type* (or *specification*) and a *body* (or *implementation*). A *process* is an instantiation of a process definition. Each process is a sequential program and has its own flow-of-control; it executes in parallel with other processes. The existence of a process definition does not automatically create a process. Instead, the programmer must explicitly create each process (except the `main` process) at run time.

One can think of each process as having its own stack, machine registers, program counter, etc. Most implementations will have some underlying scheduler that runs these processes on the available processors. Concurrent C does not define the scheduling policy, except to say that the scheduling policy should be fair; scheduling is regarded as an implementation detail.

Concurrent C processes interact with each other by means of *transactions* which are associated with processes. Transactions can be thought of as the mechanisms for getting (accessing) services. Processes requesting services may be thought of as "client" processes and processes offering (and accepting requests for) services may be thought of as "server" processes.

There are two kinds of transactions: synchronous (blocking) and asynchronous (non-blocking). A process calling a synchronous transaction is blocked until the called process accepts the transaction, executes the code associated with the transaction, and returns the transaction result, if any. Synchronous transactions allow bidirectional communication between the interacting processes. They can also be used for process synchronization. The calling and receiving processes synchronize at the transaction call; they are free to resume independent execution after the transaction call has been accepted.

A process calling an asynchronous transaction is allowed to continue immediately after making the call. The transaction is accepted by the called process whenever it is ready to do so. An asynchronous transaction can be used only for unidirectional information transfer: from the calling process to the sender; no result can be returned.

2.1 Shared Memory

If shared memory is available (e.g., if processes occupy the same address space or the processors access common memory) then processes can also communicate by updating shared objects, i.e., objects pointed to by common pointers or global objects. It is the programmer's responsibility to synchronize access to the shared data, e.g., to ensure that the shared data is updated in mutual exclusion. Concurrent C does not have explicit facilities for synchronizing access to shared data; this must be done by using synchronous transactions.

3. Process Types and Transaction Declarations

The process type (specification) is the public part of a process definition; only information specified in the process type is visible to other processes. The process type contains declarations of the transactions associated with processes of this type. Each transaction declaration consists of the name of the transaction, the parameter declarations (or just the parameter types), and the result type, if any.

A process type[1] can be used wherever a C type specifier is allowed, and has the general form[2]

> *type-specifier:*
>> process spec *identifier*(*parameter-decl-list$_{opt}$*) *transaction-part$_{opt}$*

where *parameter-decl-list* is a comma-separated list of parameter declarations or types, as in

> process spec generator(int count, int size);

The parameter names serve as comments to indicate the purpose of the parameter. The names can be omitted, as in

> process spec generator(int, int);

The transaction declaration part of a process type has the following syntax:

> *transaction-part:*
>> { *trans-decl-list* }
>
> *trans-decl-list:*
>> *trans-decl*
>> *trans-decl trans-decl-list*
>
> *trans-decl:*
>> trans *trans-type-specifier trans-declarator-list*;
>
> *trans-type-specifier:*
>> async
>> *type-specifier*
>
> *trans-declarator-list:*
>> *trans-declarator*
>> *trans-declarator, trans-declarator-list*
>
> *trans-declarator:*
>> *declarator*(*parameter-decl-list$_{opt}$*)
>> *declarator*

Here are some examples of transaction declarations:

---

1. The keyword spec (short for specification) in a process type declaration represents the fact that a process type can also be viewed as the syntactic specification of a process.

2. Subscript *opt* associated with an item indicates that the item is optional.

```
process spec sample()
{
    trans void init(int x, double y);
    trans int up(), down();
    trans char *alloc(int len);
    trans async sendInt(int c),
                sendFloat(float c);
};
```

The same transaction name can be used in several process types, and these transactions can have different parameters and return value types.

4. Process Bodies

A process body contains the code (and the associated declarations and definitions) that is executed by a process; it is analogous to a function body, which it resembles. A process body is an external definition (just like a function definition), and has the form

> *external-definition:*
>> process body *identifier* (*param-list$_{opt}$*) *process-body*
>
> *process-body:*
>> *function-statement*

The *param-list* is a comma-separated list of names of the process process parameters. The types of the process parameters are given only in the process type (specification); to avoid unnecessary verbosity, they are not repeated in the process body. The number of names in the *param-list* must match the number of parameters declared in the process specification. These parameters are local variables within the process body, and their initial values are those given when the process was created.

Process bodies can contain any legal C statement, plus the Concurrent C extensions. Executing a *return* statement in a process body completes the process. This is equivalent to running off the end of the process body. Note that a process, unlike a function, cannot return a value.

5. Process Creation

When a Concurrent C program starts executing, there is only one process running: the main process, which calls the main function; this process must then create all other processes.[3] Processes (process instances to be precise) are created with the create operator; they become eligible for execution immediately. The created process is called a *child* process of the creating, or *parent*, process. Processes that have the same parent process are called *sibling* processes.

The create operator is an expression, and has the general form

expression:
    create *identifier* (*expression-list*$_{opt}$)
                     processor-clause$_{opt}$ *priority-clause*$_{opt}$

processor-clause:
    processor (*expression*)

priority-clause:
    priority (*expression*)

The processor and priority expressions must be integer or integer coercible.

The *identifier* must be the name of a process type. The *expression-list* is a comma-separated list of expressions. The number of expressions, and their types, must match the process parameter types declared in the process specification. The values of these expressions will become the initial values of the parameters of the new process.

The create operator returns the process id of the newly created process. The expression has the type process *identifier*.

A process can be in one of two states: active and completed. A process becomes *active* upon creation and remains in this state while executing the statements specified in the corresponding process body. A process becomes *completed* when it executes a *return* statement in its process body, or when it reaches the end of its body.

5.1 Priority Specification

By default, each process is assigned priority zero. An alternative priority can be specified explicitly with the priority clause when creating a process. The integer expression in the priority clause specifies the new priority relative to the standard priority. Positive values specify higher priority; negative values specify lower priority.

---

3. Thus every C program (modulo those that have conflicts with Concurrent C reserved keywords) is a trivial (from a concurrent programming viewpoint) Concurrent C program which consists of just the main process.

Process scheduling is done on a per processor basis subject to the following rules:

1. When selecting a process for execution, from the set of processes ready for execution, a higher priority process is always given preference over a lower priority process.

2. No process is indefinitely denied execution because of processes with the same or lower priority.

Priorities should be used to give more execution time to some processes at the expense of others but *not* for synchronizing processes. For example, programmers should *not* assume that a higher priority process will immediately preempt all lower priority processes. Note that transactions calls made by higher priority processes are not given preference over calls made by lower priority processes.

5.2 Processor Specification

In a multiprocessor implementation, if the processor clause is omitted, the implementation can place a newly created process on any processor. Typically this will be a processor that maximizes concurrency or minimizes the communication cost, e.g., a new process may be placed on a processor with the lightest load. If it is important for a process to reside on a specific processor, then this information can be explicitly specified by using the processor clause. Processors are identified by small non-negative integers, whose values are implementation-dependent.

The value −1 means "pick any processor," and is equivalent to omitting the processor clause. Uniprocessor implementations of Concurrent C accept but ignore the processor clause.

6. Process Types And Ids

Process types can be used like other C types to declare and define identifiers, e.g.,

```
process consumer c;
process buffer b, bufarr[ 10 ], *pb;
process relation rel_id( );
```

A process value (identifier, or just id) identifies a specific process instance. Legal process ids are the ones returned by the create operator. The special null process value 0 can be assigned to any process variable. Dereferencing (i.e., referencing a process with) an illegal process value or 0 will result in an error.

Process ids can be stored in process variables provided their types match, e.g.,

```
process buffer b;
b = create buffer(128);
```

If the same process id is stored in several process variables, then these variables will all refer to the same process. As with pointer values, care must be taken to avoid dangling references. Process ids can be compared for equality or inequality.

6.1 Process Anytype

The predefined type `process anytype` is a "wild card" process type. It is used to declare or define objects that may be associated with different processes types during program execution. For example, it is used to specify the return type of function `c_mypid`.

In general, an expression of any process type can be given wherever a `process anytype` value is expected. Going the other way, a `process anytype` value can be used wherever a specific process type is expected; Concurrent C generates an implicit cast to the target type. However, a `process anytype` value cannot be used directly as the process id in a transaction call, because this can be ambiguous if several process types have a transaction with the same name.

7. Transaction Pointers

A transaction pointer refers to a specific transaction of a specific process instance. Transaction pointer declarations and definitions have the same syntax as the transaction declarations in a process specification, except that the type must be "pointer to function."

As an example, consider the following transaction pointer declarations:

```
trans void (*tp)();
trans int (**ptp)();
trans async (*atp)(int);
```

`tp` is declared as a pointer to a `void` transaction, `ptp` as a pointer to an `int` transaction pointer, and `atp` as a pointer to an asynchronous transaction with one `int` parameter.

---

3. Thus 0 is to process values as the null pointer constant 0 is to pointers.

A transaction pointer is an ordinary variable, and is very much like a function pointer. Transaction pointers can be declared wherever a variable declaration is allowed: as a local variable for a function, as a global variable, as a member of a structure, etc.

Provided the parameter and return value types match, an expression of the form *p . t* or *pp->t*, where *p* is a process-valued expression, *pp* is an expression of type pointer to process, and *t* is the name of a transaction associated with the process in question, can be used wherever a transaction pointer value is expected and vice versa. For example, the following assignment sets `tp` to point to the `put` transaction of process `b`:

```
tp = b.put;
```

The null pointer constant 0 is guaranteed to be an invalid transaction pointer value. 0 can be assigned to or compared against a transaction pointer.

The transaction pointer syntax does not allow the direct declaration of a pointer to a transaction that returns a transaction pointer. However, this can be done in two steps by using an intermediate *typedef* statement to define the return-value type:

```
typedef trans int (*tp_type)(int, int);
trans tp_type (*xtp)(int);
```

8. Transaction Calls

A transaction call is the caller's side of a transaction. Transaction calls are expressions, and have the following forms:

primary:
    tc-primary (*expression-list*$_{opt}$)
tc-primary:
    primary . name
    primary-> name
    (*expression*)

When used with the dot (.) operator, *primary* must be a process-valued expression for a process whose specification has a transaction named *name*. When used with the right arrow (->) operator, *primary* must be a pointer to such a process value. In the last form, *expression* must be a transaction pointer value.

The *expression-list* is a comma-separated list of expressions. The number of expressions, and their types, must match the parameter types declared for transaction *name* in the process specification.

The type of a transaction call expression is the return-value type declared for the transaction specified in *tc-primary*.

Here are some examples of transaction calls:

```
b.new_move(rn, x, y);
pos = dbase.next_position(rn);
(*tp)('a');
```

Note that `tp` is a transaction pointer. The syntax of a transaction call using a transaction pointer is identical to that of a function call using a function pointer.

8.1 Timed Transaction Calls

A timed transaction call allows the calling process to withdraw a synchronous transaction call provided the call has not been accepted within a specified period. A timed transaction call is an expression, and has the syntax

expression:
    `within` *duration* ? *tc-primary* (*expression-list*$_{opt}$) : *expression*

where *duration* is an integer or floating-point expression. The type of *expression* must match the return type of the transaction specified by *tc-primary*. If the process specified by *tc-primary* accepts this transaction call within *duration* seconds, then the value returned by this process becomes the value of the timed transaction call. In this case, *expression* is not evaluated. Otherwise, the transaction call is withdrawn, *expression* is evaluated, and its value becomes the value of the timed transaction call.

The timeout period *duration* refers to the waiting time until the called process *accepts* the call, and not to the time until the called process returns the result. Once accepted, a transaction call cannot be withdrawn.

9. Accept Statements

The *accept* statement is the called process' side of a transaction. It contains code to process the transaction call and return the result. An *accept* statement has the form

statement:
    `accept` *identifier* (*param-list*$_{opt}$) *by-clause*$_{opt}$ *suchthat-clause*$_{opt}$
        statement

by-clause:
    `by` (*expression*)

suchthat-clause:
    `suchthat` (*expression*)

An *accept* statement can only appear in the body of a process whose specification has a transaction named *identifier*. The *param-list* is a comma-separated list of names of parameters for that transaction. The number of names in the *param-list* must match the number of parameters given in the declaration for the transaction *identifier*. Note that only parameter names, and not parameter declarations, are given in the *accept* statement.[4]

The by expression must be an arithmetic expression and the suchthat expression must be an integral or integral coercible expression. These expressions should involve the parameters of the *accept* statement (they may also use variables in the process body, function calls, etc.).

The *statement* is the body of the *accept* statement. Execution of an *accept* statement completes after its body has been executed or by executing a *treturn* statement.

If the suchthat and by clauses are not present, then transaction calls are accepted in FIFO order. If a process has one or more transaction calls pending for a specific transaction, then an *accept* statement for this transaction accepts one of them immediately. If there are no pending transaction calls for this transaction, then the process blocks until such a call arrives.

Once a transaction call has been accepted, the body of the *accept* statement is executed. Within the *accept* statement body, the parameter names represent local variables that are initialized to the values of the corresponding transaction call arguments. The scope of the *accept* parameters is limited to the body of the *accept* statement. To retain parameter values beyond the scope of the *accept* statement body, these values must be stored in variables global to the *accept* statement.

Here are some examples of *accept* statements:

```
accept pick_up();
accept init(rn, x, y) {
    rs[rn].r_curx = x;
    rs[rn].r_cury = y;
}
accept move_done(rn)
    rs[rn].r_moving = 0;
```

---

4. We recommend, but do not require, that the parameter names in an *accept* statement match the names given in the transaction declaration.

9.1 The Suchthat and By Clauses

If a `suchthat` clause is present, then the *accept* statement accepts the first transaction call for which the `suchthat` expression is true (non-zero). If this expression is false (zero) for all the pending transaction calls, then execution of the *accept* statement is delayed until an appropriate transaction call arrives. Pending transaction calls for which the `suchthat` expression is false are not discarded; they are held, and may be accepted at some later time. As an example, the following *accept* statement accepts the first `lock` call for which the expression `isfree(id)` is true:

```
accept lock(id) suchthat(isfree(id))
    { ... }
```

Note that the argument `id` given in the call to function `isfree` is the parameter `id` of the `lock` transaction call.

If there is a `by` clause, then the `by` expression is evaluated for each pending transaction call, and the call with the minimum value for the `by` expression is accepted. As an example, in a disk driver process, the following statement accepts the `diskop` transaction for the cylinder (`cyl`) that is closest to the current disk arm position (`curpos`):

```
accept diskop(cyl, ...) by(abs(cyl-curpos))
    { ... }
```

The `suchthat` and `by` clauses can be given together. There are no guarantees as to how often these expressions will be evaluated, so side effects should be avoided. Transaction calls and process creations are not allowed within the `suchthat` and `by` expressions.

9.2 Treturn Statements

The *treturn* statement is used to complete execution of a *accept* statement and, if appropriate, to return a value to the calling process. This statement has the form

   `treturn` *expression*$_{opt}$;

The type of *expression* must match or be coercible to the corresponding transaction's return value type.

10. Delay Statements

A process can delay itself by executing a statement of the form

   `delay` *expression*;

where *expression* is a floating-point expression specifying the amount of the delay in seconds. (Negative delay values are treated as zero delays). The actual delay may be more, but not less, than the requested delay.

11. Select Statements

The *select* statement allows a process to wait for the first of several events. It has the following syntax:

statement:
      select { *guard-alternative-list* } ;

guard-alternative-list:
      guard$_{opt}$ alternative
      guard$_{opt}$ alternative or *guard-alternative-list*

guard:
      (*expression*) :

alternative:
      statement-list
      terminate;

A *guard* is an integral or integral coercible expression. The order in which guards are evaluated is unspecified, and there is no guarantee that all the guards will be evaluated. Consequently, side effects should be avoided in guards. As in the case of suchthat and by expressions, transaction calls and process creation are not allowed within guards.

A *select* statement can appear only in a process body.

The first statement of a *select* alternative determines its type:

1. an *accept* statement, optionally followed by other statements (an *accept* alternative),

2. a *delay* statement, optionally followed by other statements (a *delay* alternative),

3. the keyword terminate followed by a semicolon (a *terminate* alternative), or

4. a list of statements, not beginning with any of the above (an *immediate* alternative).

The *select* statement executes one and only one of the alternatives. Once chosen, all statements in the selected alternative are executed, and flow resumes after the *select* statement. The following rules determine which alternative is taken; alternatives with false guards are not considered in the execution of the *select* statement.

1. . If there is an *accept* alternative, and if there is a pending call for this transaction, accept the call and take the corresponding alternative. If the

accept statement has a suchthat clause, take the alternative only if there is a call that satisfies the suchthat clause.

2. Otherwise, if there is an *immediate* alternative, take it.

3. Otherwise, if there is a *terminate* alternative and if there are no *delay* alternatives, then wait until

    i. a transaction arrives that can be accepted, or

    ii. all other processes have completed or are waiting at a *terminate* alternative, in which case the entire Concurrent C program terminates normally.

4. Otherwise, if there are *delay* alternatives but no *terminate* alternatives, let x be the lowest delay specified by a *delay* alternative. Then if a transaction call that can be accepted by an *accept* alternative arrives within x seconds, take this *accept* alternative. If not, take the *delay* alternative with the lowest delay.

5. Otherwise, if there are *delay* alternatives and *terminate* alternatives, the implementation has a choice:[5]

    i. If a transaction call arrives that can be accepted by an *accept* alternative, take this *accept* alternative. If all active processes are waiting at a *terminate* alternative, terminate the entire Concurrent C program. Let x be the lowest delay specified by a *delay* alternative. If neither of the above two events occurs within x seconds, take the *delay* alternative with the lowest delay.

    ii. Alternatively, the implementation may choose to ignore the *terminate* alternative (i.e., treat the *select* statement as if the *terminate* alternative had a false guard).

An error condition occurs if all the guards are false.

12. Preprocessor

The Concurrent C compiler defines the preprocessor symbol c_CONCURRENT. For example, you can use this in a header file that is included from both C and Concurrent C programs to prevent the C compiler from seeing (and complaining about) Concurrent C definitions, as in

---

5. The first option is the preferred one. We allow the implementers a choice because (a) it is rare for a process to have *delay* alternatives and *terminate* alternatives in the same *select* statement, and (b) in some implementations, it can be very expensive to implement the first option correctly (this can slow down *all* processes, not just those with *delay* and *terminate* alternatives).

```
typedef struct {...} JobData;

#ifdef c_CONCURRENT
process spec JobManager(JobData job);
#endif
```

13. Library Functions

The library functions discussed here are part of Concurrent C's standard environment. A few of these functions are implementation dependent, and they will be identified as such.

We will use C++ (ANSI C) syntax to describe the parameter types and return value types of a function. For example, the declaration

```
int c_active(process anytype pid);
```

declares `c_active` to be a function with one parameter of `process anytype` that returns an `int` value.

External names that start with "c_" are reserved for the Concurrent C implementation. Users should avoid such names.

13.1 Include Files

The standard header file `concurrentc.h` contains the declarations of the Concurrent C library functions. It also contains the definition of the null process id `c_nullpid`.

13.2 Process Abortion

Processes can be aborted by calling function `c_abort`. This function is declared as

```
void c_abort(process anytype pid);
```

and it aborts process `pid`. Aborting an active or completed process terminates a process. That is, `c_abort` terminates all children (and grandchildren, etc.) of the indicated process. If the process being aborted has made a transaction call that has not been accepted, then the call is withdrawn. If the processes being aborted are engaged in transaction calls among themselves, all such calls will be terminated. However, the caller must ensure that none of these processes are in the middle of a transaction call (either as client or server) with a process that is *not* being aborted. Otherwise, the result will be undefined.

13.3 Self Identity

A process can determine its process id by calling function `c_mypid` which is declared as

```
process anytype c_mypid();
```

c_mypid returns the id of the process calling it.

13.4 Process States

The following functions check the state of a process or test the validity of a process id:

```
int c_active(process anytype pid);
int c_completed(process anytype pid);
int c_valid(process anytype pid);
```

c_active returns 1 if process pid is active; otherwise it returns 0. c_completed returns 1 if process pid has completed; otherwise it returns 0. c_valid returns 1 if pid is a valid process id (i.e., the process is active or has completed); otherwise it returns 0.

13.5 Process Priorities

The following functions manipulate and query process priorities:

```
int c_changepriority(process anytype pid, int p);
int c_setpriority(process anytype pid, int p);
int c_getpriority(process anytype pid);
```

c_changepriority changes the priority of process pid by the signed integer value p and returns its old priority. c_setpriority sets the absolute priority of process pid to value p and returns its old priority. c_getpriority returns the priority of process pid.

13.6 Number of Pending Transaction Calls

The number of pending calls for a particular transaction of a process can be determined by calling function c_transcount which is declared as

```
int c_transcount(trans int (*tp)());
```

where transaction pointer tp specifies the transaction and process to which calls have been made (the argument can really be a transaction pointer of any type). The value returned by c_transcount includes pending timed transaction calls. Because such transaction calls can be withdrawn by the calling process, the value returned may be only an approximate indication of the number of pending calls.

13.7 Processor Identification

The processor id used in the processor clause of the create statement is a small integer that identifies a logical processor. The mapping of the processor id values to logical processors depends on the implementation. Programs can obtain valid processor id values by calling the following functions (for compatibility, uniprocessor implementations provide trivial versions of these functions):

```
int c_processorid(process anytype pid);
int c_bestprocessor();
int c_giveprocessors(int n, int arr[]);
```

`c_processorid` returns the id of the processor on which the Concurrent C process `pid` is running.

`c_bestprocessor` returns the id of the "best" processor for creating a new process. The definition of "best" depends on the implementation, but it could be a processor that is lightly loaded, or one that has an efficient communication path to the processor which is calling `c_bestprocessor`.

`c_giveprocessors` returns the total number of processors, and stores their ids into the integer array `arr`. This array must have space for at least *n* integers. If n is less than the number of processors, then only the first n processor ids are copied into `arr`.

13.8 Symbolic Process Names

A symbolic name can be attached to a specific process. Concurrent C uses these names to identify processes in error messages. These names are useful for distinguishing between multiple processes of the same type. There are two functions for manipulating these names:

```
void  c_setname(process anytype pid, char *name);
char *c_getname(process anytype pid, char *name);
```

`c_setname` sets the name of the process `pid` to the string `name`. Only the first `c_NAMELEN`−1 characters of the name are used (`c_NAMELEN` is defined in `concurrentc.h`). `c_getname` copies the name of the process `pid` into the character array `name`, and returns a pointer to this array. The `name` argument should point to an array of at least `c_NAMELEN` characters. When a process is created, its symbolic name is initialized to the name of its process type.

13.9 Defining Logical Processors

Our LAN multiprocessor implementation of Concurrent C provides the following functions to define the logical processors which the Concurrent C program will use:

```
int c_processor(char *machine, char *program);
int c_startprocessors(char *list);
```

`c_processor` creates a new logical processor and returns its processor id. Parameter `machine` is the processor name (i.e., the processor's Ethernet host name) and parameter `program` is the path name of a load module on this processor. The user must ensure that this load module is identical to the load module executed when starting the Concurrent C program.

`c_startprocessors` is an alternative to `c_processor`. The single argument is a pointer to a string of the form

$$machine_1 : program_1 \quad machine_2 : program_2 \quad ... \quad machine_n : program_n$$

Function `c_startprocessors` scans this string, calls `c_processor` for each machine/program pair, and returns the number of successful calls.

Implementations may provide alternative functions for defining and initializing the multiprocessor hardware.

13.10 Process Stack Size

Our Concurrent C implementations provide two functions for changing and determining the process stack size:

```
int c_setstksiz(int);
int c_getstksiz();
```

Each process has a "create-stack-size" attribute, which specifies the stack size used for all child processes created by the process. Function `c_setstksiz` can be used to change this attribute for the calling process. Once a process has been created, its stack size cannot be changed. Typically `c_setstksiz` is called in the `main` process, before it creates any other processes. If this is done, then all processes will have the specified stack size.

`c_getstksiz` returns the value of the create-stack-size attribute for the calling process. When a process is created, its create-stack-size attribute is set to that of its parent.

The stack size of the `main` process (and only the `main` process) is specified by the external `int` variable `c_stksiz`. The user may define and initialize this variable. Otherwise, the definition and a default initial value are taken from the run-time library.

Please note that the stack size manipulation facilities are implementation dependent.

13.11 Interrupts and Transactions

On some implementations, hardware interrupts can be associated with transactions. This done by calling the implementation-dependent function `c_associate` which is declared as

```
void c_associate(trans async (*tp)(), int addr, ...);
```

When the interrupt associated with the specified address `addr` occurs, Concurrent C generates a call to the transaction specified by `tp`. This must be an asynchronous transaction. Parameter `addr` and the following parameters define the interrupt, and these are implementation dependent.

14. Syntax Summary

We will not give you the complete Concurrent C syntax; instead we will omit the C syntax [Ritchie 1980], listing only the items related to Concurrent C, i.e., syntactic items that we have added or C syntax items that we have extended. New syntactic items will be marked by the word "**new**" and additions to existing C items will be marked by the word "**addition**".

14.1 Expressions

expression: (**addition**)
    `within` *expression* ? *tc-primary* (*expression-list$_{opt}$*) : *expression*
    `create` *identifier* (*expression-list$_{opt}$*) *processor-clause$_{opt}$* *priority-clause$_{opt}$*

primary: (**addition**)
    tc-primary (*expression-list$_{opt}$*)

tc-primary: (**new**)
    primary . *name*
    primary-> name
    (*∗expression*)

processor-clause: (**new**)
    `processor` (*expression*)

priority-clause: (**new**)
    `priority` (*expression*)

14.2 Declarations

type-specifier: (**addition**)
    `process` `spec` *identifier* (*parameter-decl-list$_{opt}$*) *transaction-part$_{opt}$*
    `process` `anytype`
    `process`$_{opt}$ *identifier*

parameter-decl-list: (**new**)
    parameter-type-decl
    parameter-type-decl, parameter-decl-list

transaction-part: (**new**)
    { *trans-decl-list* }

parameter-type-decl: (**new**)
    type-name
    decl-specifier declarator

trans-decl-list:

$$trans\text{-}decl$$
$$trans\text{-}decl \ trans\text{-}decl\text{-}list$$

(new)

trans-decl: **(new)**
    `trans` *trans-type-specifier*$_{opt}$ *trans-declarator-list* ;

trans-type-specifier: **(new)**
    `async`
    type-specifier

trans-declarator-list: **(new)**
    trans-declarator
    trans-declarator, trans-declarator-list

trans-declarator: **(new)**
    declarator (*parameter-decl-list*$_{opt}$)
    declarator

14.3 Statements

statement: **(addition)**
    `select` { *guard-alternative-list* }
    `delay` *expression* ;
    `treturn` *expression*$_{opt}$;
    `accept` *identifier* (*param-list*$_{opt}$) *by-clause*$_{opt}$ *suchthat-clause*$_{opt}$ *statement*

by-clause: **(new)**
    `by` (*expression*)

suchthat-clause: **(new)**
    `suchthat` (*expression*)

guard-alternative-list: **(new)**
    guard$_{opt}$ *alternative*
    guard$_{opt}$ *alternative* `or` *guard-alternative-list*

guard: **(new)**
    (*expression*) :

alternative: **(new)**
    statement-list
    `terminate` ;

14.4 External Definitions

external-definition: **(addition)**
    `process body` *identifier* (*param-list*$_{opt}$) *process-body*

process-body: **(new)**
    function-statement

Appendix B

Concurrent C: Design and Implementation

To give the readers a better understanding of Concurrent C, we will discuss some of the rationale behind its design and give an overview of its implementations on different types of computers, i.e., uniprocessors and multiprocessors.

1. Design

The C programming language does not have concurrent programming facilities. However, concurrent programs can be (and have been!) written in C, using multiple UNIX processes and UNIX operating system calls. However, we chose to not use this approach as the basis of Concurrent C because it suffers from several disadvantages:

1. Only limited interaction is possible between UNIX processes.

2. While the UNIX shell provides an elegant interface for using pipes, the underlying system calls—`fork`, `exec`, `pipe`—are not easy to use. Errors can be very hard to find.

3. Some versions of the UNIX system do provide message passing facilities However, these messages are arbitrary byte strings, and do not allow compile-time checking of message types.

4. A fast process context switching mechanism is important. This encourages programmers to write small, simple, modular processes—just as a fast function call mechanism encourages programmers to write small, simple, modular functions. The UNIX system gives each process its own virtual address space. Because the UNIX system must change address spaces, the UNIX process context switch time is rather high. Concurrent C processes running in the same program can share the same address space; hence a scheduler designed for Concurrent C processes should have much lower overhead.

5. Many versions of UNIX enforce a limit on the number of processes that one user can run at a time. Typically this limit is about 20 processes, which is too small for many concurrent programming applications.

1.1 Design Considerations

In this section, we will discuss the rationale for several of the design decisions that we made for Concurrent C. The most important decision, of course, was the choice of the rendezvous model; this was discussed earlier.

1.1.1 Language Extensions versus Library Functions: A major question was, why provide language extensions at all? A simpler alternative would be to write a function package that provides some form of concurrent processing. However, such a library package would have the following limitations:

1. It would be clumsy and inelegant to provide some of the facilities of Concurrent C, e.g., the *select* statement.

2. The concurrent parts of a program would not be easily identifiable— either to a compiler or to another programmer.

3. It is difficult to design a set of functions that can be implemented efficiently on a wide class of machines.

4. A compiler may not be easily able to optimize concurrent programs well, because it will be tuned to optimizing sequential programs [Pratt 1983].

1.1.2 Transaction Pointers: Transaction pointers were included because they allow the dynamic specification of process interaction points. For example, a server manager process can give a client process a transaction pointer which the client can use to call the process that will actually perform the service. The client does not need to know the type of the server process.

Because transaction pointers are very similar to function pointers, we could have used function pointers to refer to transactions also. We decided against this for the following reasons:

1. Using function pointers to point to transactions would have a negative impact on program clarity. It would not be possible, in general, to statically determine whether a function pointer referred to a function or to a transaction.

2. It would complicate the implementation because it would force us to determine at run-time whether a function pointer points to a function, or to a transaction. Moreover, it might make it necessary to use an additional byte or word to implement the extended function pointers.

1.1.3 Suchthat Clause: At first, we resisted adding a suchthat clause to the *accept* statement, because of the complexity and potential inefficiency. What changed our minds was the lock manager example given in Chapter 2. Our first lock manager did not use suchthat, and was extremely complicated; we discovered the suchthat clause greatly simplified the lock manager and the interaction with it.

1.1.4 Types in Accept Statements: In their stripped form, Concurrent C *accept* statements (i.e., without the suchthat or by clauses) are similar to those in Ada. The major difference is that Ada requires the return value and parameter types to be repeated in the *accept* statement, while our *accept* statement gives just the parameter names. We originally required the types; like the Ada designers [DoD 1979] we felt that the redundancy was useful. This was fine for our first examples, which had only one or two simple parameters, and which returned simple types. However, for practical programs, with transactions with five parameters of complicated types, the *accept* statements became unreadable. The return value type obscured the transaction name, and the parameter names were buried in the type declarations. Furthermore, we found that the parameter declarations ran off the right edge of the page, because *accept* statements generally appear inside loops and are already indented. For these reasons, we (reluctantly) decided to omit types from *accept* statements.

1.1.5 Nested Processes: We decided not to allow processes to be syntactically nested within functions or within other processes. This is in the spirit the C language, which does not allow nested functions. This allows each process to have its own independent stack, which simplified the implementation. We did not really appreciate this simplification until we saw how an Ada implementation needs "cactus stacks".

1.1.6 Process Anytype: Process values in Concurrent C are strongly typed. We have found this very helpful when interacting with processes. However, we also found that the strong typing got in the way when performing general operations on an arbitrary process. We added the built-in type process anytype to solve these problems. To see the difficulty, consider the built-in function c_mypid, which returns the process value of the calling process. In the current version of Concurrent C, c_mypid is an ordinary function that returns a process anytype value. However, before we added process anytype, c_mypid was a pseudo-function, in that it was only allowed inside a process body, and the compiler made the return type match that of the enclosing process body. This was unsatisfactory first because c_mypid could not be called from a function, and second because the compiler had to treat c_mypid specially. We ran into similar problems with the parameter types for functions which abort processes or which manipulate process priorities; it was annoying to change the compiler each time we added such a function. The process anytype concept provided a neat, extensible solution to these problems.

1.1.7 Asynchronous Transactions: Concurrent C initially provided only synchronous message facilities (transactions). We selected synchronous message passing in preference to the asynchronous message passing because we felt that it was simpler to understand and implement. We felt that a language should have either synchronous or asynchronous message passing facilities but that both facilities were not necessary because they are theoretically equivalent. As discussed in Chapter 7, both synchronous and asynchronous facilities have their advantages and we eventually extended Concurrent C to provide asynchronous transactions.

1.2 Open Issues

There are several areas where we feel that Concurrent C can be extended or improved. For example, Concurrent C does not provide facilities for data abstraction. There was another research project which was investigating how to add data abstraction facilities to C, and we did not want to duplicate that effort. Instead, we decided that we would use the results of this effort. This effort eventually resulted in the design of C++ [Stroustrup 1986]. We eventually merged Concurrent C with C++ to produce Concurrent C++ (see Chapter 5).

Currently *accept* statements can only appear inside process bodies (Ada has a similar restriction). In theory, at least, it would be nice to allow them to appear inside arbitrary functions. However, recall that an *accept* statement gives just the transaction name. This is ambiguous without the name of the process type containing that transaction. We could extend the *accept* statement, perhaps by allowing *processtype*: : *transname* for the transaction name. However, this raises several questions, such as what is to be done if the function is not called by a process of the specified type.

Instead of trying to answer these questions immediately—and perhaps making an unfortunate choice—we instead decided to disallow *accept* statements in functions, and see how painful this restriction would be. As it turns out, it has not been a significant limitation: we have not seen any programs that would be simplified by this feature. The typical structure of a process is a single *select* statement in a loop, with *accept* alternatives for that process' transactions, and guards expressing when each transaction can be accepted. These alternatives then call functions as necessary (e.g., see the lock manager example).

Section 2.5 of this Appendix discusses some additional ways in which Concurrent C might be extended.

1.3 Problems With Using Some C Library Functions

We would like Concurrent C programs to be able to directly call standard C library functions such as `malloc` and the `stdio` library. However, some of these functions are not reentrant because they update global variables or `static` variables. These functions will have to be modified before they will work in a concurrent environment. For example, suppose that the scheduler decides to switch processes in the middle of a `malloc` call, just after `malloc` has partially updated its storage allocation data. If the next process also calls `malloc`, the result will be chaos. (In theory, the same problems can occur in ordinary sequential C programs that use signals. E.g., suppose a signal interrupts a `malloc` call, and somehow `malloc` is called again before the first call is resumed. In practice, typical signal handlers are very simple, so this does not happen.)

There are several solutions. One solution is to provide a library with concurrent versions of functions like `malloc`. For example, the concurrent `malloc` could issue a transaction call to a storage allocator process, which is the only process that updates the storage allocation data. Unfortunately, this solution requires us to identify those library functions that use shared data, and to maintain separate versions of these functions. Furthermore, the concurrent versions of these functions would be less efficient than the simple sequential versions.

Another solution is to make all calls to sequential C library functions that update shared memory be *atomic* so that they are never interrupted. Our current implementation of Concurrent C makes all sequential C library functions atomic by ensuring that the Concurrent C scheduler never dispatches away from a process when it is in such a function. (In our current uniprocessor UNIX implementations, the scheduler is invoked once every second, by means of a UNIX alarm signal. The scheduler normally suspends the currently running Concurrent C process and starts another. However, if at the time of the alarm signal the program counter is in a UNIX library function, then the scheduler does not do a process switch.)

2. Implementation Overview

Concurrent C has been implemented on several uniprocessors and multiprocessors running the UNIX operating system [Cmelik, Gehani & Roome 1988b]. In this section, we will give you an overview of three different Concurrent C implementations: a uniprocessor implementation, a multiprocessor implementation in which processors communicate by sending messages, and a shared memory multiprocessor implementation. We will also discuss some of our experiences with these implementations.

2.1 Implementation Strategy

In designing Concurrent C, our primary goal was to provide a tool for distributed programming (i.e., programming a network of computers that do not share memory). We first implemented a uniprocessor version of Concurrent C. As discussed in the preface, a concurrent programming facility on a uniprocessor is an important program structuring facility in its own right even though the lack of a multiprocessor may not give you much computational advantage.

Our decision to first implement Concurrent C on a single computer was pragmatic and based on the following reasons:

- Implementing Concurrent C on a uniprocessor would be easier than implementing it on a multiprocessor. This would allow us to get relatively quick feedback on the design of Concurrent C and techniques for implementing it.

- Focusing our efforts on the uniprocessor implementation would allow us to postpone worrying about the multiprocessor aspects of the implementation until after we had understood the uniprocessor implementation.

- A uniprocessor implementation was likely to be much more portable than a multiprocessor implementation. This is because a uniprocessor implementation depends only on the type of operating system and computer; installing it at a new site requires no more effort than reading in a set of binary files from tape (or whatever). The distributed version, however, depends critically on the networking facilities, and these vary substantially between computer installations. Very few sites will have multiprocessor architectures like ours; consequently, installing a distributed implementation of Concurrent C at a new site could require substantial effort.

- Finally, we correctly anticipated that the uniprocessor implementation would serve as the basis of the multiprocessor implementations.

After acquiring experience with the uniprocessor implementation, we extended the uniprocessor Concurrent C implementation to run on two types of multiprocessors: object-code compatible computers connected by a local area network (Ethernet) and a shared-memory multiprocessor.

2.2 Uniprocessor Implementation

The uniprocessor implementation we will describe runs on top of the UNIX system and does not require any changes to the UNIX kernel. Each Concurrent C program is implemented as one UNIX process:

UNIX Process

○   Concurrent C process

Within the UNIX process, each Concurrent C process has its own stack and machine registers. The Concurrent C run-time library provides a process scheduler which switches between Concurrent C processes by saving and restoring registers. This context switching is done purely at the user level, without invoking the operating system. The Concurrent C process scheduler is invoked at process interaction points and at regular intervals (time slicing). The latter ensures that no CPU- or I/O-greedy process starves other processes with equal or higher priorities.

There are several reasons why we put all Concurrent C processes in one UNIX process instead of putting each Concurrent C process in a separate UNIX process:

- The cost of switching between Concurrent C processes is substantially less than that of switching between UNIX processes. Each UNIX process has its own virtual address space; context switching is slow because changing address spaces is slow (about 1 ms on a VAX 11/780). Switching between Concurrent C processes is fast (about 50 μs) because these processes share the same address space (i.e., the address space of the containing UNIX process). A fast process context switch mechanism will encourage programmers to write small, simple, and modular processes—just as a fast function call mechanism encourages programmers to write small, simple, and modular functions.

- Because all Concurrent C processes are packed within one UNIX process, they have the same address space. Our implementation exploits this fact; e.g., instead of copying messages between processes, we pass pointers.

- Having a separate, user-level scheduler for Concurrent C processes allows us to experiment with different scheduling strategies.

For portability reasons, we do not encourage the use of shared memory between Concurrent C processes. We do not provide facilities for synchronizing access to shared memory. However, shared memory does allow efficient (and sometimes convenient) data access. It is the programmer's responsibility to ensure consistency of the shared data.

2.3 Local Area Network (LAN) Implementation

Our first multiprocessor implementation was targeted for a set of object-code compatible computers (VAX 11/780s and 8600s) connected by an Ethernet local area network (LAN) and the Berkeley 4.2 BSD UNIX system. In this implementation each Concurrent C program is implemented as one or more UNIX processes which are connected by socket streams (full-duplex communication channels):

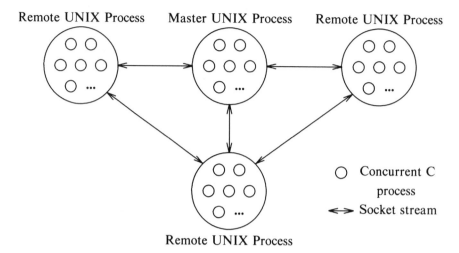

Remote UNIX Process

As in the uniprocessor implementation, each UNIX process contains a set of Concurrent C processes, and an internal scheduler switches between these processes. Normally each UNIX process runs on a separate physical processor, and can be regarded as a logical processor. Of course, for testing in a single processor environment, all the UNIX processes can be placed on one processor. Each UNIX process executes a copy of the same load module. The main process is executed only on the "master" UNIX process—the one on which execution of the Concurrent C program is initiated. When a new Concurrent C process is created, it is assigned by the user to a logical processor and remains on this processor until it terminates (i.e., we do not support process migration).

Each UNIX process contains a Concurrent C process which handles messages from other processors—a "message reading daemon" process. This daemon process periodically examines all input streams to the UNIX process. If any messages are waiting, it takes the appropriate action. In most cases, these actions involve putting messages and results on the appropriate queues and changing the states of the Concurrent C processes. Like the uniprocessor implementation, the distributed implementation does not require any changes to the UNIX kernel.

As an example, suppose that a Concurrent C process c calls a synchronous transaction of another process s. If they are in the same UNIX process, the call works just as in the uniprocessor version: the internal scheduler saves c's registers and switches to the next ready process. After s completes execution of c's transaction call, it reactivates c and calls the scheduler. If c and s are on different UNIX processes, the internal scheduler saves c's registers, sends a message to the UNIX process which contains s, and then switches to another

Concurrent C process. S's daemon process eventually reads the message and sets the state of S to active. When S gets to execute and it completes executing the transaction, the Concurrent C run-time system sends a message back to C with S's reply; C's daemon process eventually reads this message and reactivates C.

2.4 Shared Memory (SM) Implementation

2.4.1 Hardware Architecture: The shared memory multiprocessor consists of several single-board computers (SBCs) and some memory, all on a common global bus. In addition, a host UNIX system can access the global bus; it acts as a debugger, monitor, and I/O server.

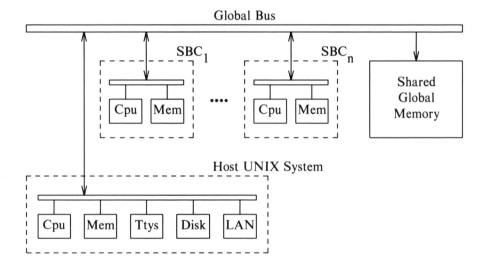

Each SBC consists of a microprocessor and some local (on-board) memory. Accesses to the local memory use the SBC's local bus, and do not tie up the global bus. If the microprocessor references a non-local memory address, the SBC places the memory reference on the global bus.

Each SBC's local memory is "dual-ported", in that the local memory is assigned an address range on the global bus, and the SBC responds as a memory slave to any bus request for these addresses. Thus the SBCs can access each other's local memory, as can the host.

A typical configuration has four SBCs and 16 megabytes of global memory, and we have assembled systems with up to eight SBCs and 64 megabytes of global memory. We have used two different SBCs: one based on the AT&T 32100 microprocessor, with one megabyte of local memory, and another SBC based on the Motorola 68020 microprocessor, with four megabytes of local memory. The local memory makes this multiprocessor practical. In general, a pure shared memory multiprocessor (one without local memory) is limited to two or three processors; at that point the common bus becomes a bottleneck. But with the local memory, we can place each processor's instruction text, stacks, and much of its data in the local memory. Thus the majority of memory references made by each processor are to local memory, which greatly decreases the load on the global bus. The bus has not been a bottleneck for most programs; we expect that up to 12 processor systems would be practical.

The host UNIX system acts as a monitor and debugger. Because the SBCs' local memories are dual-ported, programs running on the host can examine or alter them. Note that the programs can be loaded into the SBCs by the host. The host can also examine and alter the global memory. Programs on the host also provide I/O services for the SBCs.

2.4.2 SBC Operating System: Each SBC has a simple multi-tasking operating system [Roome 1986]. This is an extension of a tasking system originally developed for a database machine [Leland & Roome 1985, 1988]. This operating system offers simple task management services, such as task creation and destruction. All tasks share the same address space. Tasks can wait for and wake up "events". An event is defined by a structure in shared memory. Tasks can also get and release locks; as with events, a lock is defined by a structure in shared memory.

The primary inter-task communication mechanism is a "stream". A stream is a buffer in shared memory, with a producer-consumer protocol defined by a set of functions. A stream is logically equivalent to a UNIX pipe. Any task that knows a stream address can read data from the stream or write data to it. A program on the UNIX host uses streams to handle I/O requests for the SBCs; the UNIX program creates a "service request" stream, and continually reads I/O requests from this stream. As an example, the `read` function used by an SBC program sends a request to the service request stream, and waits. The host program eventually reads the request from the stream, does the I/O, and then wakes up the waiting task.

2.4.3 Concurrent C: Concurrent C is implemented on top of the SBC operating system. Unlike the UNIX implementations, in the shared memory multiprocessor, each Concurrent C process is mapped to a task (process) of the underlying operating system. As a result the context switching overhead is slightly higher in the SM implementation than in the uniprocessor implementation. However, the SBC operating system is very simple, and its context switch time is much less than that in a full UNIX system. The advantage is that this scheme allows Concurrent C processes to use the underlying SBC operating system facilities in a natural fashion.

Like the uniprocessor implementation, the SM Concurrent C implementation uses shared memory for passing transaction arguments and return values, and uses a process table in shared memory. As an example, consider a simple synchronous transaction call. The calling process locks the process table, places itself on a queue of processes waiting to call the called process, wakes up the called process if it is waiting, releases the process table, and waits. (All this is done by Concurrent C run-time functions, of course; the user does not see these operations!) After the called process accepts the call and completes the transaction, it wakes up the calling process, which will eventually be rescheduled by the operating system. The calling process passes arguments by saving the global address of the arguments in its process table entry, using the dual-ported aspects of the processor's local memory. Similarly, the caller provides the address of an area into which the called process can store the value returned, if any, by the transaction call.

The result of all this is that the shared memory multiprocessor version is much closer to the uniprocessor version of Concurrent C than to the LAN multiprocessor version.

2.5 Language Issues

2.5.1 Transaction Arguments: C (and therefore Concurrent C) supports only the "call-by-value" argument passing mode; C does not support the "result" or the "value-result" modes. This is not a problem in C, because programmers can pass variables "by reference" by passing a pointer to the variable. Using pointers works in the uniprocessor and in the SM multiprocessor Concurrent C implementations, but it does not work in the LAN implementation. The use of pointers in Concurrent C programs to pass transaction arguments is the single most important reason why these programs may require substantial modification before they can be ported from the uniprocessor and SM implementations to the LAN distributed implementation.

One solution would be to add out (result) and in out (value-result) parameter modes to Concurrent C. In these modes, the called process would allocate a temporary variable of the appropriate length, and would copy data from the caller at the start of a transaction (for value-result mode) and would copy the results back to the caller at the end of the transaction (for both modes). The Concurrent C run-time system can do this copying automatically. This would work (modulo aliasing problems) because the caller is suspended during the transaction call.

Unfortunately, this does not solve the problem of passing variable amounts of data, e.g., variable length arrays. In C, array names are really pointers to the beginning of the array. Consequently, the compiler is not able to determine how much of the data is to be copied. Of course, if the array length was available to the compiler then this problem would disappear. We have not come up with a satisfactory notation for doing this as yet.

On top of that, there is the question of what semantics should be assigned to these modes when shared memory is available, for example, when the processes are on the same processor. We have two choices. We can replace the value-result mode with true reference mode or we can actually copy the data. Thus the question is, can we live with a hybrid reference/value-result mode, in which an implementation can use either mode, or must we guarantee value-result semantics? The problem is one of efficiency versus purity: there is no question that the pure value-result mode is cleaner, but it is much less efficient. Furthermore, if we insist on copy semantics, programmers would be tempted to write two versions of such transactions: one with pointer parameters, which will be used for local calls, and another with value-result parameters, which will be used for remote calls, and they would decide which to use at run time.

Yet another question is the impact of these new modes on the sequential part of the language. For example, one can argue that to be consistent, the new parameter passing modes should also be allowed for function parameters. However, these modes are only needed when passing arguments across processor boundaries; this happens with process and transaction arguments, but not with function arguments. For functions, reference mode (implemented with pointers) seems to be sufficient; remember that the reason for adding the new modes is that we cannot provide a true reference mode for transaction arguments in the LAN multiprocessor implementation.

We intend to implement the value-result argument passing mode just for transaction calls. If shared memory is available, then a compiler will be free to pass arguments by reference provided it can guarantee value-result semantics.

2.5.2 Global Variables: Programs depending upon shared memory may not work on multiprocessors without shared memory. In our first version of Concurrent C, we attempted to discourage the use of shared memory by prohibiting process bodies from accessing global variables. This was not an outright prohibition, because process bodies could bypass this restriction by calling functions that referenced global variables. Also, we did not add language constructs for dealing with shared memory, or for simulating shared memory in a non-shared-memory environment.

However, in the uniprocessor implementation, we discovered that this restriction was very annoying in practice, primarily because many of the C standard library routines, such as the I/O routines, are macros that use global variables. Furthermore, it seemed pointless to forbid programmers from using shared memory when it exists. We were afraid that if we prohibited the use of available shared memory, then programmers would just refuse to use Concurrent C. As a result, we dropped the restriction, and allowed process bodies to access global variables, trusting that the programmers who did this would be mature enough to accept the resulting limitations on portability.

In the LAN implementation of Concurrent C, only processes on the same logical processor truly share global variables. We decided not to attempt to simulate shared variables in the LAN implementation (for example, by some copy-on-write scheme), primarily because we object to inherently inefficient things. However, the LAN implementation does allow constants to be shared. Because all UNIX processes execute the same load module, any initialized global variable which is not changed during execution can be safely accessed by any process. Thus addresses of string constants, constant tables, function pointers, etc., can be safely passed between processes.

The SM multiprocessor offers two classes of global variables: *fully-shared* (or just *shared*) variables which are shared by all processes and *partially-shared* variables which are shared only by processes on the same processor. The former would be in the global memory that is shared by all processors; the latter would be in each processor's local memory. The default is for all global variables to be partially shared. At first this seems counter intuitive, because making all variables be fully shared would come closest to the semantics of ordinary C programs. However, sharing all variables would greatly increase the load on the global bus, which would limit the number of processors. For now, programmers use loader commands to designate variables as processor-shared; eventually, we will add some syntactic sugar to Concurrent C for specifying shared variables.

Programmers using shared memory need a mechanism for synchronizing access to it. In case of the SM multiprocessor implementation, programmers can use the locking mechanisms provided by the underlying operating system. However, at present no special facilities are provided with the LAN and uniprocessor implementations. Processes can be used to synchronize access to shared memory but this can be expensive because of the context switch overhead associated with synchronizing processes. We are currently investigating the incorporation of a shared-memory mechanism called the *capsule* [Gehani 1988b].

2.5.3 Termination: The Concurrent C *select* statement allows a process to wait for a set of events. When we first designed Concurrent C, the *terminate* alternative of the *select* statement was used for specifying collective termination of sibling processes. In this version, these processes would collectively terminate when all of them were ready to terminate, when their children had terminated, and when their parent process had completed execution or was waiting to terminate.

Implementing that version of collective termination was relatively simple on a uniprocessor: it just required keeping track of the parent and sibling process relationships and examining their states at specific points. The implementation on a SM multiprocessor was similar. However, implementing that version of collective termination on the LAN multiprocessor was extremely complicated. Among other things, it involved a two-phase commit protocol to ensure that a process would not change its state after it had indicated that it was ready to terminate but before it was told to terminate.

The semantics and implementation (especially in the LAN multiprocessor) of that initial version of our *terminate* alternative were not as simple as we would like. We were uncomfortable with the semantics of collective termination and wanted to simplify its semantics (and hopefully the implementation). After having written several programs that used collective termination, we noticed that collective termination was always used to terminate the entire program and not just a set of sibling processes. This provided a basis for the current simpler semantics of collective termination: if all processes of a program are ready to terminate, then the whole program will terminate. These semantics have lead to a simpler implementation. Note that with the simplified semantics, once the collective termination conditions have occurred—that is, once all processes are waiting at a *select* statement with a *terminate* alternative or have completed—then the program will stay in that state forever. Thus the run-time system starts a low-priority process which periodically checks the state of all other processes. When that process detects that the collective termination conditions have occurred, it terminates the program.

2.6 Files

2.6.1 Reading from Slow Devices: In the UNIX-based Concurrent C implementations (uniprocessor and LAN), putting several Concurrent C processes into one UNIX process creates a problem when a Concurrent C process reads from a slow device, such as standard input. If we let a Concurrent C process do an ordinary UNIX read, the Concurrent C process would block, blocking the entire UNIX process, until the arrival of input. This means that all Concurrent C processes in the blocked UNIX process will block until the process doing the read gets its data and unblocks the UNIX process.

Fortunately, the Berkeley UNIX system provides a `select` system call (different from the Concurrent C *select* statement) which can be used to determine if input is available. By using this, we can allow a read request to block only the Concurrent C process requesting the read, but not other processes. We do this by supplying our own version of the `read` system call. Our version calls the Berkeley UNIX `select` system call to determine if input is available. If it is, our version reads the data and returns to the calling processes; otherwise, our version of `read` marks the Concurrent C process as waiting for input on the specified file descriptor, and invokes the Concurrent C scheduler. The scheduler periodically checks for input availability, and activates the waiting Concurrent C process when input is available.

In the shared memory system, reading from a slow device does not require any special treatment. Each Concurrent C process is a separate process under the control of the underlying operating system. Thus if one Concurrent C process reads from a file, then this Concurrent C process will block, but the others will not.

2.6.2 Reading from Standard Input and Writing to Standard Output: In the uniprocessor implementation, all Concurrent C processes share the single UNIX process' standard input and output. Input for and output from different processes can be multiplexed using windows. Thus input and output present no difficulties, except for the problem of blocking reads as discussed above.

In the LAN implementation, each UNIX process has its own standard input and output. To give the illusion of a single standard input and output, standard input and output for all processes is redirected to the master processor, i.e., the processor where execution of the Concurrent C program was initiated. Redirecting all standard input and output to one processor allows the program to be controlled from one terminal and facilitates debugging.

For the SM implementation, all I/O requests go through the host UNIX system, so there is naturally only one standard input and output, and they are shared by all Concurrent C processes.

2.6.3 File Access: The lack of a distributed file system is sorely felt in the LAN Concurrent C. For example, it is the users responsibility to copy the load module on to the different processors. In the SM multiprocessor, the host computer acts as the central file server.

2.7 Comparison of the Uniprocessor and Distributed Versions

Here are some times for typical Concurrent C operations in the various implementations discussed in this paper. The uniprocessor and LAN systems use VAX 11/780 computers; the SM multiprocessor uses AT&T 32100 microprocessors running at 14 Mhz.[1]

---

1. The times given for the uniprocessor and LAN implementations are user plus system times, while the times given for the SM Concurrent C are elapsed times. The user time is the total amount of time spent in executing user code (Concurrent C program plus run-time system code; note that the Concurrent C run-time system runs on top of the UNIX system as user code). The system time is the total amount of time spent in the UNIX system kernel executing on behalf of the user. User plus system time should equal real time if the UNIX system was dedicated to just executing the Concurrent C program.

action	uniprocessor (VAX 11/780)	LAN multiproc. (VAX 11/780)	SM multiproc. (AT & T 32100)
function call	27 μs	27 μs	10 μs
context switch	50 μs	50 μs	140 μs
local transaction call & return	270 μs	550 μs	670 μs
remote transaction call & return	–	31 ms (local) 15 ms (remote)	490 μs
create local process	18 ms	18 ms	0.8 ms
create remote process	–	13 ms (local) 39 ms (remote)	1.3 ms

In the transaction call tests, the transaction takes one argument, and returns it. The called process loops on an *accept* statement. Only two processes, the caller and the called process, are active. Note that in the uniprocessor implementation, this action involves two context switches, and is equivalent to two message send/receive pairs. The local transaction call and return time is higher in the LAN implementation than in the uniprocessor implementation because of the additional checks to determine whether a call is local or remote, and because it was not feasible to do some optimizations.

The context switches are slower in the shared memory system because each Concurrent C process is a separate task managed by the underlying operating system. Thus context switches are done by the operating system. In the other systems, context switching is done purely at a user level. This is also why local transaction calls in the shared memory system are slower. The advantage of using the operating system is that each Concurrent C process can use operating system services, such as I/O, in a simple, natural fashion. We considered this advantage well worth the slight increase in context switch and transaction call times.

For the SM multiprocessor, remote calls are actually *faster* than local calls. The reason for this is that much of the time for the call is spent in context switching. For the local case, all switches are done by the same processor. But for the remote case, much of the context switch overhead can be done in parallel. That is, one processor can save the calling process' registers while the other processor is loading the called process' registers.

2.8 Debugging in a Distributed Environment

Debugging a distributed Concurrent C program is much more difficult than debugging a uniprocessor Concurrent C program. The main reason for this is that in the uniprocessor world, there is only one process that is executing at any give time. Stopping this process stops the whole Concurrent C program. This allows the user to get a consistent view, or snapshot, of the state of the Concurrent C program. We can come close to getting a consistent view in the SM multiprocessor because we keep all the process state information in shared memory. In case of the LAN multiprocessor, without special hardware, it will not be possible to stop all the processes instantaneously. Consequently, it is not possible to get a consistent snapshot of a Concurrent C program.

In the LAN implementation, we found it somewhat beneficial to use a single processor to debug multiprocessor programs for the following reasons:

- In the absence of a distributed file system, it is easier to examine the debug output stored in files on the same processor.

- It is easier to monitor the UNIX processes containing the Concurrent C processes if all of the UNIX processes are on the same processor.

- There is no need to worry about remote processor or network failure.

2.9 Coping with Partial System Failure

A Concurrent C program is a collection of processes cooperating to achieve a common goal. In the uniprocessor implementation and in our current distributed implementation, processor failure terminates the Concurrent C program. However, in a fault tolerant distributed implementation, failure of one processor should not stop the whole program. Processes on the remaining processors can continue to execute. But, how should they react to the partial failure of the program? And what should be done with processes on the failed processors? We are addressing these and related issues by providing facilities to handle partial hardware failure [Cmelik, Gehani & Roome 1988a].

2.10 Conclusions

We chose the Ethernet/LAN environment for our first distributed implementation because it was readily available and we wanted to get an implementation working quickly. Experience gained with this implementation has facilitated the implementation of Concurrent C on other types of multiprocessors. The Ethernet/LAN environment is not ideal for Concurrent C because Concurrent C processes are tightly coupled and they tend to exchange short messages frequently. The Ethernet/UNIX environment was not designed for such process interaction. The inter-processor communication cost is high relative to the normally short messages exchanged by Concurrent C processes. For the LAN multiprocessor, the high inter-processor communication cost reduces the number of applications that can benefit from LAN Concurrent C. Applications that can use the LAN multiprocessor advantageously are those in which processes on different processors exchange messages infrequently. One such application is Concurrent Make [Cmelik 1986] which was described in Chapter 4.

The shared memory multiprocessor is an appropriate multiprocessor architecture for Concurrent C. The shared memory makes this implementation more efficient than the LAN implementation, and it makes it easier to implement Concurrent C.

Experience with the multiprocessor implementations has confirmed the need for making some changes to Concurrent C. For example, the `create` operator was extended to allow for processes to be placed on remote processors. The complicated termination semantics made it expensive to implement termination, which gave us another reason for simplifying the termination semantics. The LAN implementation confirmed the need for adding the value-result parameter transmission mode for transactions, while the shared memory implementation pointed out the need for facilities to specify shared variables and facilities for synchronizing access to shared memory.

Finally, the LAN implementation has lead us to move in a new research direction: the design and implementation of a fault tolerant version of Concurrent C, called Fault Tolerant Concurrent C [Cmelik, Gehani, Roome 1988a], which will allow a program to continue operating despite the failure of some processors. Fault tolerance is particularly important for computer systems engaged in "continuous" real-time applications such as switching, process control, on-line databases and avionics. Even a temporary failure of one of the computers can cause breakdown of the system and could lead to disaster or require extensive work to repair the breakdown. Unfortunately, even the most reliable components are susceptible to failure.

FT Concurrent C supports fault tolerance by allowing the programmer to replicate critical processes. A program continues to operate with full functionality as long as at least one of the copies of a replicated process is operational and accessible. All details of interaction with replicated processes are handled by the FT Concurrent C run-time system. As far as the user is concerned, interacting with a replicated process is the same as interacting with an ordinary process. FT Concurrent C also provides facilities for requesting notification upon process termination, detecting processor failure during process interaction, and automatically terminating slave processes.

A replicated process behaves like a single process. Its replicas cannot, in general, be referenced individually. Interaction with a replicated process automatically implies interaction with all the surviving replicas. The replicas interact with each other (this is transparent to the user) to ensure that they all do the same thing (replicas can lag behind as long as the implementation ensures that they eventually do what the other replicas did). This is accomplished, in presence of processor failure, by using a distributed consensus protocol [Arevalo & Gehani 1988]. FT Concurrent C does all of this automatically.

Cost is an important factor in the design of fault tolerant systems. To reduce the cost of fault tolerance, our emphasis is on the design of fault tolerant programs with selective fault tolerance, i.e., programs in which only the critical parts are made fault tolerant. Besides the cost of the redundancy (i.e., replication of the processes and interacting with the replicas), the main cost is that of the consensus between the replicas. For real-time applications, hardware support may be necessary to handle the extra communication and to do the consensus between the replicas within real-time constraints.

Appendix C

Comparison with Concurrent Programming in Ada

Concurrent programming facilities in Concurrent C and Ada [DoD 1983] are both based on the rendezvous concept. Concurrent C's facilities were designed keeping in perspective the concurrent programming facilities in Ada and their limitations. The facilities in Concurrent C were also modified as a result of feedback and experience with the initial implementations of Concurrent C. Although the concurrent programming facilities in Concurrent C and Ada are similar, there are substantial differences. We will compare the concurrent programming facilities in the two languages and show that it is easier to write a variety of concurrent programs in Concurrent C than in Ada.

1. Terminology

There are some differences in the terminology used in Ada and Concurrent C. The following table contains the list of the corresponding terms:

Ada	Concurrent C
task	process
extended rendezvous	synchronous transaction
entry declaration	transaction declaration
entry call	transaction call
access types	pointers

We will use these terms interchangeably, although we will in general use Concurrent C terminology.

2. The Rendezvous Model

Ada processes interact by means of entry calls, which are similar to the synchronous transactions in Concurrent C. An Ada entry call is syntactically similar to a procedure call while a Concurrent C transaction call is syntactically similar to a function call. Unlike entry calls which can only be synchronous, Concurrent C transaction calls can be either synchronous or asynchronous. Transaction calls, like entry calls, can be used for bidirectional information transfer. However, asynchronous calls can be used only for unidirectional information transfer: from the caller to the callee. Unless explicitly qualified with the adjective asynchronous, we will use the term

251

transaction call to refer to a synchronous transaction call.

3. An Example

To give the reader a taste of Ada and to compare it with Concurrent C, we will
rewrite in Ada the producer-consumer program (from Chapter 1):

File: `pc-sync.h`

```
process spec consumer( )
{
    trans void send( int c );
};
process spec producer(process consumer cons);
```

File: `pc-sync.cc`

```
#include <stdio.h>
#include "ctype.h"   /*for islower( ), toupper( )*/
#include "pc-sync.h"
process body producer(cons)
{
    int c;
    while ((c = getchar( )) != EOF)
        cons.send(c);
    cons.send(EOF);
}
process body consumer( )
{
    int xc;
    for (;;) {
        accept send(c)
            xc = c;
        if (xc == EOF)
            break;
        if (islower(xc))
            xc = toupper(xc);
        putchar(xc);
    }
}
main( )
{
    create producer(create consumer( ));
}
```

Here is the Ada version of the producer-consumer program (from Chapter 6):

| **File:** pc.ada |

```
with TEXT_IO; use TEXT_IO;
with ISLOWER, TOUPPER;
procedure MAIN is
   task PRODUCER;
   task CONSUMER is
      entry SEND(C: in CHARACTER);
   end CONSUMER;

   task body PRODUCER is
      C: CHARACTER;
   begin
      while not END_OF_FILE(STANDARD_INPUT) loop
         GET(C); CONSUMER.SEND(C);
      end loop;
      CONSUMER.SEND(ASCII.EOT);
   end PRODUCER;

   task body CONSUMER is
      X: CHARACTER;
   begin
      loop
        accept SEND(C: in CHARACTER) do
           X := C;
        end SEND;
        if X = ASCII.EOT then exit; end if;
        if ISLOWER(X) then X=TOUPPER(X); end if;
        PUT(X);
      end loop;
   end CONSUMER;
begin      --PRODUCER and CONSUMER become active
   null; --subprogram body must have a statement
end MAIN;
```

Even in this simple example, some differences are noticeable.[1] For example:

1. In Concurrent C, processes are created by first declaring process types, then using these process types to instantiate processes and finally, if

---

1. We will not discuss the differences in the sequential programming facilities in Ada and Concurrent C, or the cosmetic syntactic differences in their concurrent programming facilities.

desired, storing the ids of the instantiated processes in process variables. In Ada, it is not necessary to declare a process type to create a process; a process can be defined directly without the use of a process type. Such a capability is convenient for one-of-a-kind processes, but it introduces an extra facility in the language.

2. Processes in Ada are not full-fledged objects; they must be components of a program component like a subprogram even though the subprogram body may consist of just a null statement.

3. Concurrent C processes must be explicitly created (activated). Ada processes are automatically activated at the end of the declaration part of the program component containing them.

4. In the Ada program, the name of the consumer process (CONSUMER) is hard-coded in the producer process (PRODUCER), i.e., in the entry call CONSUMER.SEND. This is because Ada processes cannot be parameterized. (*Note*: As shown, the Ada program is written in a straightforward manner in the typical Ada style. Ada tasks cannot directly have parameters; the generic facilities in Ada can be used to implement limited process parameterization, i.e., specifically, they can be used to implement compile-time process parameterization).

3.1 Asynchronous Producer Process

In the example shown above, the producer process must operate in lock-step with the consumer process, i.e., it must wait for the consumer process to accept the last character before it can read the next one from standard input. In Concurrent C, the producer process can be "freed' from this lockstep mode of operation by simply declaring transaction send of the consumer process to be asynchronous:

```
process spec consumer( )
{
    trans async send(int c);
};
```

Now the producer process will not have to wait for the consumer process to accept the send transaction. It can just call the send transaction to pass on the character read by it to the consumer process, and then read the next character (see Chapter 2 for more details).

4. Process Parameters

Unlike Concurrent C processes, Ada tasks cannot be parameterized. Parameters are allowed for structured types such as arrays and records, and are also allowed for subprograms, but they are not allowed for process types.

This design decision in Ada is not only inconsistent with the rest of the language, but it also has the following ramifications from a concurrent programming viewpoint:

- Parameter values can be supplied by using a special entry call. Not only does this require an extra rendezvous, but it also requires more code.

- To avoid an extra initialization rendezvous, programmers may refer to global names; e.g., notice that in the Ada task PRODUCER, the name CONSUMER is hard-coded.

From an implementation viewpoint, there is no reason for not allowing Ada tasks to have parameters. In the Concurrent C implementation, process parameters are put on a process' stack when it is created.

5. Process Specification And Creation

In Concurrent C, to create a process, its type is first specified and then the create operator is used to instantiate a process with this type.

In Ada, on the other hand, you can specify a process type and use this type to declare process variables. Processes denoted by these variables become active at the end of the declaration section (before the first executable statement). An effect similar to the Concurrent C create operator can be realized in Ada by declaring pointers to process types, and then allocating storage for them with the new operator. Processes referenced by pointers are activated when storage is allocated.

Ada also allows you to directly declare one-of-a-kind processes without the need of an explicitly specified type (such processes are said to have *anonymous* task types). These processes become active at the end of the declaration section.

Ada is complicated by the fact that there are two flavors of tasks (with explicit and anonymous types) and there are two ways of creating instances of tasks with explicitly specified types. Moreover, tasks with anonymous types cannot be passed as arguments.

6. Synchronous versus Asynchronous Transaction Calls

Concurrent C supports both synchronous and asynchronous transaction calls. However, Ada supports only synchronous transaction calls. As discussed in detail in Chapter 7, both kinds of transactions are necessary. Synchronous transactions provide a higher level of abstraction than asynchronous transactions, and are especially efficient for bidirectional information transfer. On the other hand, asynchronous transactions provide maximum flexibility because processes can compute and make transaction calls in parallel in any way they want. A process making a transaction call is not blocked until the receiver gets around to accepting the call; this allows the caller to attend to other events quickly. Asynchronous transactions become particularly important when the inter-process communication time is high, as in a loosely coupled computer network. Asynchronous transactions also allow pipelining of multiple transactions from the same process and allow the receiving process to accept the transactions in the most appropriate order.

7. Ordering Process Interaction Requests

Facilities in Concurrent C for accepting transaction calls in a user-specified order and for specifying asynchronous transactions represent the most important differences between the concurrent programming facilities in Concurrent C and Ada. In Ada, entry calls are accepted in FIFO order. In Concurrent C, by default, transaction calls are accepted in FIFO order, but this order can be altered easily by using the by and suchthat clauses. These clauses allow a transaction call to be accepted based on the values of the transaction arguments.

The transaction mechanism is the synchronization and communication mechanism in both Concurrent C and Ada. According to Bloom [1979], a synchronization mechanism is fully expressive[2] only if it allows synchronization requests to be accepted by a process based on the following information:

1. Name of the synchronization operation.
2. The order in which requests are received.
3. Arguments of the operation.
4. State of the called process.

According to these criteria, Concurrent C, but not Ada, is fully expressive. Ada does not allow the selection of entry calls to be based upon the entry arguments; in Concurrent C, such selection can be made by using the by and suchthat clauses. Nevertheless in Ada, it is possible to simulate selection of entry calls based upon entry arguments, albeit in a roundabout way. The simulation is accomplished by using two rendezvous and an entry array. In the first rendezvous, the server (or accepting) process records the entry arguments and gives a "ticket" to the calling process. The calling process uses this ticket to call the corresponding member of an entry array belonging to the server for the second rendezvous. The calling process waits until the server decides to accept the second call.

---

2. A language is *expressive* if it allows you to solve relevant problems in a straightforward way [Andrews & Olsson 1985].

7.1 Prioritizing Requests — The By Clause

The Concurrent C *accept* statement with the by clause has the form

```
accept transaction-name(p₁, ..., pₙ) by(e)
    { ... }
```

where e is an arithmetic expression involving some or all the transaction parameters, p_1 through p_n, and the local process variables. Expression e is evaluated for each pending transaction call, and the call with the minimum value is accepted [Andrews 1981-82]. The other calls are not discarded; they are held and may be accepted at some later time.

7.1.1 Priority Scheduler Example: The by clause can be used to implement priority scheduling. As an example, consider a transaction parameter urgency that is used to indicate the urgency of a transaction call. In Concurrent C, the by clause

```
by(-urgency)
```

will ensure that the transaction call accepted first is the one with the highest value for the parameter urgency:

File: service.cc

```
process spec service()
{
    trans result get(int urgency, data d);
};
process body service()
{
    for (;;) {
        accept get(urgency, d) by(-urgency)
            { perform request }
    }
}
```

A Concurrent C process makes only one call to get service:

```
s.get(u, d)
```

s is of type process service.

Now here is the Ada version:

File: `service.ada`

```
task SERVICE is
   entry REGISTER(URGENCY: in INTEGER;
                  I: out ID);
   entry GET_SERVICE(ID)(D: DATA;
                         R: out RESULT);
end SERVICE;

task body SERVICE is
begin
   loop
      for J in 1..REGISTER'COUNT loop
         accept REGISTER(URGENCY: INTEGER;
                         I: outID) do
            return service ticket in I;
         end REGISTER;
      end loop;

      if any job is waiting for service then
         J := service ticket for next job to be served;
         accept GET_SERVICE(J)(D: DATA;
                               R: out RESULT) do
            perform service;
         end GET_SERVICE;
      end if;
   end loop;
end SERVICE;
```

An Ada client process, unlike the corresponding Concurrent C process, will have to make two calls to get service:

```
SERVICE.REGISTER(U, I);
SERVICE.GET_SERVICE(I)(D, R);
```

GET_SERVICE is an array of entries; the client must call the element I of GET_SERVICE where I is the ticket supplied to the client by task SERVICE when it registered its request.

It is important that the client process follow this protocol to get service; otherwise, the server process may be blocked indefinitely. To ensure that each client makes both entry calls, the client's interface must be a procedure containing the two calls. Moreover, entries of the server process must not be directly callable by the client processes. This is accomplished by putting the process within a package which provides the procedure containing the two entry calls as an interface.

This solution works as long as the calling process is not aborted. However, if the calling process is aborted after the first call has been accepted, then the server process will hang waiting for the second call. To avoid this problem, an agent process must be created by the interface procedure for each client process to make the calls on behalf of the client process.

The cost of an additional rendezvous may be significant if the two processes are on different machines that do not share memory. It is necessary to use a two-rendezvous solution if the range of the urgency level values is large. For small ranges, a one-rendezvous solution will work: the client calls element *i*, where *i* is the urgency level, of an entry array. However, the general way of accepting arbitrary calls to an entry array requires polling which can be wasteful of resources [Gehani & Cargill 1984]. For very small ranges, polling can be avoided by writing a *select* statement that has an explicit *accept* alternative for each element of the entry array.

7.2 Conditional Acceptance—The Suchthat Clause

A Concurrent C *accept* statement with the `suchthat` clause has the form

```
accept transaction-name(p₁,  ...,  pₙ) suchthat(e)
    { ... }
```

where *e* is an logical expression involving some or all the transaction parameters p_1 through p_n and the local process variables. The first pending transaction call satisfying expression *e* is accepted. If *e* is false for all pending transaction calls, then the execution of the *accept* statement is delayed until an appropriate transaction call arrives. Pending transaction calls for which *e* is false are not discarded; they are held, and may be accepted at some later time.

As in the case of the `by` clause, an Ada program can use an entry array to simulate the Concurrent C `suchthat` clause. However, as before, this requires two entry calls.

7.3 An Example Using Both the Suchthat and By Clauses

In Chapter 2, we presented a disk scheduler process which implements the "elevator" algorithm. This process used both the `suchthat` and `by` clauses. We will implement this algorithm in Ada, but first here again is the Concurrent C version:

File: `disk.h`

```
typedef enum {D_READ, D_WRITE} opcode;
process spec diskScheduler()
{
    trans void request(long blkno,
                    opcode op, char *buf);
};
```

File: `disk-elev.cc`

```
#include "disk.h"
#define BLK_CYL (19*32)      /*blocks per cyl*/
#define CYL(x) ((x)/BLK_CYL)   /*cyl number*/
#define ABS(x) ((x)>0?(x):-(x))
process body diskScheduler()
{
    int pos = 0, phase = 1, dir;

    for (;;)
        select {
            accept request(blkno, op, buf)
                suchthat(phase == 1
                    || CYL(blkno) == pos
                    || CYL(blkno)>pos == dir)
                by(ABS(CYL(blkno)-pos)) {
            if (CYL(blkno) != pos) {
                dir = CYL(blkno) > pos;
                phase = 2;
                pos = CYL(blkno);
                seek to pos;
            }
            start disk operation;
            wait for disk operation to complete;
            }
        or (phase == 2):
            phase = 1;
        }
}
```

The Ada version, given below, uses an entry array which it polls continuously
to accept pending calls:

File: `disk-elev.ada`

```
task DISK_SCHEDULER is
   entry REQUEST(CYLINDER)(BLK: INTEGER;
                          OP: OPCODE;
                          B: BUFFER);
end DISK_SCHEDULER;

task body DISK_SCHEDULER is
   I: CYLINDER; STEP: INTEGER := 1;
   CYL: CYLINDER := CYLINDER'FIRST;
begin
   loop
      for I in CYLINDER loop
         select
            accept REQUEST(CYL)(BLK: INTEGER;
                               OP: OPCODE;
                               B: BUFFER) do
               start disk operation;
               wait for disk operation to complete;
            end REQUEST;
         else
            null;
         end select;
         CYL := CYL + STEP;
      end loop;
      STEP := -STEP;
   end loop;
end DISK_SCHEDULER;
```

Note the difference in the interface of the Concurrent C and Ada programs. In the Concurrent C program, transaction `request` is called with the block number; the disk scheduler calculates the cylinder number. In the Ada program, each element of the entry array REQUEST is called with the cylinder number and the block number, even though the cylinder number could be computed from the block number. This is because an entry is provided for each cylinder and not for each block. An entry can be provided for each block but that will make the entry array REQUEST be very large. Even if the Ada implementation allows large entry arrays, this will significantly increase the amount of polling performed. Again, by using two rendezvous, polling can be avoided. However, the programmer will have to explicitly write code to determine, based on the information supplied in the first rendezvous, which request should be accepted next by the disk scheduler.

8. Process Priorities

In Ada, all processes of the same type must have the same priority because the priority is associated with the process type. Moreover, process priorities are compile-time suggestions to the compiler; the compiler is free to ignore these suggestions (i.e., a compiler is not required to implement priorities).

In Concurrent C, process priorities are assigned dynamically at process creation time. This allows different instances of the same process type to be assigned different priorities. For example, different device drivers, which are instances of the same process type, can be given different priorities. Process priorities can also be changed dynamically and can be queried by means of standard library functions.

Concurrent C facilities are more flexible because process priority can be specified and changed in several ways. The priority of a process can be specified by its parent process at creation time. A process can change its own priority; the priority can also be changed by another process.

9. Transaction Pointers

Concurrent C provides the notion of a *transaction pointers* (similar to the notion of function pointers). A transaction pointer consists of the process id plus the name of the transaction. A transaction pointer is like a capability which can be passed to other processes. There is no such notion in Ada.

To make a transaction call, a process needs to know the type and the id of the called process, and the name of the transaction in question. This information is encapsulated in a transaction pointer. Consequently, when using a transaction pointer to make a transaction call, it is not necessary for the calling process to know the type and id of the called process or the name of the transaction call. If transaction pointers are not being used, the process type and the transaction name must be "hard-wired" in the calling process.

Transaction pointers are useful in several ways:

1. *As a capability*: A server manager can return a transaction pointer specifying the transaction (and the associated process) that should be called to get service. Transaction pointers give the ability to call different transactions belonging to different types of processes, provided that they have the same argument and result types.

2. *As a call back mechanism*: A transaction pointer can be given to another process for call back at a later time. The process to be called back can be of any type and an arbitrary transaction can be called, provided that the argument types and result type match those of the transaction pointer. Without transaction pointers, a general call back mechanism cannot be implemented.

10. Immediate Alternative of the Select Statement

Concurrent C allows a *select* statement to have an *immediate* alternative, which consists of sequential code that is executed whenever an *accept* alternative cannot be taken immediately. Ada's *select* statement has an *else* clause, which is similar to the *immediate* alternative. One difference is that a guard can be attached to the Concurrent C *immediate* alternative, but not to the Ada *else* clause. To see why this is useful, consider a server process that accepts calls from clients, but also has a queue of background work. If there are calls pending, the process wants to accept them. However, when there are no pending calls, the process wants to wait only if there is no background work. In Concurrent C, this can be done with a guarded *immediate* alternative:

```
while (1)
   select {
      accept req1(...) { ... }
   or
      accept req2(...) { ... }
         ...
   or (haveWork):
      do some background work;
   }
```

In Ada, that could be simulated by using a *delay* alternative with a small, perhaps zero, time limit. However, the semantics of a "zero length" delay are not clear, e.g., is executing such a statement like executing the null statement, or does it mean that the process executing this statement will be descheduled and another process allowed to run? An alternative method is to switch between two *select* statements:

```
loop
   if HAVEWORK then
      select
            accept REQ1(...) ...;
         or
            accept REQ2(...) ...;
         ...
      end select;
   else
      select
            accept REQ1(...) ...;
         or
            accept REQ2(...) ...;
         ...
         else
            do some background work;
      end select;
   end if;
end loop;
```

Except for the *else* clause, the two *select* statements must be identical. Therefore the Ada version will be harder to maintain because programmers will have to remember to change both the *select* statements. For example, if an *accept* alternative for a new entry is added only to the first *select* statement, then this new entry will only be handled when the server does not have any background work. This could be a very difficult bug to detect.

11. Collective Process Termination

The *select* statements in both Concurrent C and Ada have a *terminate* alternative that allows a group of processes to terminate collectively. In Concurrent C, the *terminate* alternative can be taken only if *all* the processes in the program have completed or are waiting at a *select* statement with a *terminate* alterative, in which case all processes terminate. That is, in Concurrent C, execution of the *terminate* alternative leads to the termination of the whole program.

However, the Ada, *terminate* alternative is much more general and more complex. An Ada process takes the *terminate* alternative if

1. all its child processes have terminated,
2. there are no pending transaction calls,
3. its parent has completed execution, and
4. all child processes of its parent have either already terminated or are waiting at a *terminate* alternative with conditions 1 and 2 satisfied.

When this happens, the processes taking the *terminate* alternative terminate normally. Meanwhile, the other processes continue execution.

The termination mechanism in Ada is much more general than the one in Concurrent C, because Ada's mechanism allows a subset of the processes in a program to terminate. However, as a result, Ada's mechanism is much more complex, and the semantics are harder to define. Furthermore, Ada's termination mechanism is very difficult to implement efficiently in a distributed multiprocessor environment in which you cannot get a consistent snapshot of the state of all processes on all processors.

12. Miscellaneous

12.1 Associating Interrupts with Transactions

In Ada, an interrupt is associated with an entry by means of a compile-time declaration, called a representation clause. In Concurrent C, this association is done dynamically by using the library function `c_associate`. Dynamic association is more flexible. For example, associations between interrupts and transactions can be made and broken dynamically. One process type can be used to specify a set of device drivers that differ only in the interrupt, buffer and status register addresses. In Ada, a new process type (or process object) must be declared for each device driver; the tedium of specifying a new process type for each device driver can be alleviated by using the generic facilities.

12.2 Nested Process Types

In Concurrent C, process definitions cannot be nested within function definitions or other process types. Consequently, a stack for a newly created process consists of just some block of storage. This design decision reflects the fact that in C, function definitions cannot be nested within other function definitions.

In Ada, the stack for a newly created process must include the stack of the enclosing program components. This makes the implementation somewhat harder because a child process shares the root portion of the parent's stack.

12.3 Process Anytype

As in Ada, process ids in Concurrent C are strongly typed, i.e., process ids must be used consistently with respect to their type. We have found this to be very helpful. However, we also found that strong typing gets in the way when performing general operations on arbitrary processes. Therefore, we added the built-in type `process anytype`, a "wild card" process type. To see the problem with strong typing, consider the built-in function `c_mypid`, which returns the process id of the calling process. In the current version of Concurrent C, `c_mypid` is an ordinary function that returns a `process anytype` value. However, before we added `process anytype`, c_mypid was a pseudo-function, that was allowed only inside a process body, and the compiler made the return type match that of the process calling the function. This was unsatisfactory because c_mypid could not be called from a function, and because the compiler had to treat c_mypid specially. We also encountered similar problems with the parameter types of the functions for aborting processes and for manipulating process priorities; it was annoying to change the compiler each time we added such a function. The process anytype concept provided a neat, extensible solution to these problems.

12.4 Placement of Processes

The Concurrent C create operator allows specification of the processor on which a process should execute. Ada does not make any provision for specifying the processor on which a process should execute. Although Ada can easily be extended to provide facilities for processor placement, Ada has been standardized and will not be changed in the near future.

12.5 Argument Passing Limitations of Concurrent C

Concurrent C lacks explicit facilities for

1. passing variable length arrays as transaction or process arguments, and

2. passing arguments with the modes in out or out.

Note these facilities are not provided in the base language C. In a shared memory implementation of Concurrent C (as in the base language C) lack of the above facilities is not a limitation because pointers can be used to implement these facilities. However, the lack of these facilities will be a handicap in distributed implementations of Concurrent C.

Ada does not suffer from the above argument passing limitations.

12.6 Determining Self-Identity

Concurrent C processes can determine their own process ids by calling the function c_mypid. They can use their process ids to construct transaction pointers that refer to their transactions. Determining its own process id allows a process to pass its id, or a transaction pointer referring to its transactions, to other processes for call back.

This identification can be simulated in Ada by using pointers to processes. Using pointers to simulate process ids may be difficult in a distributed environment without shared memory, because it requires that each process pointer value contain an indication of the processor on which the process resides. To make process pointers work in such an environment, the Ada implementation will have to treat process pointers differently from other pointers because a processor identifier would have to be embedded in the process pointer.

13. Summary

We have compared the concurrent programming facilities in Concurrent C and Ada, and shown that it is easier to write a variety of concurrent programs in Concurrent C than in Ada. Several facilities in Concurrent C contributed towards this end, e.g., the ability to parameterize process types, the `by` and `suchthat` clauses for selectively accepting transaction requests, asynchronous transactions, transaction pointers, and `process anytype`. Although these facilities could be simulated in the Ada language, simulation requires an extra rendezvous or results in a polling program. Furthermore, the Ada program is often not as flexible as the corresponding Concurrent C program.

Appendix D

C: A Synopsis

The C programming language [Kernighan & Ritchie 1978, Ritchie 1980] was originally designed and implemented by Dennis Ritchie in 1972 at AT&T Bell Laboratories. The goal was to design a systems programming language that would replace assembly language programming at AT&T Bell Labs. The phenomenal success of this goal is reflected by the widespread use of C. In this section, we will give you a brief overview of C.

1. Examples Illustrating the Language

We will first give you a flavor of the C programming language by showing you two programs written in C: a function `sine` that computes the *sine* and a main program that acts as an interface between the user and the `sine` function.

1.1 The Main Program: User Interface to the Sine Function

```
                                                File: sine-main.c
    #include <stdio.h>
    #define PR ':'
    #define EPS 0.001      /*desired accuracy*/

 5  main()
    {
        float x;
        double sine();

10      while (putchar(PR), scanf("%f",&x)!=EOF)
            printf("result is %f\n",sine(x, EPS));
    }
```

Lines 1-3 are C preprocessor instructions. Each C program is processed by the C preprocessor before it is compiled. The preprocessing is done automatically when the C compiler is invoked.

The first preprocessor instruction

```
#include <stdio.h>
```

tells the preprocessor to include the file `stdio.h` which contains appropriate declarations for the standard input/output library functions. File `stdio.h` also contains the definition of the constant `EOF`.

The second preprocessor instruction

```
#define PR ':'
```

defines identifier `PR` as the colon character; it will be used to prompt the user for data.

The third preprocessor instruction

```
#define EPS 0.001      /*desired accuracy*/
```

defines identifier `EPS` as the constant 0.001. The character pair "`/*`" begins comments while the pair "`*/`" ends comments.

Line 4 is blank and it is simply ignored by the C compiler. Line 5 specifies the beginning of the special function `main`, which is the first function that is called when a C program is executed. The body of the `main` function, like that of all C functions, is enclosed within curly braces (`{ }`).

The first line in the body of `main` (line 7) defines `x` as a floating point variable; the second line (line 8) declares `sine` as a function which returns a double precision floating point result. Note that all definitions, declarations and statements, with the exception of statements that end with a right curly brace, must be terminated by semicolons.

The next statement (line 10) is a *while* loop of the form

```
while (exp)
    statement
```

Expression *exp* is a compound expression formed from the two expressions

```
putchar(PR)
```

and

```
scanf("%f", &x) != EOF
```

by using the comma operator. The value of this compound expression is the value returned by the last expression, which in this case is the result of comparing the value returned by function `scanf` against the constant `EOF`. The value returned by the function `putchar` is ignored. Note that `scanf` returns `EOF` upon encountering the end of input. All arguments in C are passed by value. Consequently, addresses of variables (e.g., `&x`) are passed to simulate the effect of passing arguments by reference.

1.2 The Sine Function [Wirth 1973, Gehani 1984]

The *sine* of a value x (in radians) is given by the series

$$sine(x) = x - \frac{x^3}{3!} + \frac{x^5}{5!} - \cdots + (-1)^{2i-1} * \frac{x^{2i-1}}{(2^i-1)!} + \cdots$$

This series consists of the recursive terms

$$t_j = -t_{j-1} * \frac{x^2}{k_j*(k_j-1)}, \quad j > 0$$

$$k_j = k_{j-1} + 2, \quad j > 0$$

$$t_0 = x$$

$$k_0 = 1$$

Computation of the sine can be terminated when the value of the last term is less than the sum of the earlier terms multiplied by eps, an arbitrarily small value.

Here is the function for computing the sine:

File: sine.c

```
#include <math.h>    /*contains decl. of fabs*/
double sine(x, eps)
    double x, eps; /*computes sine of "x" with*/
                   /*an accuracy of "eps"      */
{
    double sum, term;
    int k;

    term = x; k = 1; sum = term;
    while (fabs(term) > eps*fabs(sum)) {
        k += 2;
        term *= -(x*x) / (k*(k-1));
        sum += term;
    }
    return sum;
}
```

2. Types

Types are classified into two categories—*fundamental* (simple) and *derived* (structured) types. The fundamental types are character, integer, enumeration, floating point, and the void types. Character, integer, enumeration and floating point types are collectively called the *arithmetic* types. Character, integer and enumeration types are also called *integral* types. Derived types are constructed from the fundamental types; they are the array, the function, the pointer, the structure, and the union types.

Before we delve into the details of C types, here is some terminology. The *declaration* of an object is used to specify only the properties of the object; no storage is allocated for the object. The *definition* of an object is used to specify the properties of the object *and* to allocate storage for the object.

2.1 Characters

Character variables are defined by using the keyword `char`; e.g.,

```
char c, d;
```

Characters can be treated as integers and vice versa. This duality is exploited in programming, e.g., functions which return character values are often declared to be of type integer so that they can return an integer, such as −1, which does not represent any character, to indicate failure or end-of-file.

2.2 Integers

Integers come in three sizes `int`, `short int` (or just `short`), and `long int` (or just `long`). Some examples of integer definitions are

```
int i, j;
short low, high;
long max;
```

If the sign bit is not needed, then type `unsigned int` (or just `unsigned`) may be used to declare an integer object. Unsigned integers are also used to access bits of a machine word.

2.3 Enumeration Types

Enumeration types allow identifiers to be used as values. For example, `jan`, `feb`, `mar`, and so on can be used to denote the months of a year instead of the integers 1, 2, 3, and so on. Here is an example enumeration tag (type) declaration:

```
enum day {mon, tue, wed, thu, fri, sat, sun};
```

The enumeration tag `day` can now be used define variables; e.g.,

```
enum day d, week_day;
```

2.4 Floating Point

There are two varieties of floating point types—`float` (single precision) and `double` (double precision). Examples of variable definitions illustrating the use of these two types are

```
float a, b;
double error;
```

2.5 Arrays

Simple array definitions have the form

type-specifier $x[n_1] [n_2] ... [n_k]$

where x is the identifier for the array name, and n_i is the size of the ith dimension of the array. The elements of the ith dimension are numbered from 0 to n_i-1.

Some examples of array definitions are

```
int page[10];   /*one dimensional array with 10*/
                /*elements numbered from 0 to 9*/
float distance[100][100],
      sales[REGION][MONTHS][ITEMS];
```

where REGION, MONTHS, and ITEMS are constant identifiers defined using C preprocessor statements.

The following examples show how array elements are referenced:

```
page[5]
page[i+j-1]
distance[i][j]
```

2.6 Structures

A *structure* (record) is a composite object that consists of possibly heterogeneous components. Structure types have the form

```
struct {
    list of declarations
}
```

For example, the definition

```
struct {
    double x, y;
} a, b, c[9];
```

defines a and b to be structures, each with two components x and y. Variable c is defined to be an array of structures; each element of c has two components.

Structure tags can be declared and these can then be used to define variables. For example, the following declaration

```
struct student {
   char name[25];
   int id, age;
   char sex;
};
```

defines student to be a structure tag. This tag can be used to define structures, as in

```
struct student s, *senior;
```

which declares s as a structure of type student and senior as a pointer to a structure of type student.

Structure components are accessed using the selected component notation; some examples are a.x, b.y, c[4].y, and s.name.

2.7 Unions

A *union* is like a structure except that only one of its components is active at any given time. As an example of a union object, consider the union geom_fig defined as

```
union {
   float r;          /*circle*/
   float l, b;       /*rectangle*/
   float side[3];    /*triangle*/
   position p;       /*point*/
} geom_fig;
```

The active component is the component last assigned a value. Union components are "overlaid". In general, it does not make sense to access the inactive components.

2.8 Pointers

A *pointer* refers to a memory address, e.g., the starting location of an object. Some examples of pointer definitions are

```
int *pi, *qi;   /*pointers to integer objects*/
struct {
   int x, y;
} *p;           /*pointer to a structure object*/
```

Pointers are used in dynamic object creation. Storage for these objects is allocated by calling the *storage allocators* malloc and calloc.

The null pointer value 0 is associated with pointers of all types. The null pointer indicates that this pointer does not reference a valid object. The null pointer value can be assigned to a pointer variable, and a pointer value can be compared with the null pointer (but only for equality or inequality). Dereferencing the null pointer value either gives garbage or else a run-time error ("memory fault"), depending on the implementation. The header file `stdio.h` defines the macro `NULL` as 0; and by convention, this name is used to refer to the null pointer.

The `sizeof` operator may be used to determine the amount of storage needed for an object of a specific type.

A value is assigned to the object pointed to by a pointer by dereferencing the pointer, e.g.,

```
*pi = 55;
```

2.8.1 Pointing to Defined Objects: Pointers can also be made to point to defined objects (i.e., objects specified in definitions). The address of a defined object is determined by using the *address operator* &. For example, the assignment

```
pi = &i;
```

allows the object with name `i` to also be referenced using the pointer `pi` by using the notation `*pi`.

2.8.2 Relationship between Pointers and Arrays: Arrays and pointers are intimately related in C; in fact, arrays may be considered to be syntactic sugar for pointers. Every array name is treated as a pointer to the first element of the array. A reference to the array element `a[i]` is equivalent to referencing the element pointed to by the pointer value `a+i`, i.e., `*(a+i)`.

2.8.3 Pointers and Structures: Consider the structure pointer `senior` defined earlier. Suppose that `senior` points to a `student` object. Then components of this object can be referenced as `(*senior).name` and `(*senior).id`. These components can also be referenced using the *right arrow* operator, as in `senior->name` and `senior->id`.

2.9 Strings

Strings are arrays of characters. By convention, the last character must be the null character `'\0'`. Because an array name is really a pointer to the first element of an array, string variables can also be considered to be character pointers.

3. Type Declarations

Type declarations are used to collect common properties of objects and give them a name. This *type name* can then be used in subsequent declarations and definitions of these objects. Type declarations have the form

```
typedef type-specifier declarator;
```

where *type-specifier* is the name of some predefined type or one that has been declared earlier; a *declarator* contains the identifier being declared (declarators will be explained in detail later).

Some examples of type declarations are

```
typedef float speed;  /*declares "speed" as a*/
                      /*synonym for "float"  */
typedef float a[5], *pf;
       /*declares type "a" to be an array type*/
       /*with 5 float elements and "pf" as a  */
       /*pointer to "float" objects*/
typedef struct { float x, y; } point;
```

These types can be used to define and declare objects just like the predefined types `float` and `int`. For example, the definition

```
point s1, s2, *p;
```

defines `s1` and `s2` to be structures of type `point` and `p` to be a pointer to a structure of type `point`.

4. Definitions

An *object* is a manipulatable region of storage. A *variable* is a name that is associated with an object. Names can be identifiers or expressions. For example, the expression

```
*p
```

is the name of the object pointed to by the pointer `p`.

Objects may be associated with identifiers using definitions of the form

storage-class type-specifier declarators;

where either of *storage-class* or *type-specifier* may be omitted. The *storage-class* and *type-specifier* apply to the declarators, each of which defines one object. Each declarator may be followed by an *initializer* which specifies the initial value of the object being defined in the declarator.

4.1 Storage Classes

Objects can have one of the following storage classes:

storage class	meaning
auto	Local variables that are allocated at block (i.e., the compound statement) entry and deallocated at block exit.
static	Local variables that exist across block invocations and global variables used for communication between functions that are defined in the same file.
extern	Global variables used for communication between functions including independently compiled functions.
register	auto variables which should be stored, if possible, in registers for fast access.

If no storage class is specified, then objects defined inside a function are assigned the storage class auto; objects defined outside functions are assigned the storage class extern. Functions without any specified storage class are always assigned the storage class extern.

For an extern object, storage is allocated only when the storage class is not specified explicitly in its definition. Explicit specification of the extern storage class implies that the object will be defined elsewhere and that no storage is to be allocated—the declaration is being given here only for type checking and code generation purposes. There must be only one definition of an extern variable.

4.2 Data Types

The data type specified in a declaration or a definition can be one of the *type specifiers*

```
char
int
short int   (or just short)
long int   (or just long)
unsigned int   (or just unsigned)
unsigned char
float
double   (or long float)
void
struct tag
union tag
enum tag
typedef-name
```

If the data type of an object is not specified, then it is assumed to be `int`.

4.3 Declarators

Each declarator contains exactly one identifier which is the name being given to the object specified in the declarator. Declarators must be separated by commas:

declarator, *declarator*, ... , *declarator*

The form and semantics of the declarators are explained in the table given below. Assume that *T* is the data type specified in the object definition or declaration, or in the type definition:

declarator	meaning
identifier	*identifier* of type *T* is being declared or defined.
(*declarator*)	Same as *declarator*.
∗declarator	Same as *declarator* in an object declaration with the data type being *pointer to T*.
declarator( )	Same as *declarator* in an object declaration with the data type *function returning a value of type T*.
declarator[*n*]	Same as *declarator* in a definition or a declaration with the data type *array of n* elements of type *T*; *n* must be a constant expression and the elements are numbered from 0 to *n*−1.

4.4 Examples of Variable (Object) Definitions

The definition

```
int i, *ip, f(), *fip(), (*pfi)();
```

declares the following variables:

`i`	an integer variable
`ip`	pointer to an integer variable
`f`	function returning an integer
`fip`	function returning a pointer to an integer
`pfi`	pointer to a function that returns an integer

The functions (`f` and `fip`) have the storage class `extern`. If this definition appears inside a function, then the variables (`i`, `ip`, and `pfi`) have the storage class `auto`; otherwise they have the storage class `extern`.

4.5 Initializers

Initializers are used in definitions to give variables initial values. An initializer for a variable follows its declarator, and has one of the following forms:

> = *value*
> = { *list of values* }

Here are some examples:

```
int low = 100, high = 0;
long arr[5] = {0, 1, 2, 3, 4 };
struct {
    char *name;
    int tag;
} entry = {"Sam", 1};
```

5. Operators

C has a rich variety of operators. In this section, we will give a brief summary of these operators.

1. Function Call and Selection Operators:

   ( ) (function call)
   [ ] (array subscript)
   .   (structure component selector)
   ->   (selecting a component of structure via a pointer)

2. Unary Operators:

   *   (dereferencing)
   &   (address of)
   –   (negation)
   !   (logical negation)
   ~   (one's complement)
   ++   (increment; postfix and prefix)
   --   (decrement; postfix and prefix)
   sizeof (storage size of a value or a type)

3. Multiplicative Operators:

   *   (multiplication)
   /   (division)
   %   (remainder)

4. Additive Operators:

> + (addition)
> − (subtraction)

5. Shift Operators:

> << (left shift)
> >> (right shift)

6. Relational Operators:

> < (less than)
> > (greater than)
> <= (less than or equal to)
> >= (greater than or equal to)

7. Equality/Inequality Operators:

> == (equality)
> != (inequality)

8. Bitwise Operators:

> & (and)
> ^ (exclusive or)
> ¦ (inclusive or)

9. Logical ("Short-Circuit") Operators:

> && (and)
> ¦¦ (or)

10. Conditional Operator: ?:. The conditional operator is the only operator that requires three operands; the result of the expression

$$a \ ? \ b \ : \ c$$

is b if a is non-zero and c otherwise.

11. Assignment Operators:

> = (simple assignment)
> $\theta=$ (compound assignment).

θ can be one of the symbols +, −, *, /, %, >>, <<, &, ^, or ¦. The assignment expression

$$v \ \theta= \ e$$

is roughly equivalent to the assignment expression

$$v \ = \ v \ \theta \ e$$

The only difference is that the $\theta=$ operator evaluates the expression v only once.

12. Comma Operator: Combines two expressions into one and the value of the combined expression is the value of the right expression.

5.1 Operator Precedence Summary

Operator precedence is summarized by the following table, the operators being listed vertically in order of decreasing precedence:

precedence	operators	symbols				associativity
1	Function Call/Selection	( )	[ ]	.	->	left to right
2	Unary	++ --	* -	& sizeof	~	right to left
3	Multiplicative	*	/	%		left to right
4	Additive	+	-			left to right
5	Shift	<<	>>			left to right
6	Relational	<	>	<=	>=	left to right
7	Equality/Inequality	==	!=			left to right
8	Bitwise *and*	&				left to right
9	Bitwise *exclusive or*	^				left to right
10	Bitwise *inclusive or*	¦				left to right
11	Logical *and*	&&				left to right
12	Logical *or*	¦ ¦				left to right
13	Conditional	? :				right to left
14	Assignment	=	$\theta=$			right to left
15	Comma	,				left to right

6. Control Structures

6.1 Null Statement

The *null* statement is denoted by a semicolon, e.g.,

```
;
```

This statement is used when a statement is required by the C syntax, but no action is logically needed. For example, a *null* statement is used as the body of the following *while* loop

```
while ((c = getchar()) == ' ')
    ;
```

which skips to the first non-blank character.

6.2 Expression Statement

An expression followed by a semicolon is a statement:

expression;

The expression is evaluated for its side-effects, and the resulting value, if any, is discarded. Normally the outermost operator in this expression is an assignment or a function call. The following are examples of expression statements:

```
j = 1;
j += k;
k++;
*qc = 'c';
printf("*qc is %c\n", *qc);
```

Something like

```
i+j;
```

is a legal—but useless—statement.

6.3 Compound or Block Statement

The *compound* or *block* statement is used to group many statements into one logical statement and to restrict the visibility of declarations and definitions to a part of the program. The *compound* statement has the form

```
{
        definitions
        statements
}
```

Variables defined inside the *compound* statement override definitions of variables with the same name for the scope of the *compound* statement.

6.4 If Statement

The *if* statement has two forms:

if (*expression*) *statement₁*

and

if (*expression*) *statement₁* else *statement₂*

If *expression* evaluates to true (non-zero) then *statement₁* is executed. Otherwise, this completes execution of the first form of the *if* statement, while in case of the second form *statement₂* is executed. *If* statements may be nested, and either form can be used. In this case, an *else* part is associated with the nearest *if* that does not have an *else*.

6.5 Loops

There are three kinds of loops—the *while*, the *for*, and the *do*. The *while* loop has the form

```
while (expression) statement
```

The *statement* is executed as long as *expression* is true (non-zero). The *expression* is tested before *statement* is executed.

The *for* statement

```
for (expression₁; expression₂; expression₃) statement
```

is a convenient abbreviation of the following paradigm using the *while* loop:

```
expression₁ ;
while (expression₂) {
    statement;
    expression₃ ;
}
```

The $expression_1$ represents the loop initialization part, $expression_2$ represents the loop test, and $expression_3$ represents the loop reinitialization.

The loop

```
do statement while (expression);
```

is executed as long as *expression* is true. The *expression* is tested after *statement* is executed.

6.6 Switch Statement

The *switch* statement is used for multiway branching. Here is an example:

```
switch (c) {
    case '+': add; break;
    case '-': subtract; break;
    case '*': multiply; break;
    case '/': divide; break;
    default: put on stack;
}
```

The *switch* branches to the statement after the `case` label whose value matches that of the *switch* expression. Execution continues from that point, disregarding any subsequent `case` labels. That is, the body of the *switch* statement is a linear string of statements. The `case` prefixes act as labels, but they do *not* divide the *switch* statement into a mutually-exclusive set of alternatives. Unless you use a *break* statement, which branches to the statement after the *switch* statement body, execution flows from one "alternative" to the next. Thus if x is 0, the following calls `printf` twice:

```
switch (x) {
    case '0': printf("x is 0\n"); /*want "break"*/
    case '1': printf("x is 1\n");
}
```

In general, you should always put a *break* statement at the end of each alternative.

6.7 The Break Statement

The *break* statement is used to exit from the immediately enclosing *while*, *do*, *for*, or *switch* statements. Control passes onto the statement following the statement exited. The *break* statement has the form

```
break;
```

6.8 The Continue Statement

The *continue* statement is used to skip the remaining portion of the current iteration of the immediately enclosing *while*, *do*, or *for* loop. The next iteration is then initiated provided it is allowed by the loop conditions; otherwise the loop is terminated. The *continue* statement has the form

```
continue;
```

6.9 The Return Statement

The *return* statement is used to return the function result to the calling program and to terminate the execution of the function. The *return* statement has two forms

```
return expression;
```

where the value of *expression* is the function result, and

```
return;
```

A function can have more zero or more *return* statements. The first form of the *return* statement should be used only in functions that return values. The second form should be used only in functions that do not return any value, i.e., `void` functions.

6.10 The Goto Statement

The *goto* statement is used to unconditionally transfer control to the statement with the specified label:

```
goto label;
```

6.11 Statement Labels

Any statement in C can be labeled by prefixing it with a label as follows:

label: *statement*

label is an identifier.

7. Functions

Control abstraction is provided in C by means of functions which have the form

static$_{opt}$ *type-specifier declarator*(*param-list$_{opt}$*)
    parameter declarations$_{opt}$
{
    function body
}

The value returned by a function cannot be an array or a function although a function can return a pointer to an array or a function. Functions that do not return a value should be specified to have the void result type.

Functions terminate by completing execution of their bodies or by executing a *return* statement. Functions that do not return a value execute a *return* statement of the form

    return;

Functions that return a value execute a *return* statement of the form

    return *e*;

which causes the function to yield the result *e*.

The storage class static is used to control the visibility of a function. A function with the storage class static is not visible outside the file containing it.

Parameter declarations are similar to definitions of ordinary variables except that the only storage class that can be specified is register. When declaring array parameters, the size of the first dimension may be omitted, as in

    int a[], b[4], d[][4];

7.1 Calling Functions

Function calls have the form

function-name(*argument-list$_{opt}$*)

where the parameters are expressions. Some examples are

```
max(a, 5)
max(max(a, 5), e)
fopen(argv[1], "r")
partition(a, 1, u, &i, &j);
quicksort(a, 1, j);
time()
```

All arguments are passed by value in C. The effect of passing arguments by reference can be achieved by passing pointers to objects.

8. Source File Organization

C source files are usually organized as follows:

> *preprocessor statements —constant and macro declarations, file inclusions*
> *external variables*
> *functions*

This structure is an informal guideline, and does not cover all cases. For example, the C preprocessor statements can be given anywhere in the file; they are not restricted to the top portion of a file.

A C program can be split across many files, for example, some of the functions may be placed in other files so that they can be compiled independently.

Annotated Bibliography

Andler, S. 1979. Predicate Path Expressions. Conference Record of the *Sixth Annual ACM Symposium on Principles of Programming Languages* (1979), pp. 226-236, San Antonio, Texas.

Andrews, G. R. 1981. Synchronizing Resources. *TOPLAS*, v3, no. 4 (October), pp. 405-430.

The concept of *synchronizing resources* is proposed to allow the writing of efficient concurrent programs for both computers with shared memory and computers that communicate by using message passing. Synchronizing resources are somewhat similar to Ada tasks. Processes within a synchronizing resource interact by means of operations (i.e., message passing) and shared variables, while those in different resources interact only by means of operations. Contains many illustrative examples.

Andrews, G. R. 1982. The Distributed Programming Language SR — Mechanisms, Design and Implementation. *Software —Practice and Experience*, v12, pp. 719-753.

Andrews, G. R. and R. A. Olsson 1985. The Evolution of the SR Language. TR 85-22, Computer Science Dept, University of Arizona, Tucson, Arizona 85721.

Andrews, G. R. and F. B. Schneider 1983. Concepts and Notations for Concurrent Programming. *ACM Computing Surveys* (March), pp. 3-43.

Detailed survey of the evolution of concurrent programming facilities. Facilities for concurrent programming languages such as Modula, Concurrent Pascal and the Ada language are summarized. Concurrent programming languages are classified into three categories: *procedure-oriented*, *message-oriented* and *operation-oriented*. In procedure-oriented languages, such as Modula, Mesa and Edison, process interaction occurs by modifying the environment such as shared variables. This category is also called the *monitor model*. In message-oriented languages, such as the Ada language, CSP, Gypsy and PLITS, process interaction occurs using messages; processes do not share variables. In operation-oriented languages, such as DP and StarMod, process interaction uses the *remote procedure* call.

ANSI C 1988a. *Draft Proposed American National Standard for Information Systems —Programming Language C.*

ANSI C 1988b. Rationale for *Draft Proposed American National Standard for Information Systems —Programming Language C.*

Arevalo, S. and N. H. Gehani 1988. Replica Consensus in Fault Tolerant Concurrent C. Submitted for Publication.

AT&T UNIX 1983. *Unix System V User Reference Manual (Release 5.2).* AT&T Bell Laboratories.

Barnes, J. G. P. 1980. An Overview of Ada. *Software—Practice and Experience*, v10, pp. 851-887.

Ben-Ari, M. 1982. *Principles of Concurrent Programming.* Prentice-Hall.

Discusses concurrent programming with an emphasis on topics such as mutual exclusion, semaphores, monitors, and the Ada rendezvous. It contains the development of Dekker's algorithm to implement mutual exclusion without the aid of any special primitives. Several initial versions of Dekker's algorithm and the dining-philosophers problem, representing initial attempts to arrive at the correct solution, are given along with the final version. Correctness of concurrent programs is also discussed.

Berkeley UNIX 1986. *UNIX Programmer's Manual (4.3 BSD).* Computer Science Division, Department of Electrical Engineering and Computer Science, University of California, Berkeley, CA 94720.

Bloom, T. 1979. Evaluating Synchronization Mechanisms. *Proceedings of the Seventh Symposium on Operating Systems Principles. ACM-SIGOPS,* December 1979.

Brinch Hansen, P. 1972. A Comparison of Two Synchronizing Concepts. *Acta Informatica*, v1, pp. 190-199.

The use of semaphores and conditional critical regions in synchronizing processes is compared with the use of conditional critical regions. Programs that use conditional critical regions are clearer and much easier to prove correct than those that use semaphores.

Brinch Hansen, P. 1973a. *Operating System Principles.* Prentice-Hall, 1973.

Brinch Hansen, P. 1973b. Concurrent Programming Concepts. *ACM Computing Surveys*, v6, no. 4 (December), pp. 223-245.

A survey of concurrent programming features from semaphores to monitors. Points out advantages of high-level features for concurrency in programming languages, e.g., easier understanding of concurrent programs and automatic checking of assertions. Features from event queues and semaphores to critical regions and monitors are discussed. Contains many examples.

Brinch Hansen, P. 1975. The Programming Language Concurrent Pascal. *IEEE Transactions on Software Engineering*, v1, no. 2 (June), pp. 199-207.

The programming language Pascal is extended for concurrency by adding processes and monitors that define the data shared by processes and synchronization procedures by which processes access this data.

Brinch Hansen, P. 1977. *The Architecture of Concurrent Programs.* Prentice-Hall.

Discusses how monitors can be used to systematically construct concurrent programs. The development of an operating system called Solo is described. The programming language Concurrent Pascal is used.

Brinch Hansen, P. 1978a. Distributed Processes: A Concurrent Programming Concept. *CACM*, v21, no. 11 (November).

Brinch Hansen proposes that processes communicate by calling procedures in other processes and synchronize by means of guarded regions. No shared variables are used. Contains many examples.

Brinch Hansen, P. 1978b. Multiprocessor Architectures for Concurrent Programs. *ACM 78 Conf. Proc.* (December), pp. 317-323, Washington, DC.

Computer architectures should be tailored to support programming languages. A hierarchical multiprocessor architecture is proposed for real-time programs written in a block structured concurrent programming language with monitors and processes.

Brinch Hansen, P. 1979. A Keynote Address on Concurrent Programming. *Computer*, v12, no. 5 (May), pp. 50-56.

First discusses history of concurrent programming. Contends that the whole concurrent programming problem was triggered by hardware developments in the early 1960's, and that cheap mini/micro computers have changed the economics, but have not posed new programming problems. However, networks will pose new problems, because they do away with shared memory, thus requiring communication via messages. What is worse, nondeterministic message passing is necessary; a process cannot always predict exactly what it must do next. Mentions several open areas in concurrent programming.

Brinch Hansen, P. 1986. JOYCE: A Programming Language for Distributed Systems. Report No. 86/5. Computer Science Dept., Univ of Copenhagen, Copenhagen, Denmark.

Bruno, G. 1984. Using Ada for Discrete Event Simulation. *Software — Practice and Experience*, v14, no. 7, pp. 685-695, July 1984.

Calingaert, P. 1982 *Operating System Elements.* Prentice-Hall, 1982.

Campbell, R. H. and A. N. Habermann 1974. The Specification of Process Synchronization by Path Expressions. *Lecture Notes in Computer Science*, v16, Springer-Verlag.

Cargill, T. A. 1981. A Robust Distributed Solution to the Dining Philosophers Problem. *Software —Practice and Experience*, v10, no. 10, October 1982.

Presents an elegant solution, written in the Ada language, in which the philosophers do not deadlock or starve. The solution is distributed in that synchronization and communication is limited to adjacent philosophers and the impact of a faltering philosopher is limited to his immediate neighborhood.

Cmelik, R. F. 1986. Concurrent Make: A Distributed Program in Concurrent C. AT&T Bell Laboratories.

Cmelik, R. F., N. H. Gehani and W. D. Roome 1988a. Fault Tolerant Concurrent C. A Tool for Writing Fault Tolerant Distributed Programs. *The 18th International Symposium on Fault-Tolerant Computing* (1988), Tokyo, Japan.

Cmelik, R. F., N. H. Gehani, and W. D. Roome 1988b. Experience with Multiple Processor Versions of Concurrent C. To be published in *IEEE Transactions on Software Engineering*.

Coffman, E. G., M. J. Elphick and A. Shoshani 1971. System Deadlocks. *ACM Computing Surveys*, v3, no. 2 (June), pp. 67-78.

A comprehensive survey of theoretical and practical analysis of the deadlock problem.

Coleman, D. 1980. Concurrent Pascal—An Appraisal. In *On the Construction of Programs*, edited by R. M. McKeag and A. M. MacNaghten, Cambridge Press, England.

Concurrent Pascal is a simple portable extension of a subset of Pascal. It is well suited to the design of simple single-user operating systems and encourages the systematic design and testing of modular programs.

Conway, M. E. 1963. Design of a Separable Transition Diagram Compiler. *CACM* (July), pp. 396-408.

Cook, R. P. 1980. *MOD—A Language for Distributed Programming. *IEEE Transactions on Software Engineering*, vSE-6, no. 6 (November), pp. 563-571.

Courtois, P. J., F. Heymans and D. L. Parnas 1971. Concurrent Control with "Readers" and "Writers". *CACM*, v14, no. 10 (October), pp. 667-668.

The problem of mutual exclusion of independent *reader* and *writer* processes is posed and two solutions presented.

Cox, I. J. and N. Gehani 1987. Concurrent C and Robotics. *1987 IEEE Conference on Robotics and Automation*, Raleigh, NC.

Cox, I. J. and N. Gehani 1988. Concurrent Programming and Robotics. To be published in *International Journal of Robotics Research*.

Dijkstra, E. W. 1968a. Cooperating Sequential Processes. In *Programming Languages*, edited by F. Genuys, Academic Press.

The concepts of concurrent statements, semaphores, and critical regions are introduced and mutual exclusion is discussed.

Dijkstra, E. W. 1968b. Structure of the "THE" Multiprocessing System. *CACM*, v11, no. 5 (May), pp. 341-346.

Dijkstra, E. W. 1971. Hierarchical Ordering of Sequential Processes. *Acta Informatica*, v1, pp. 115-138.

Dijkstra, in this classic paper, states that concurrency in an operating system should be controlled in steps which will lead to a layered design of an operating system. Processes in each layer should harmoniously cooperate with each other. A key problem in implementing this cooperation is *mutual exclusion.* Mutual exclusion is discussed in detail with many examples. Correctness of these examples of concurrent programming is also discussed. It is in this paper that Dijkstra first posed the dining-philosophers problem.

DoD 1979. *Rationale for the Design of the Ada Programming Language. SIGPLAN Notices*, v14, no. 6 (June), part B.

A comprehensive document that provides justification for the design of the preliminary version of the Ada language. This document is a must for all those interested in language design and those who want to know more about the Ada language.

DoD 1983. *Reference Manual for the Ada Programming Language.* United States Department of Defense.

Feldman, J. A. 1979. High Level Programming for Distributed Computing. *CACM*, v22, no. 6 (June), pp. 353-368.

Describes the message-module-transaction key paradigm used in University of Rochester's distributed computation experiments. A "module" seems to be analogous to a process. It can send messages to other modules, with optional "transaction keys". A message consists of a set of slot-value pairs. When receiving a message, a module can specify an optional sender, an optional key, both, or neither. all messages for a given sender or receiver will be kept in order.

He discusses "distributed jobs" which are arbitrary collections of modules, all "owned" by the same "user", running on one or more machines, and communicating via messages.

Feldman, S. I. 1979. Make—A Program for Maintaining Computer Programs. *Software — Practice and Experience*, v9, pp. 255-265.

Feuer, A. 1982. *C Puzzle Book.* Prentice-Hall.

Franta, W. R. 1977. *The Process View Of Simulation.* North-Holland.

Gehani, N. H. 1984a. *Ada: Concurrent Programming.* Prentice-Hall.

Gehani, N. H. 1984b. Broadcasting Sequential Processes (BSP). *IEEE Transactions on Software Engineering*, vSE-10 (July).

Gehani, N. H. and T. A. Cargill 1984. Concurrent Programming in the Ada Language: The Polling Bias. *Software—Practice and Experience*, v14, no. 5, pp. 413-427, May 1984.

Ada language concurrent programming facilities lead to and encourage the design of programs that use polling rather than non-polling paradigms.

Gehani, N. H. 1985. *C: An Advanced Introduction*. Computer Science Press.

Gehani, N. H. and W. D. Roome 1985. Concurrent C—An Overview. *Proc. of the Winter 1985 Usenix Conference*, Dallas, Texas, pp. 43-50.

Gehani, N. H. and W. D. Roome 1986. Concurrent C. *Software—Practice & Experience*, v16, no.9 (September), pp. 821-844.

Gehani, N. H. 1988a. Message Passing: Synchronous vs Asynchronous. Submitted for Publication.

Gehani, N. H. 1988b. Capsules: A Shared-Memory Mechanism. Submitted for Publication.

Gehani, N. H. 1988c. *C: An Advanced Introduction (ANSI C Edition)*. Computer Science Press.

Gehani, N. H. and W. D. Roome 1988a. Rendezvous Facilities: Concurrent C and the Ada Language. To be published in *IEEE Transactions on Software Engineering*.

Gehani, N. H. and W. D. Roome 1988b. Concurrent C++: Concurrent Programming With Class(es). To be published in *Software—Practice & Experience*.

Gentleman, W. M. 1981. Message Passing Between Sequential Processes: The Reply Primitive and the Administrator Concept. *Software—Practice and Experience*, v11, pp. 435-466.

The issues in message passing as a means of communication and synchronization between processes are discussed. The use of the *administrator* concept as a concurrent programming style is advocated and illustrated with many examples.

German, S. M. 1984. *Monitoring for Deadlock and Blocking in Ada Tasking*. *IEEE Transactions on Software Engineering*, vSE 10, no. 6 (November), pp. 764-777.

Describes techniques to transform an Ada program into an equivalent one that detects whenever the tasks have deadlocked. The basic idea is to insert calls to a separate monitor task before each interaction; the monitor keeps the graph of interactions and determines whether tasks have deadlocked. Cannot handle tasks that use the terminate alternative.

Habermann, A. N. and D. E. Perry 1983. *Ada for Experienced Programmers*. Addison-Wesley.

Havender, J. W. 1968. Avoiding Deadlock in Multi-Tasking Systems. *IBM Systems Journal*, v2, pp. 74-84.

Designers and users of concurrent programs must be aware of the deadlock problem. Conditions that lead to deadlock and techniques to avoid deadlock are discussed.

Hoare, C. A. R. 1962. Quicksort. *Computer Journal*, v5, no. 1, pp. 10-15.

Hoare, C. A. R. 1974. Monitors: An Operating System Concept. *CACM*, v17, no. 10 (October), pp. 549-557.

The monitor is proposed as a method of structuring an operating system. Contains several illustrative examples.

Hoare, C. A. R. 1978. Communicating Sequential Processes. *CACM*, v21, no. 8 (August), pp. 666-677.

Proposes a concurrent programming model in which parallel processes communicate and synchronize by using input and output commands. Combined with Dijkstra's guarded commands, this idea becomes very powerful and versatile. Structuring programs as a composition of communicating sequential processes is advocated by Hoare as fundamental. Contains many excellent examples.

Holt, R. C. 1972. Some Deadlock Properties of Computer Systems. *ACM Computing Surveys*, v4, no. 3 (September), pp. 179-196.

Discusses deadlock in the context of operating systems, although the discussion extends easily to programming languages with concurrency in them. Deadlock is discussed in terms of a graph-theoretic model and efficient algorithms for deadlock detection and prevention are given.

Kapilow D. A. 1985. Real-Time Programming in a UNIX Environment. *1985 Symposium on Factory Automation and Robotics*, Courant Institute of Mathematical Sciences, New York University.

Kaubisch, W. H., R. H. Perrot and C. A. R. Hoare 1976. Quasiparallel Programming. *Software—Practice and Experience*, v6, pp. 341-356, 1976.

A concurrent programming language Simone, an extension of Pascal, is described. Simone is designed primarily for programming simulation applications.

Kernighan, B. W. and D. M. Ritchie 1978. *The C Programming Language.* Prentice-Hall.

Kieburtz, R. B. and A. Silberschatz 1979. Comments on "Communicating Sequential Processes". *TOPLAS*, v1, no. 2, pp. 218-225.

They discuss communicating sequential processes [Hoare 1978] In particular, they mention several problems caused by the process sending a message is blocked until the process receiving the message is read to receive the message.

Kleinrock, L. 1975. *Queueing Systems: Volumes I and II*. John Wiley & Sons.

Lampson, B. W. and D. D. Redell 1980. Experience with Processes and Monitors in Mesa. *CACM*, v23, no. 2 (Feb), pp. 105-117.

Leland, M. D. P. and W. D. Roome 1985. The Silicon Database Machine. *Database Machines: Fourth International Workshop* edited by D. J. DeWitt and H. Boral. Springer-Verlag, pp. 169-189.

Leland, M. D. P. and W. D. Roome 1988. The Silicon Database Machine: Rationale, Design, and Results. *Database Machines and Knowledge Base Machines* edited by M. Kitsuregawa and H. Tanaka. Kluwer Academic Publishers, pp. 311-324.

Liskov, B. and R. Scheifler 1983. Guardians and Actions: Linguistic Support for Robust Distributed Programs. *ACM TOPLAS*, v5, no. 3 (July), pp. 381-404.

"Robust" means crash recovery provided automatically, by the underlying language support system. This is based on *atomic types*, *nested actions* and *guardians*.

An atomic type is an abstract data type whose operators are *indivisible*. An action may contain any number of nested actions; the nested actions can be executed sequentially or concurrently. A guardian is an abstraction of a node of a distributed computer system. It encapsulates one or more resources, and provides controlled access to those resources. The external interface of a guardian consists of a set of operations called *handlers*, which may be invoked by other guardians. Internally, a guardian contains data objects and processes. After a crash of the guardian's node, the language support system re-creates the guardian using stable memory.

Liskov, B., M. Herlihy and L. Gilbert 1986. Limitations of Remote Procedure Call and Static Process Structure for Distributed Computing. *Proceedings 13th ACM Symp. on the Principle of Programming Languages*. St. Petersburg, Florida.

Liskov, B., T. Bloom, D. Gifford, R. Scheifler and W. Weihl 1987. Communication in the Mercury System. MIT.

Liskov, B. Distributed Programming in Argus. *CACM*, v31, no. 3 (March) pp. 300-312.

Pratt, V. 1983 Five Paradigm Shifts in Programming Language Design and Their Realization in Viron, a Dataflow Programming Environment. *Conference Record of the Tenth Annual ACM Symposium on Principles of Programming Languages* (January), Austin, Texas.

Ritchie, D. M. 1980. The C Programming Language—Reference Manual. AT&T Bell Laboratories.

Roome, W. D. 1986a. Discrete Event Simulation in Concurrent C. AT&T Bell Laboratories.

Roome, W. D. 1986b. The CTK: An Efficient Multi-Processor Kernel. AT&T Bell Laboratories.

Smith-Thomas, B. 1984. Managing I/O in Concurrent Programming. The Concurrent C Window Manager. AT&T Bell Laboratories.

Stroustrup, B. 1986. *The C++ Programming Language*. Addison Wesley.

Tanenbaum, A. S. and R. V. Renesse 1985. Distributed Operating Systems. *Computing Surveys*, v17, no. 4 (December).

UNIX 1983a. *UNIX System User's Manual (Release 5.3)*. AT&T Bell Laboratories.

UNIX 1983b. *UNIX Programmer's Manual (4.2 BSD)* 1983. Computer Science Division, Department of Electrical Engineering and Computer Science, University of California, Berkeley, CA 94720.

Welsh, J., A. Lister and E. J. Salzman 1980. A Comparison of Two Notations for Process Communication. In *Language Design and Programming Methodology*, edited by J. Tobias, *Lecture Notes in Computer Science Series*, No. 79, Springer-Verlag.

Comparison of Hoare's "Communicating Sequential Processes" and Brinch Hansen's "Distributed Processes".

Welsh, J. and A. Lister 1981. A Comparative Study of Task Communication in Ada. *Software—Practice and Experience*, v11, pp. 257-290.

Compares the mechanism for process communication in Ada with those in Hoare's "Communicating Sequential Processes" and Brinch Hansen's "Distributed Processes".

Wirth, N. 1982. *Programming in Modula-2*. Springer-Verlag.

Woo, N. S. and R. Sharma 1987. An AND-OR Parallel Execution System for Logic Program Evaluation. *Proc. of 1987 International Conference on Parallel Processing*.

Index

& operator 275
-> operator 275
. operator 275
.cc for Concurrent C source files, suffix 2
_Null process 20
0, null pointer value 274
0, null process value 216, 34
0, null transaction pointer value 218, 55
32100 microprocessor, AT&T 239, 245
68020 microprocessor, Motorola 240

a

abortion, process 80, 224
accept alternative 43
accept statement 9, 39, 219
accept statement, general form of a 219
  possible extensions to 234
  rationale for 233
accessing components of a `struct` 274, 275
accessing components of a `union` 274
active state 79, 215
Ada 165, 166, 167, 251
Ada sol. for *producer-consumer* example 165, 253
Ada, comparison of Concurrent C and 251
address of operator 275
alternative, *select* statement 43
ANSI C 211, 224
`anytype, process` 35, 217, 265
argument declarations, process 213
argument passing modes for functions 270, 286
argument passing modes for transactions 241, 266
arguments, process 4, 11, 254
arguments, transaction 10
arithmetic types 271
array declarations, omitting dimensions of 285
array references 273
array types 273
arrays and pointers, relationship between 275
asynchronous & synch. message passing, eq. of 154, 173
asynchronous message passing 153, 167, 168
asynchronous message passing models 154
asynchronous message passing, advantages of 172
  cost of 175
asynchronous transactions 6, 55, 212, 255
asynchronous transactions, when to use 56

AT&T 32100 microprocessor 239, 245
`auto` storage class 277
automobile cruise controller example 87

b

betting processes example 23
block statement 282
body, process 11
break statement 283, 284
built-in functions 33
busy waiting, definition of 187
`by` clause 40, 220, 221, 257

c

C functions 90
C operator precedence, summary of 281
C operators, summary of 279
C preprocessor 269, 286
C++ 133
C++ class declarations 133
C++ class declarations, private components 133
  public components 134
C++ constructors 134, 135, 148, 151
C++ derived classes 143
C++ destructors 134, 142, 145, 148, 151
C++ friend functions 134
C++ member functions 134
C++ member functions, inheritance of 143
C++ virtual functions 143
C++, brief summary of 133
  comments in 135
C, comments in 270
call-by-reference 270, 286
call-by-value 270, 286
calling a function 285
`calloc` function 274
CCC, Concurrent C compiler 2
chain line printer driver example 45
`char` type 272
character strings 275
child process 11, 215

class declarations 133
class declarations, private components 133
           public components 134
cmake program 114
collective process termination 11, 49, 223, 243, 264
comments in C 270
comments in C++ 135
Communicating Sequential Processes (CSP) 162, 166
comparison of Ada and Concurrent C 251
compiling and running a Concurrent C program 9
completed state 34, 79, 215
components of a struct, accessing 274, 275
components of a union, accessing 274
compound statement 282
concurrency, maximization of 185
Concurrent C compiler CCC 2
Concurrent C shared memory multiproc. impl. 239, 248
Concurrent C, comparison of Ada and 251
        debugging programs in 246
        Fault Tolerant 248
        file access from 244
        implementation of 235
        LAN implementation of 237, 247
        multiprocessor impl. of 237, 239, 247
        possible extensions to 234, 241
        timings for various operations of 246
        uniprocessor implementation of 236
Concurrent C++ 133
concurrentc.h, standard header file 34, 79, 224
concurrent make example 114
concurrent readers and writers example 69
conditional acceptance of transaction calls 40, 221, 259
conditional critical regions 159
constructors 134, 135, 148, 151
context switching 231, 240
context switching, timings for 246
continue statement 284
continuous time simulation 189
cost of asynchronous message passing 175
cost of synchronous message passing 175
create operator 3, 255
create operator, general form of the 11, 215
creation, process 2, 11, 254, 255
creation, timings for process 246
critical reg. sol. for *producer-consumer* example 159
critical regions 159, 166
CSP 162, 166, 167
CSP solution for *producer-consumer* example 162
cumulative time drift 38
c_, global names starting with 33
c_abort function 35, 80, 224
c_active function 80, 225
c_associate function 86, 227
c_bestprocessor function 85, 226
c_changepriority function 82, 225
c_completed function 80, 225
c_CONCURRENT 223
c_getname function 84, 226
c_getpriority function 82, 225
c_getstksiz function 90, 227

c_giveprocessors function 85, 226
c_mypid function 33, 79, 224, 233, 265, 266
c_NAMELEN macro 226
c_nullpid, null process value 34, 224
c_processorid function 85, 226
c_processor function 226
c_setname function 84, 226
c_setpriority function 82, 225
c_setstksiz function 90, 227
c_startprocessors function 226
c_transcount function 82, 225
c_valid function 80, 225

d

deadlock 172, 174, 175, 181
deadlock, conditions necessary for 181
        definition of 181
        effective 183
        example of 182
debugging 246
declaration of an object 272
declaration, transaction 10
declarations, process 9
declarators 278
define preprocessor instruction 270
definition of an object 272, 276
definition process 4
definitions, scope of 282
delay alternative 43, 222
delay statement 36
delay statement, general form of a 221
dereferencing a pointer value 275
derived classes 143
derived types 271
destructors 134, 142, 145, 148, 151
dining philosophers example, *mortal* 26
discrete event simulation 189
discrete event simulation, inter-arrival times for 190
        service times for 190
disk scheduler example, *elevator algorithm based* 47
        simple 41
Distributed Processes (DP) 164, 166
do statement 283
dot operator 275
double type 272
DP 164, 166
DP solution for *producer-consumer* example 164
drift, cumulative time 38

e

effective deadlock   183
else part, associating with *if* statement   282
entry calls   251
entry point in C, main function as   270
enum types   272
Ethernet   237, 247
Ethernet implementation of Concurrent C   237
example, async. sol. for the *producer-consumer*   58
    automobile cruise controller   87
    buffered sol. for the *producer-consumer*   15
    betting processes   23
    chain line printer driver   45
    concurrent make   114
    concurrent readers and writers   69
    deadlock   182
    desirable polling   187
    elevator algorithm based disk scheduler   47
    implementing sets as processes   185
    job-shop scheduling   73
    lock manager   40
    mortal dining philosophers   26
    parallel quicksort   28
    performing requests in parallel   60
    priority scheduler   46
    producer-consumer   12
    producer-consumer   155
    protocol simulation   93
    robot controller   103
    synch. sol. for the *producer-consumer*   13
    simple disk scheduler   41
    simulating semaphores   66
    traffic light   82
    window manager   124
examples of variable definitions   278
exec system call   231
exponential distribution   195, 198
expression statement   282
extended rendezvous   154, 168
extern storage class   277

f

fault tolerance   247, 248
Fault Tolerant Concurrent C   248
feedback queueing networks   208
file access   244
file organization, suggested source   286
float type   272
flow-of-control   1
for statement   283
fork system call   231
friend functions   134
FT Concurrent C   248
function and transaction calls, similarity between   8

function and transaction pointers, similarities between   54
function body, syntax of   285
function calls, timings for   246
function prototype   79
functions and processes, analogy between   4
functions, argument passing modes for   270, 286
    built-in   33
    calling   285
    overloading   134
    returning values from   285
fundamental types   271

g

global names starting with c_   33
global variables   242
global variables, problems with   234
goto statement   284
guard   222
guard, *select* statement alternative   43

h

hello.cc   2

i

if statement   282
immediate alternative   43, 222, 263
implementation, process   4
implementing sets as processes example   185
include preprocessor instruction   270
information polling   187
inheritance of member functions   143
initializers   276, 279
initializers, examples of   279
int type   272
integral types   271
inter-arrival times   190
interrupts, associating with transaction calls   86, 227, 265

j

job-shop scheduling example   73

k

keywords, reserved   211

l

labels, statement   285
LAN implementation of Concurrent C   237, 247
library functions, problems with standard C   234
lock manager example   40
long type   272

m

main function   270
main process   2, 214
main process stack size   90, 227
make program   114
malloc function   274
malloc function, problems with   234
mean value   198
member functions   134
member functions, inheritance of   143
members of a struct, accessing   274, 275
members of a union, accessing   274
message passing models   153
monitor sol. for *producer-consumer* example   160
monitors   160, 166
Motorola 68020 microprocessor   240
multiprocessor impl. of Concurrent C   237, 239, 247
multiprocessor, processor selection in a   11, 85, 286

n

nested *if* statements   282
nested processes   233, 265
null character value '\0'   275
null pointer value NULL   275
null process value 0   34, 216, 274
null process value c_nullpid   34, 224
null statement   281
null transaction pointer value 0   55, 218
NULL, null pointer value   275

o

object   276
object definitions, examples of   278
operator precedence, summary of C   281
operator<<   150
operator=   149
operator>>   150
operators, overloading   134, 145
operators, summary of C   279
order of acceptance of trans. calls   40, 220, 256
organization, suggested source file   286
overloading functions   134
overloading operators   134, 145

p

p operation, the semaphore   66
packages and processes, similarities between   185
parallel quicksort example   28
parameter declarations, process   213
parameter passing modes for functions   270, 286
parameter passing modes for transactions   241, 266
parameters, process   4, 11, 254
                 transaction   10
parent process   3, 11
pending transaction calls, number of   225
performing requests in parallel example   60
pipe system call   231
PLITS   167
pointer types   274
pointer value 0, null   274
pointer value NULL, null   275
pointer value, deferencing a   275
pointers and arrays, relationship between   275
pointers, transaction   54, 217, 262
Poisson distribution   195
polling   170, 171, 187
polling example, desirable   187
polling, definition of information   187
              definition of rendezvous   187
preprocessor, C   269, 286
priority clause   11, 215
priority scheduler example   46
priority, process   81, 215, 262
process abortion   80, 224
process anytype   35, 217, 265
process anytype, rationale for   233
process arguments, passing   11
process body   4, 11, 211
process body, general form of a   214
process completion   34
process creation   2, 11, 254, 255
process creation, timings for   246
process declarations   9
process definition   4, 211

process identifier values 11
process ids 11, 12, 79, 216
process ids, use of 12
process implementation 4
process instantiation 4
process interaction 6
process parameter declarations 213
process parameters 4, 11, 254
process priority 81, 215, 262
process priority at process creation, specifying 11
process priority, functions manipulating 225
process scheduling, policy for 212
       rules for 216
process specification 4
process specification, general form of a 213
process stack size 90, 227
process state, functions returning 225
process states 34, 79, 215
process termination, client counts for 51
       collective 11, 49, 223, 243, 264
process type 4, 10, 211, 216
process type and process specification 10
process type before declaring it, using a 23
process type, general form of a 213
process value 0, null 34, 216
process value c_nullpid, null 34
process values 12, 216
process variables 5
process, child 11
       parent 11
       sibling 11
process-interaction model of simulation 190
processes 1
processes and functions, analogy between 4
processes and packages, similarities between 185
processes calling each other's transactions, two 23
processes, naming 84
       symbolic names of 226
processor failure 247, 248
processor id values 216, 225, 226
processor id values, functions returning 226
processor selection in a multiprocessor 11, 85, 266
processor clause 216, 225
producer-consumer example 12, 155
producer-consumer example, Ada sol. for 165, 253
       async. sol. for the 58
       buffered sol. for the 15
       critical reg. sol. for 159
       CSP solution for 162
       DP solution for 164
       monitor sol. for 160
       semaphore sol. for 158
       synch. sol. for the 13
program organization, Concurrent C 23
protocol simulation example 93
prototype, function 79

q

queueing networks 189, 192, 208
quicksort example, *parallel* 28

r

random number generator 198
read system call 244
register storage class 277, 285
relationship between pointers and arrays 275
remote procedure calls 166, 168
rendezvous 154, 168
rendezvous polling 187
rendezvous, extended 154
reserved words 211
return statement 284, 285
return statement in process body 214
right arrow operator 275
robot controller example 103
run-time function declarations 79

s

scheduler 1
scheduler process for discrete event sim. 191, 194, 206
scheduling policy 212
scheduling, rules for process 216
scope of variables 282
select alternative 222
select statement 42, 243
select statement alternative 43, 222
select statement, choosing alternatives of 222
       general form of a 222
       guard in 222
select system call 244
semaphore sol. for *producer-consumer* example 158
semaphores 158, 166
semaphores, binary 67
       disadvantages of 67
       integer 68
semaphores example, *simulating* 66
service times 190
shared memory 212, 239, 242, 248
shared memory hazards 21
shared memory models 153, 155
shared memory multiproc. impl. of Concurrent C 239, 248
shared-memory models 154
short type 272
sibling process 3, 11, 215
sim., simulated time scheduler process for 206
simulated time 191, 194
simulation, continuous time 189

discrete event 189
    inter-arrival times for 190
    process-interaction model of 190
    service times for 190
simulation, sim. time scheduler process for 191, 194
source file organization, suggested 286
specification, process 4
SR 167, 172
stack size, process 90, 227
    process `main` 90, 227
standard C library functions, problems with 234
standard deviation 198
standard header file `concurrentc.h` 224
standard input 245
standard output 245
statement labels 285
statement, *accept* 39
    delay 36
    select 42
`static` storage class 277, 285
`stdio.h` header file 270, 275
storage allocators 274
storage class 276, 27
storage classes, list of 277
strings, character 275
`struct` types 273
subscripts, array 273
`suchthat` clause 40, 220, 221, 259
`suchthat` clause, rationale for 232
suffix `.cc` for Concurrent C source files 2
switch statement 283
switch statement, use of *break* in 283
synchronous & asynch. message passing, eq. of 154, 173
synchronous message passing 153, 167, 168
synchronous message passing models 154
synchronous message passing, advantages of 169
    cost of 175
synchronous transactions 6, 212, 255

t

tags, `enum` 272
    `struct` 273
terminate alternative 43, 49, 222, 243, 264
terminate alternative, limitations of the 51
termination, client counts for process 51
    collective process 11, 49, 223, 243, 264
thread-of-execution 1
timed transaction calls 38, 219, 225
timed transaction calls, general form of 219
timeouts 171
timings for various Concurrent C operations 246
traffic light example 82
transaction and function calls, similarity between 8
transaction and function pointers, similarities between 54
transaction argument passing modes 241, 266
transaction calls 6, 212

transaction calls, assoc. interrupts with 86, 227, 265
    conditional acceptance of 40, 221, 259
    general form of 218
    number of pending 82, 225
    order of acceptance of 40, 220, 256
    timed 38, 219, 225
    timings for 246
transaction declaration 10
transaction declaration, general form of a 213
transaction parameters 10
transaction pointer declarations 217
transaction pointer value 0, null 55, 218
transaction pointers 54, 217, 262
transaction pointers, rationale for 232
    use of 218
transactions 212
transactions, asynchronous 6, 55, 212, 255
    synchronous 6, 212, 255
    when to use asynchronous 56
treturn statement 9
treturn statement, general form of a 221
type declarations 275
type specifiers, list of 277
type, process 4, 10
`typedef` declarations 276
types in C 271

u

union types 274
uniprocessor implementation of Concurrent C 236
UNIX file access 244
UNIX functions 90
UNIX library functions, problems with 234
UNIX system calls 244
`unsigned` type 272

v

v operation, the semaphore 66
variable 276
variable definitions, examples of 278
variables, process 5
    scope of 282
virtual functions 143
`void` type 285

W

while statement 283
window manager example 124